Tort Law in Poland

Tort Law in Poland

Second Edition

Ewa Bagińska
Magdalena Tulibacka

This book was originally published as a monograph in the International Encyclopaedia of Laws/Tort Law.

Founding Editor: Roger Blanpain
General Editor: Frank Hendrickx
Volume Editor: Britt Weyts

Wolters Kluwer

Published by:
Kluwer Law International B.V.
PO Box 316
2400 AH Alphen aan den Rijn
The Netherlands
E-mail: lrs-sales@wolterskluwer.com
Website: www.wolterskluwer.com/en/solutions/kluwerlawinternational

Sold and distributed by:
Wolters Kluwer Legal & Regulatory U.S.
7201 McKinney Circle
Frederick, MD 21704
United States of America
E-mail: customer.service@wolterskluwer.com

Printed on acid-free paper

ISBN 978-94-035-4961-3

e-Book: ISBN 978-94-035-4722-0
web-PDF: ISBN 978-94-035-4483-0

This title is available on www.kluwerlawonline.com

Printed in the United Kingdom.

The Authors

Ewa Bagińska is a full professor at the Faculty of Law and Administration of Gdansk University, Poland, where she holds the Chair of Civil Law. She specializes in Tort Law, Medical Law, Consumer Protection Law and Comparative Law, and she is a member of the European Group on Tort Law, fellow of the European Centre of Tort and Insurance Law in Vienna, Member of the Advisory Board of the European Review of Private Law.

Magdalena Tulibacka has a PhD and is an independent researcher and a Visiting Research Fellow at the Centre for Socio-Legal Studies of the University of Oxford. Former Senior Lecturer in European and Comparative Law at the University of Westminster. She has published books and articles on the law of product liability of Central and Eastern Europe, on Polish law and civil procedure, and on the European Union law and civil procedure.

The Authors

Table of Contents

List of Abbreviations

Dz. U.	Dziennik Ustaw (Official Journal of Laws)
EC	European Community
ERPL	*European Review of Private Law*
EU	European Union
JETL	*Journal of European Tort Law*
KC	Civil Code
KPP	Kwartalnik Prawa Prywatnego
OSA	Reports of the Courts of Appeal
OSN/ OSNC	Reports of the Supreme Court Cases (Civil Chamber)
OSNC ZD	Reports of the Supreme Court Civil Chamber Cases – Supplementary Collection
OSP	Reports of the Polish Courts
OSPiKA	Reports of the Polish Courts and Arbitration Panel Cases
OTK	Orzecznictwo Trybunalu Konstytucyjnego (Judgments of the Constitutional Tribunal)
PiM	Prawo i Medycyna (Law and Medicine)
PiP	Panstwo i Prawo (State and Law)
PS	Przeglad Sadowy (Judicial Review)
SA	Sad Apelacyjny (Court of Appeals)
SN	Sad Najwyzszy (the Supreme Court)
TK	Trybunał Konstytucyjny (the Constitutional Tribunal)

List of Abbreviations

General Introduction

§1. General Background of the Country

I. Geography

1. Poland is one of the larger European countries, covering an area of over 322,000 square kilometres.[1] It is located in the north-central part of the continent. In the North it borders the Baltic Sea, and in the South the border runs along the Beskid, Sudeten and Carpathian mountains. It neighbours the following countries (West to East): Germany, the Czech Republic, Slovakia, Ukraine, Belarus, Lithuania and Russia (through Kaliningrad Oblast). Its population as of 31 March 2011 was over 38,511,800.[2] More than 99.8% of those residing in Poland are Poles, and only 0.15% (57,500) are foreigners. Among those, the largest group are Ukrainians, followed by Germans and Russians.[3] The capital of Poland is Warsaw (Warszawa), with a population of over 1.7 million.[4]

Both the territory of Poland and its demographic structure changed very significantly within the past century. Before World War II, Poland extended much further to the East (covering lands now within the territories of Lithuania, Ukraine, Belarus, Russia and Slovakia), and some of its current western parts belonged to Germany. The current small percentage of minorities is in stark contrast to the Polish population in the interwar period (1918–1939), when over 30% of residents included Ukrainians, Jews, Belarusians, Germans, Lithuanians, Czechs, Armenians, Russians and Gypsies.

Poland became a Member State of the European Union (EU) on 1 May 2004, in the process of the Union's extension to the east to include former socialist states of Central and Eastern Europe. Following this momentous event, large numbers of

1. This number includes parts of the Baltic Sea belonging to Poland, as well as Poland's waterways. The administrative area is over 312,000 square kilometres.
2. Source: the Main Statistical Office (*Główny Urząd Statystyczny*), '*Ludność. Stan i struktura demograficzno-społeczna. Narodowy Spis Powszechny Ludności i Mieszkań 2011*' (Population. The condition and the demographic and social structure. The National Census of Population and Housing), Warszawa: 2013. Available at: http://www.stat.gov.pl/cps/rde/xbcr/gus/LUD_ludnosc_stan_str_dem_spo_NSP2011.pdf. Accessed on 11 Nov. 2013.
3. GUS – Główny Urząd Statystyczny (the Main Statistical Office) 'Ludność. Stan i struktura w przekroju terytorialnym. Stan w dniu 30.06.2012' (Population. The state and structure by territorial division as of 30 Jun. 2012). Warszawa 2012. Available at: http://www.stat.gov.pl/cps/rde/xbcr/gus/l_ludnosc_stan_struktura_30062012.pdf. Accessed on 11 Nov. 2013.
4. GUS – Główny Urząd Statystyczny 'Ludność. Stan i struktura w przekroju terytorialnym. Stan w dniu 30.06.2012', p. 82.

Poles temporarily left Poland to find employment in other EU countries, especially the United Kingdom and Ireland. Further, an increasing number of citizens of other EU countries live in Poland. However, it still remains largely an ethnically homogenous state inhabited in very significant majority by Poles.

II. Political and Legal History

A. *Early History*

2. The date from which Poland started its existence as a state is not easy to ascertain. Most historians take the year 966 (or 965) C.E.,[5] when the ruler Mieszko I officially accepted Latin Christianity and therefore imposed it upon the territories of what was to be later known as Poland, as the 'start date'.[6] Mieszko was a member of what historians named the 'Piast dynasty', albeit only a small number of Piasts were actually crowned kings. Mieszko and his son Boleslaw continued to extend the borders of Poland using marriage alliances and military power. Between 1039 and 1058, during the reign of Kazimierz Odnowiciel ('The restorer') Krakow (Cracov) became the capital. Between then and the late thirteenth century, however, the territories of Poland were often subjected to internal conflicts, pagan unrests, invasions and wars with neighbours. Lacking natural barriers which would separate it from neighbours, it was naturally an area of international conflict. Thus, what actually amounted to the Polish territory was an extremely fluid concept.

B. *The Republic of Two Nations: Until 1795 and the Partition*

3. In 1385 Poland, having concluded a union with the Grand Duchy of Lithuania, became the largest European state. It spread from the Baltic Sea to the borders of the Ottoman Empire. Initially, this impressive structure, based on personal rather than political or legal ties, was quite unstable. As the Jagiellonian dynasty governing Poland at the time was approaching extinction (the King Zygmunt II August had no heir) the efforts to reform the current political structure intensified. In 1569 the union between the Kingdom of Poland and the Duchy of Lithuania became formalized and the newly reformed state was referred to as *Rzeczpospolita Obojga Narodow* – the Republic of Two Nations. The Republic had one King, one Parliament, a common foreign policy and common currency. Strengthened by the stable political arrangements, the Republic became one of the most politically, economically and culturally important European states. The capital was moved to the more geographically convenient Warsaw in 1596. The political system between the late sixteenth century and the eighteenth century was a very interesting mixture of monarchy and a decentralized form of democracy referred to as democracy by nobles (*demokracja*

5. 965 as per N. Davies, *Heart of Europe. The Past in Poland's Present*, 249 (Oxford University Press, 2001); and 966 as per J. Lukowski, H. Zawadzki, *A Concise History of Poland*, 3 (Cambridge University Press, 2001).
6. Lukowski, Zawadzki, *A Concise History of Poland*, 3.

szlachecka). Polish and Lithuanian gentry constituted a relatively large percentage of the population. The nobles were represented in the General Assembly (Parliament) by representatives elected during meetings of local assemblies (*sejmiki*). The General Assembly consisted of the King, *Senat* – the highest monarchy officials, and the Chamber of Representatives (170 representatives of local nobles). Interestingly, kings were elected by the General Assembly of all gentry, and their powers were limited. The legal system at the time was a complex blend of very different systems of rules: land law used by nobles, the laws used by municipalities, canon law used by the church and extremely diversified local rules, mostly based on custom, used by the general population. Following the golden age in the history of the Republic (first half of the seventeenth century), wars with neighbours became very difficult to contain and Poland lost some of its territories and much of its political influence. Its position became increasingly precarious, especially that it found itself surrounded by very strong empires governed by absolute monarchs. Polish and Lithuanian nobles resisted attempts to strengthen the monarchy and limit their privileges. Economic and financial problems added to the picture of a state in chaos. The Republic became an easy target for growing foreign influences. The first partition of parts of the Republic by the Russian, Prussian and Austrian empires took place in 1772. It triggered a very significant effort to reform and save the ailing state. Under the reign of Stanislaw August Poniatowski the 'Four-Year-Parliament' attempted a very comprehensive reform, including enacting a Constitution. The Constitution of 3 May 1791, the first written Constitution in Europe and only the second in the World (after the Constitution of the United States of America of 1787), radically changed the political system of the Republic. In spite of these efforts, the Constitution lost its force and the Republic was finally and totally partitioned for the third time in 1795.

Poland ceased to exist as a state for 123 years. During the time of partition, it was under the influence of a number of legal systems. The Prussian Civil Code (BGB), the Collection of Laws of the Russian Empire (especially volume X on private law) of 1835, the Austrian Civil Code (ABGB), as well as the Code Napoleon were all official sources of law.

C. The Interwar Period: Regained Independence and the Period of Unification

4. In 1918 Poland regained its independence following World War I and the collapse of the empires. The Second Republic was established. Poland was initially a parliamentary republic, but economic and political pressures led to unrest and a political coup. After an overturn of government the political system of Poland became presidential and authoritarian. These internal difficulties did not, however, stifle the process of administrative and legal reform in the interwar period. The extent of the necessary reforms was very substantial. While other civil law systems, those of Western Europe, established their unified and mature legal systems through nineteenth-century codifications, Poland emerged from the domination of the empires as a blend of legal systems and cultures. It inherited a true 'tower of Babel' of legal systems and traditions.[7] The process of unification and reform started very soon after the country gained its independence back. The codification process included the law of obligations and several other areas of law. The Code of Obligations of 1933 and the Code of Commercial Law of 1934 were drafted by legal scholars who were very well read in the current European codifications, and drew inspiration from them. The Codes were hailed as sophisticated and coherent pieces of legislation. However, crucial areas of law were not codified, hence an important role of judicial decisions and scholarly writings which sought unity and consistency among differing legal rules.[8]

D. 1945–1989: Socialism

5. The reforms towards creating a fully coherent and comprehensive legal system were curtailed by World War II and the change of political and economic order of Poland after the War. Socialism took over Polish political thought and political order, economic and social relations and law as well. The socialist government was formed and the Polish United Workers' Party (PZPR) started dominating political and social life. The new Constitution of 1952 constituted the legal basis for the functioning of the socialist state. It formally established Poland as a socialist state which was governed by the PZPR and which rejected the principle of division of powers opting for the dominant role of the Parliament.

Together with other countries of Central and Eastern Europe within the scope of power of the Soviet Union, Poland became part of what comparative law scholars named the 'socialist legal family'. Private law was effectively marginalized in socialist systems. A remarkable feature of the socialist ideology was its overwhelming influence on market relations, and thus on the rules governing those relations. Socialist civil laws were alienated from the reality of social and economic life. Most legal relationships (in particular – those between businesses, most of which were state-owned) were governed by rules deriving from sources not related to or deriving from the code-based law of obligations: by the acts of central planning, 'normative acts'. As far as legal thought and legal culture were concerned, socialism had a stifling effect on both. While legal scholars offered comprehensive legal treatises and analyses, their effect on legal practice, judicial decisions and everyday life of the socialist society was weak. Judicial decisions suffered from a very peculiar form of formalism referred to as 'bound judicial decision-making'.[9] Judges tended to rely on written law, refraining from dynamic interpretation or exercising discretion.[10]

The socialist period in Poland's history was a time of turmoil, massive socio-economic change engineered by the socialists, ineffective reforms, the economy of shortages, as well as massive protests and strikes. It was also, however, the time of

7. D. Lasok, *Polish Civil Law,* in, *Law in Eastern Europe*, 2 (A.W.Sijthoff, 1973).
8. *Ibid.*, 2.
9. Z. Kühn, Worlds Apart: Western and Central European Judicial Culture at the Onset of the European Enlargement, 52 Am. J. of Comp. L. 531–567, 540–544 (2004).
10. M. Tulibacka, Product Liability Law in Transition: A Central European Perspective, 25–34 (Ashgate, 2009).

increased civic awareness and an active opposition movement embodied in Solidarity. The latter was an independent trade union which reflected and inspired anti-socialist sentiments in Polish society. These sentiments were grounded in the emphasis of links with Western European states, especially the common roots of the legal, economic and social systems. Legal scholars emphasized the links with the 'good old law' of the interwar period: the time when Poland was evolving as an independent state and freely drew from examples of Western European legislation in drafting its own laws. Although remaining socialist until 1989, Poland always remained in a relatively close relationship with the 'West'. These links and common elements, as well as the civil law roots which remained in legislation and legal thought, meant that the way ahead for Polish law was clear. As socialism weakened and the opposition to it strengthened during 1980s, the phenomenal characteristic of the socialist legal culture were also disappearing.

The very strong public support for the opposition, the weakening of the socialist party in Poland and also in Russia led to the peaceful transition into democracy.

E. After 1989: The Great Transition

6. The round-table discussions between the socialists and the opposition, the parliamentary elections and the total defeat of the socialists meant a new chapter in Poland's history. In common with other post-socialist countries, Poland needed to change virtually the entire political and economic system, and most of its legal framework. Reforms started with fundamental concepts such as the rule of law or constitutionality. The small Constitution (which was a transition document), and subsequently the new Constitution of 1997[11] established the general principles and fundamentals of the Polish state, including democracy, human rights and division of powers. Poland went through a very rapid economic and social transformation, and the legal system needed to adapt to the new reality. A further challenge has been the association and the membership of the EU.

The process of joining the Union started formally with the conclusion of 'Europe Agreements' (Association Agreements between the EU and Poland as well as other Central and Eastern European states) in December 1991. Poland applied for EU membership in 1994, and the accession negotiations began in 1998. The 2001 Gothenburg European Council concluded that the accession negotiations would be completed in 2002. The 2002 Copenhagen European Council formally welcomed the new Member States (Poland and nine other Central and Eastern European countries), the membership to be confirmed by their national referenda. The Treaty of Accession was signed in 2003, and the date for the formal accession was set at 1 May 2004. Since then, Poland is bound by the EU law and remains a very active member of the organization.

The transition from socialism to free market, democracy and an active civic society is still ongoing. The legal system and legal culture need time to mature. The plethora of new laws and regulations which appeared in Poland within a relatively

11. Published in Dziennik Ustaw (Journal of Laws, here: Dz.U.) of 1997, No. 78, item 483.

short period of time somewhat overwhelmed the legal system and the justice system. Both the new administrative infrastructure and public law enforcement system, as well as the civil justice system, continue to evolve. There is a need for more consistency within substantive and procedural law. Work on greater harmonization and coherence is progressing steadily. Within the area of civil law the process of drafting a new, more coherent Civil Code commenced ten years ago. The judiciary, which during socialism suffered from lack of social trust, lack of dynamism and initiative in legal interpretation, is now in the process of re-establishing their position. This is a systemic transformation within Polish legal culture and it has been taking time. Judges, especially those in lower courts, tend to continue refraining from using their own discretion and flexibility inherent in some legal provisions. Hesitant to take decisions based on their own judgment, they tend to use expert opinions in order to support their position in a case. With the current shortage of experts, waiting time for their statements can be long indeed. This judicial restraint is one of the key reasons for delays in Polish civil proceedings. The 'bound judicial decision-making', formalism and lack of initiative are only very gradually giving way to tendencies observed in the West of Europe: judicial activism, dynamic interpretation and even managerialism. The latter phenomena can already be observed in higher courts, and especially the Supreme Court and the Constitutional Tribunal.

III. Political System

7. According to the Constitution of 1997, Poland is a parliamentary republic,[12] although it leans slightly towards a presidential system. The President of Poland is elected in a direct, universal ballot. The leading principles which lie at the foundation of the Polish state are:

- sovereignty of the people (Article 1 of the Constitution);
- independence and sovereignty of the state (Articles 1 and 2);
- democracy (Article 2);
- rule of law (Articles 2 and 7);
- civil society (Articles 1 and 12);
- separation of powers (Article 10);
- plurality (Article 11);
- social market economy (Article 20); and
- respect for human rights and for the environment (Article 5).

Poland is a unitary state where powers are divided between the central government and the local level authorities. Some of the local authorities are directly elected

12. The Constitution of the Polish Peoples' Republic was adopted by the National Assembly on 2 Apr. 1997 and endorsed by a general referendum in May 1997. It is also referred to as the 'Fundamental Law' (*ustawa zasadnicza*), as it is the most important source of law in Poland.

on the local level. Following the administrative reform of 1 January 1999, the country's administrative structure is based on three levels of localities: from the smallest *gmina*, through *powiats*, to larger districts (*wojewodztwa*, of which there are sixteen).

Today Poland firmly endorses the principle of separation and balance of powers (Article 10 of the Constitution). The president is head of state, and apart from the power to propose and veto legislation his role is mostly a representative one. The executive power is exercised by the government: the Council of Ministers headed by the prime minister, and by the president. The legislative power is entrusted to the Parliament; and judicial power: to courts and tribunals.

Legislation can be proposed by the government, by the president, by the Parliament and by at least 100,000 citizens who have the right to vote.

A. *Legislative Power*

8. Members of the bicameral Parliament (representatives and senators) are directly elected, and enter the Parliament using the system of proportionate representation, every four years. Candidates in parliamentary elections run in multi-seat constituencies, with a 5% threshold for entry for each party and an 8% for a coalition of parties. The lower Chamber of the Parliament is *Sejm,* which adopts legislation and plays a supervisory role over the Council of Ministers. The higher chamber –*Senat,* takes part in appointing certain high civil servants and state officials: for instance the Ombudsman (citizens' rights Ombudsman). The key role of the *Senat* is to approve, amend or reject legislation adopted by the *Sejm.* Both chambers take part in adopting statutes ratifying international treaties. If the international treaty transfers sovereign state powers to an international organization or an international body, the majority required in both chambers is two-thirds, with the presence of at least half of the statutory number of representatives and senators.

The Constitution prescribes that in matters important for the state a referendum can be called by the qualified majority of the *Sejm* members, or by the president with the consent of the *Senat.* The results of a referendum are binding if at least half of all citizens entitled to vote actually took part in it (Article 125).

B. *Executive Power*

9. The executive power is exercised by the government and by the president. The directly elected president, whose term of office is five years, represents the Republic of Poland and guarantees the continuity of the state. The key function of the president is proposing, approving or vetoing legislation. However, the veto can be overturned by a qualified majority vote in the *Sejm.* The president plays an important role in appointing the prime minister and approving the members of the Council of Ministers. However, this power is to some extent counterbalanced by the constitutional requirement that almost all official acts of the president ought to be signed by the prime minister. By signing such official acts the prime minister assumes responsibility for them before the *Sejm* (Article 144 of the Constitution).

The Council of Ministers (appointed by the president with the approval of the *Sejm*) is headed by the prime minister who is nominated by the largest parliamentary group. The government performs most executive tasks, except for those which were entrusted by law to other bodies, especially local authorities and local self-governance bodies. It manages internal affairs as well as foreign policy. Its main tasks include: implementation of acts of Parliament, issuing regulations to this effect, supervising administrative authorities, drafting the general budget and ensuring its proper implementation, safeguarding internal and external security of Poland (including control of national defence), ensuring smooth running of international relations, concluding international agreements which require ratification and accepting other international agreements (Article 146).

C. *Judicial Power*

10. According to Article 175 of the Constitution, judicial power is vested in: the Supreme Court, the common courts, the administrative courts and the military courts. The Polish judicial system is thus based on a multi-pillar structure. The Supreme Court and the common courts constitute one pillar, and the Chief Administrative Court and administrative courts – the second pillar. The military courts form an independent system regulated by statute, but they remain under the jurisdiction of the Supreme Court (Military Chamber). Separation of courts from other branches of power is granted by the Constitution, which emphasizes their organizational and functional independence (Article 173).

The judicial system of Poland also includes two important Tribunals: the Constitutional Tribunal, and the Tribunal of the State. The Constitutional Tribunal was established in 1985 in order to examine conformity of acts of Parliament, other legal acts and international agreements, and official aims and official activities of political parties with the Constitution. It also examines conformity of regulations and other official acts issued by central state authorities with the Constitution, and with acts of Parliament and international agreements. The Tribunal of the State was established in 1982 in order to adjudicate in cases where persons exercising the highest official roles (the President, the Prime Minister and Ministers, the President of the National Bank and the Head of the Supreme Audit Chamber) are accused of having infringed the Constitution or an act of Parliament.

IV. Economic and Social Values

11. According to Article 20 of the Constitution, Polish socio-economic system is grounded in social market economy which encompasses freedom of economic activity, protection of private property and solidarity, dialogue and cooperation of social partners. Poland is a developing economy, in transition from the 1945 to 1989 period of socialism and central planning. During the latter period, which culminated in agrarian reform and nationalization of all companies with more than fifty employees, central planning dealt with production, supply and demand. The result of more than forty years of socialism was persistent shortages of basic consumables, underdeveloped industry and infrastructure, and a low standard of living of the majority of the population. After the end of socialism Poland rejected the approach of some other Eastern European states seeking the 'third way' of building more democratic and market-oriented systems, rejecting both real socialism and capitalism.[13] In common with Hungary and Czechoslovakia (now the Czech Republic and Slovakia), it focused on building 'overt capitalist' institutions in both politics and the economy.[14] Whole areas of industry were privatized. Competition law, employment law, tax law, business law and consumer law were rewritten and were being dynamically enforced. However, the new Poland certainly did not reject the ideas of welfare state but rather embraced them fully. While immediately after the end of socialism state benefits were being limited, the system has become more stable now and remains relatively comprehensive.[15] The state provides an array of benefits to citizens in various situations. Article 67 of the Constitution provides each citizen with the right to social security benefits in cases of inability to work on account of sickness or disability, and to pension on account of old age. To name just a few examples of other benefits: state-funded health care and education (also specified in the Constitution – Articles 68 and 70), unemployment benefits (albeit relatively limited) and subsidized job training, or various family and child benefits including an annuity on account of each child, and a lump sum on the occasion of childbirth. The social security insurance system is very comprehensive indeed. It is partly funded by the beneficiaries. It includes pensions and annuities, benefits for those injured on the job or who suffer from occupational diseases, family members' benefits (for loss of a breadwinner) and disability benefits.

The Polish Constitution puts significant emphasis on the human rights of each citizen, including personal rights, political rights, social, economic and cultural rights. The basis for the protection of these rights is Chapter II of the Constitution. They are reinforced by the membership in the EU with its own Charter of Human Rights,[16] and in the Council of Europe with its European Convention of Human Rights. As regards civic life and activities, there is plenty of anecdotal evidence of Polish eagerness to enforce the law in the courts – thus their legendary litigiousness, and to get involved in public life. With the present onset of non-governmental organizations, other organizations representing various interests, campaigns and activities of central and local governmental bodies, civic awareness is growing significantly.

---

13. H. Izdebski, General Survey of Developments in Eastern Europe in the Field of Civil Law, in The Revival of Private Law in Central and Eastern Europe: Essays in Honor of F.J.M. Feldbrugge 3–14, at 4 (Ginsburgs, Barry, and Simmons eds, Institute of East European Law and Russian Studies, Leiden University Faculty of Law, No. 46, The Hague, London and Boston, MA, Martinus Nijhoff Publishers and Kluwer, 1996).
14. *Ibid.*, 6.
15. *See* R. Siemieńska, A. Domaradzka *Welfare State in Poland: Transformation with Difficulties,* in *The Handbook of European Welfare Systems,* 378–397 (Klaus Schubert, Simon Hegelich, Ursula Bazant eds, Routledge, 2009).
16. Charter of Human Rights of the European Union, OJ 30.03.2010, C 83/391.

§2. Legal System

12. Poland began rebuilding its laws after the end of socialism by reaching to the legislation and scholarly writings of the pre-War period, as well as by looking at examples of successful laws and regulations in other legal systems. It also returned to the civil law family, with its private law (and especially the Civil Code of 1964) modelled to some extent on French law, and less so on German, Swiss and Dutch law. The remaining specificities of the Polish legal system result from its complicated legal and socio-economic history, as well as long-standing customs and traditions.

I. Primacy of Legislation and Codification

13. As is typical of a civil law system, written laws are key sources of law in Poland. The contemporary Polish law is a code-based system of legislative acts and regulatory instruments. The Constitution of 1997, which is the most important source of law in Poland, sets out the political and legal framework for the functioning of the Polish state and Polish law. It is also a very important source of human rights. The Constitution is directly applicable and directly effective in horizontal and vertical relations, provided the provision involved is precise enough to warrant enforceability. Article 87 of the Constitution sets out the catalogue of other sources of Polish law. They are acts of Parliament (statutes), international treaties, regulations and local laws. These sources of internal law are binding once they are published in *Dziennik Ustaw* (Dz. U.) – the official Journal of Laws, and local laws: in *Wojewodzki Dziennik Urzedowy* for the particular district. Other legal acts, such as Presidential and ministerial decrees, judgments of the Constitutional Tribunal and parliamentary resolutions are published in *Monitor Polski.*

The Constitution as the fundamental law has primacy over all other legal sources, including international law and, interestingly enough, also the law of the EU. The latter point is elaborated below. As far as other sources of internal law are concerned, statutes are given most prominence. This is in contrast with the socialist period, where administrative acts ('normative acts') enjoyed the most important status. Those normative acts were issued by administrative authorities and regulated various areas of life, in line with socialist principles and plans. At present, in compliance with the requirements of the principle of rule of law, acts of the democratically elected Parliament which can be subject to review by the Constitutional Tribunal are key sources of law. Among those statutes, the most comprehensive and prominent are codes of various areas of law. They are drafted over prolonged periods of research, consultations and negotiations, with a very significant participation of scholars. The main aim is containing rules pertaining to a particular area of law in one coherent piece of legislation. In practice the codes are supplemented by a number of more detailed statutes and regulations concerning specific issues. In spite of their size and prominence, codes do not enjoy a legal status above other acts of Parliament and are formally seen as equal with any other statutes.

The remaining sources of internal law in Poland are regulations and local laws. Regulations are sources of law which must have a legal basis in an act of Parliament that also normally set out their scope. Local laws enacted by local authorities are sources of law within the geographical area of the authorities' competence.

Polish law and practice are experiencing unprecedented transformations at present, partly due to the recent transition to market economy, and partly as a result of direct influences of the pan-European legal harmonization project coordinated by the EU and of other international laws. In early 1990s Poland began the process of preparation for the membership in the EU and started approximating its law to EU standards. Since 1 May 2004 it has membership obligations which include acceptance of supremacy of EU law over Polish law and its direct applicability. These obligations have been reaffirmed in Article 91 §3 of the Constitution. Interestingly, the Constitutional Tribunal emphasized primacy of the Polish Constitution over EU law on numerous occasions.[17] This is not a unique position among the EU Member States, and yet it is somewhat problematic.

The last point may well introduce some confusion into the general understanding of legal force of international law, and especially EU law, in Poland. Generally, international conventions signed and ratified (if ratification is required by internal Polish law, which is the case if rights and obligations of Polish citizens, membership in an international organization or other important matters are concerned) become binding sources of Polish law once they have been published in Dz. U. Thus, Poland is a monist system as regards its relationship with international law. International conventions also have primacy over acts of Parliament. Other sources of international law which are binding include agreed international customs.[18] EU law is a new and unique system of international law, the key features of which are supremacy over domestic law of Member States and, under specific conditions, direct effect. Its sources, apart from the Treaty on the Functioning of the European Union (TFEU), are regulations, directives and decisions. Further, the decisions of the European Court of Justice are binding as regards their interpretation and application of EU law. The official position in current political and judicial writings is that while EU law is supreme over secondary law of Poland (statutes, regulations, local laws), it does not take precedence over the Constitution. The Constitutional Tribunal, in the decision mentioned above, held that in order to fulfil EU membership obligations, the legislative authorities needed to rectify the inconsistency between EU law and the Polish Constitution by amending the latter each time to ensure compliance with the relevant EU laws.

As a civil law system, Poland undoubtedly gives written law the greatest level of importance. Are there any other sources which can be found outside the scope of written law? Below we consider the role of customs, and the role of judicial decisions is examined in the further section.

---

17. For instance: Constitutional Tribunal decision of 16 Nov. 2011, SK 45/09, Dz.U. of 2011, No. 254, item 1530.
18. *See* M. Safjan *Źródła Prawa Prywatnego,* in M. Safjan (ed.) *System Prawa Prywatnego. Tom I. Część Ogólna*, 2nd Edition (CH Beck, Instytut Nauk Prawnych PAN, 2012), 191.

14. Customs, while not officially a source of law, play a key role in the interpretation of certain legal provisions, and in the application of general clauses (these are analysed below and include 'principles of community life' and 'proper conduct'). Civil law appears to be a particularly fertile ground for application of customs as it uses those general clauses, as well as general principles such as freedom of contract, sparingly. There are also a number of provisions in the Civil Code which expressly refer to customs: such as those which specify contents of a legal relationship or contents of a legal act[19] (Article 56 of the Code), or the provision concerning the manner in which obligations ought to be performed, including obligations resulting from tort law (Article 354).

II. Position of the Judiciary

15. Judges are appointed by the president following a recommendation by the National Council of the Judiciary (*Krajowa Rada Sadownictwa).* They have no definite period of appointment and are career judges, commencing their functions very often in late twenties or early thirties. Their independence and impartiality is confirmed by the Constitution, through provisions on their irremovability and immunity (Articles 180 and 181).

The structure and organization of the common court system in Poland are regulated by the Act on the Organization of Common Courts.[20] The common courts consider all cases which have not been placed within the jurisdiction of administrative courts or military courts. They are structured into a three-tier system: there are 299 district courts (*sady rejonowe*), 41 regional courts (*sady okregowe*) and 10 appellate courts (*sady apelacyjne*). Common courts are organized into specialized departments – dealing with civil, criminal, and depending on the needs also labour relations, family and custody, business and social security insurance cases. The Regional Court of Warsaw also has a specialized department for considering cases involving competition and consumer protection – the 'Court for the Protection of Competition and Consumers' (*Sad Ochrony Konkurencji i Konsumentow*).

District courts consider all cases with the exception of those expressly reserved for the regional courts (Article 16 of the Code of Civil Procedure – KPC).[21] The latter cases are, among others, proceedings where a non-pecuniary claim is sought together with the pecuniary one, intellectual property and patent rights cases and almost all cases where a pecuniary claim is sought the value of which exceeds PLN 75,000 (Polish Zloty) (Article 17 KPC). Further, district courts may transfer every case in which a legal issue giving rise to important legal questions appears to regional courts, although a justification must be given and the regional courts may always refuse the transfer if they conclude that no such questions arose (Article 18 KPC). Appellate courts consider appeals from judgments of regional courts.

19. The concept of a 'legal act' is at the basis of Polish civil law. It is an action which has legal consequences not only for the person acting but also for others. Examples of legal acts are: the making of a will, a public promise, or a contract.
20. Act on 27 Jul. 2001 (*Prawo o ustroju sądów powszechnych),* Dz.U. 2001, No. 98, item 1070. Later amended.
21. The Act of 17 Nov. 1964, Dz.U. 1964, No. 43, item 296. Later amended.

The Supreme Court – the highest judicial authority in Poland – exercises supervisory function over adjudication conducted by common courts and military courts. The Head of the Court is appointed by the president from candidates presented by the General Assembly of Supreme Court judges. The court operates in four chambers: the Civil Chamber, the Labour, Social Insurance and Public Affairs Chamber, the Criminal Chamber and the Military Chamber. The key function of the court is considering cassations from certain final decisions of common courts and military courts. Cassations are brought by the parties to the proceedings, and in circumstances specified by law by the Public Prosecutor, the Ombudsman and the Children's Ombudsman, in cases which involve a possible infringement of substantive law (its interpretation or application) or procedural law (as long as the latter could have had a material impact on the outcome of the case). If during cassation proceedings an important legal issue arises, or if there is a need to provide interpretation of a legal provision, the proceedings in the case can be suspended in order to consider the issue by a larger panel of Supreme Court judges. Some decisions concerning such legal issues are given the status of a 'legal principle' by the court, and thus become generally binding. They are taken in panels of at least seven judges, and sometimes even in an entire Chamber or joint Chambers of the court. They cannot be challenged except in another case by a larger number of judges than the panel where the principle originated. Other decisions of the Supreme Court are only binding on the parties and the court involved in a particular case.

The administrative court system consists of regional administrative courts and the Chief Administrative Court. The military courts are garrison and provincial courts (they are regulated by the Act on Military Courts).[22]

A very significant element of the Polish legal culture, somewhat stifling the impact of judicial decisions, has been the fact that most lower and even appeal court judgments are not published. It is extremely difficult to find any official transcripts of these judgments in the official domain. Analyses of judicial approaches and tendencies are normally conducted using decisions of higher courts, especially the Supreme Court.

16. What is the place of judicial decisions in the Polish legal system? In common with other codification-based abstract (civil law) systems, judicial decisions are persuasive but not authoritative sources of law. They have a very significant, although largely informal impact on the law enacted by legislators and on general tendencies in legal practice. Judicial decisions, even those of the Supreme Court, are normally not binding beyond the specific case which they concern. However, the tendency to observe these decisions and their approach to specific legal provisions, and to treat them as essential parts of the Polish legal system is clearly discernible. It appears that an analysis of a legal concept is only complete if, in addition to analysis of written law commented upon by scholars, it refers to judicial decisions on the subject. Decisions are becoming more comprehensive and descriptive, and they increasingly use dynamic and creative methods of interpretation of written law. The gradual shift in approach to legal interpretation is away from the position of the

---

22. The Act of 21 Aug. 1997. The Law on the Organization of Military Courts. The amended version published in Dz.U. of 2012, item 952.

Polish judiciary of the socialist period with the very peculiar lack of judicial activism and somewhat extreme forms of formalism. The shift commenced among judiciary in higher courts, especially the Supreme Court, during the later stages of socialism (late 1980s). Not only have judicial decisions interpreted written law in the manner consistent with the transforming socio-economic reality, but they also created specific legal approaches and concepts in the face of the existing written law which was seen as insufficiently addressing the situation. Product liability and state liability (for both of which courts effectively established strict liability systems), and liability for damage caused to a *nasciturus* (in the light of lack of a legal provision to this effect in Polish civil law at the time) are good examples. These are analysed in further parts of this study. With regard to all these examples, judicial activism served as an inspiration for later legislative amendments.

17. There are two judicial institutions in Poland, the decisions of which have a more formal impact on law without necessarily being formally referred to as sources of law. The Supreme Court, apart from considering cassations, has the power to issue binding 'legal principles' if a significant legal issue arises or if there are serious discrepancies in interpretation of a legal provision. The Constitutional Tribunal's role was also introduced above (no. 10). The Tribunal's law-shaping function is very significant. In exercising its responsibility of ensuring compliance of statutes and regulations with the Constitution Tribunal can effectively strike down a legal provision. Such decisions of the Tribunal often have repercussions on a much wider scale within the entire area of law concerned.

III. Distinction Between Public and Private Law

18. The distinction has been fundamental in Polish legal thought during the period of rebuilding national identity and establishing a unified legal framework for the newly restored Polish state (1918–1939). It was sanctioned by Article 3 of the Constitution of 1921, which stated that: 'The scope of state legislation encompasses all possible private and public laws and the manner in which they are executed.'

The socialist authorities after the War did not, for ideological reasons, accept the distinction. Legislation enacted during the era as well as doctrinal writings reflected this approach.

Following the end of socialism, the Polish legal thought is returning to its roots and re-emphasizing the different roles and nature of public and private law. Private law is growing in scope and importance. It has recently been defined as a branch of law containing principles and rules aimed at shaping legal relations and based on the need to protect individual interests, in harmony with wider social interests and using a regulatory method based on cooperation.[23] Private law respects the principle of autonomy of will (the expression of which are: the constitutional principles of individual freedom and freedom to pursue economic activity, as well as the principle of freedom of contract contained in Article 353[1] KC) and of equal treatment

23. Andrzej Bierć, in: *System Prawa Prywatnego: Część Ogólna* (Wolters Kluwer, 2012), 37.

of all individuals (based on the provisions of the Constitution concerning non-discrimination – Article 32 §1). Another standard of private law is safety and certainty of legal transactions (legal certainty). It finds its basis in the Constitutional guarantee of trust towards the state and the law (Article 2). In the Civil Code the principle of legal certainty is realized through general rules containing moral and ethical guidelines of conduct. These are contained in general clauses such as 'proper conduct' and 'principles of community life'. The general clauses which are important for civil law and tort law are analysed briefly below, in the part concerning sources of private law (no. 20–22).

IV. Sources of Private Law in General and of Tort Law in Particular

19. With regard to its approach to private law and its contents, the Polish legal system follows other civil law systems. Private law includes in particular civil law, family law, trade law and intellectual property law. The sources include the Constitution, the Civil Code, a number of other codes and statutes.

The Constitution, while being the fundamental source of Polish law in general, is also a very important source of private law and civil law. It sets out the structure and the main features of private law, and establishes it as a guarantor of some fundamental constitutional principles: freedom of contract and of economic activity, and protection of private property.[24] It also contains many individual rights which have significance in the private law area: protection of life of a person (Article 38), protection of a person's dignity (Article 47), or protection of private property (Article 64). While most of these rights are expressed in very general terms and thus require a more precise description in other legal provisions, including the provisions of the Civil Code, some rights can derive and can be applied directly using the Constitution. These are the concept of personal freedom expressed in Article 31 of the Constitution, the freedom to determine one's personal life, to bring up one's children according to one's personal preference and the right to privacy (Articles 47 and 48).[25] These rights are often also expressed in other legal provisions, but their constitutional framework is sufficient to provide protection for individuals. Further, it is certainly possible to envisage a civil law remedy for breaches of someone's constitutional rights (both by the public authorities – in the vertical dimension, and by other individuals – in the horizontal dimension).[26] Another crucial role of the Constitution is that of providing the source of inspiration and guidance as to the meaning of the general clauses used by civil law (these are mentioned below), especially the 'principles of community life' and 'proper conduct'.

20. The key source of private law in general and also civil law including tort is the Civil Code of 1964.[27] The Code constitutes a sort of a private law map, with most private law areas regulated at least to some extent, and references to further,

24. M. Safjan, *Źródła Prawa Prywatnego,* 168.
25. *Ibid.*, 181.
26. *Ibid.*
27. Act of 23 Apr. 1964 *Kodeks Cywilny*, Dz.U. 1964 No. 16, item 93.

more detailed regulations outside the Code. Unlike many classic civil codes, however, it does not regulate family law. The Civil Code contains four Books: General Provisions (Book One), Property and Other Rights in Rem (Book Two), Obligations (Book Three) and Wills (Book Four). There also are individual codes concerning family law (Family and Care Code of 1964) and parts of trade law (Trading Companies Code of 2000). Specific aspects of private law are also regulated by a large number of separate legislative acts. While the Civil Code is the main source of private law, its formal status as a source of legal rules is not above these other codes or pieces of legislation.

In common with the civil law systems of Western Europe and contrary to common law jurisdictions, Polish law views tort as part of the wider conceptual category of the 'law of obligations'. Indeed, the concept is referred to as 'delict' *(delikt)* (this in scholarly writings) or 'prohibited act' (in written law). Chapter VI of the Civil Code employs the term 'prohibited conduct (act)' (*czyn niedozwolony*), which corresponds to the German *unerlaubte handlung*. This technical term was criticized in legal writings due to the fact that it does not always correspond to its meaning in contemporary language. This terminology dates back to the 1933 Code of Obligations and it was maintained in the Civil Code of 1964 as no better alternative could be agreed upon. There is no doubt that the rules on torts relate not only to human behaviour that is contrary to law or principles of community life, but also to damage inflicted by animals, things, or damage brought about by legal conduct. Thus, they refer to liability for any damage that has been brought about irrespective of a legal relation that previously linked the victim to the person liable for the damage.[28] The term 'prohibited conduct' hence extends to cases of liability based on fault, on risk and on equity. Nevertheless, for reasons of coherence and consistency with the nomenclature used in the rest of Europe, this study uses the notion 'tort'.

In the area of tort law, code-based general rules on tortious liability are supplemented by a number of code-based specific liability rules and by separate statutes which establish other forms of tort liability[29] or regulate specific elements of general tortious liability.

The Civil Code was enacted during the time socialist legal philosophy and doctrine exerted an overwhelming influence on Poland. Thus, while some of its substantive provisions concerning specific legal concepts – including tort liability – were relatively unaffected by the political theme, the spirit and some general provisions of the Code were no doubt products of socialist legal culture. After 1989 the Code was amended a significant number of times. The purpose of these amendments, some of which were very comprehensive, was to eliminate the socialist provisions, to adjust the Code to the developing democratic system and market economy, and also more recently to ensure compliance with the relevant EU laws. Polish private law is increasingly complex and its scope and contents are much greater. The Civil Law Codification Commission – the law reform body presided by the late Professor Zbigniew Radwański embarked on a long process of drafting an

28. *See* in general Z. Radwański, *Zobowiązania – część ogólna* (C.H. Beck, 2004); W. Czachórski, *Zobowiązania. Zarys wykładu (*Lexis Nexis, 2004), M. Nesterowicz *Kodeks cywilny z komentarzem*, Vol. 1 (Warszawa, 1989), W. Warkałło, *Odpowiedzialnosc odszkodowawcza* (Warszawa, 1972).
29. For instance: environmental liability, liability for genetically modified products, or nuclear liability.

entirely new Civil Code. The Commission adopted a very systematic approach, with a number of separate subject committees consisting of prominent scholars working on specific subject matters. 'The Green Paper' specifying the starting points of analysis and aims of the new codification was adopted by the Commission in 2006.[30] While the new Code is meant to coherently and concisely regulate most areas of civil law, its contents are not dissimilar to the current Code. Often the former simply reorders and reorganizes the latter.

21. Private law features strongly within the legislative interests of the EU, and various EU law instruments are also sources of private law in Poland. This includes the Treaty on European Union and the Treaty on the Functioning of the European Union,[31] EU regulations, as well as EU directives which have been implemented into Polish law, in particular Consumer Contracts Directives and the Product Liability Directive.[32]

22. Last but not least, it is important to briefly examine here the concept of 'general clauses', as they play an important role within private law as well as tort law. The concept and framework of Polish general clauses are outside the scope of direct sources of law, and yet they are relevant with regard to the contents of some legal provisions, their legal effects and interpretation.

During socialism the general clauses used before World War II (especially 'proper conduct') were replaced by clauses which were seen as more suitable for a socialist legal and a social order. The most prevalent clauses were the principles of community life (which can also be translated as principles of social coexistence). Indeed, the Constitution of 1952 contained a general requirement for all citizens to respect the principles of community life (Article 90). Another clause was the socio-economic aim of a right – used, alongside the principles of community life, in the provision of the Civil Code regulating abuse of rights (Article 5). The notion of abuse of rights is examined in some detail in a further part of this study (*see* General Introduction, Chapter 2. §7).

Perhaps surprisingly both these clauses remain in the Civil Code until today, although the new Constitution of 1997 no longer contains the general requirement to respect the principles of community life. It appears that after the amendments of the Civil Code in 1990[33] all the political undertones of the principles of community life and the socio-economic aim of a right disappeared. This was confirmed and the status of these two was clauses reaffirmed in a recent decision of the Constitutional Tribunal. The decision concerned the concept of abuse of rights, but the main issue were the two clauses which set the limits of application of Article 5 of the Civil

30. The Green Paper adopted by the Polish Civil Law Codification Commission (2006) is available online in English at: <http://www.ejcl.org/112/greenbookfinal-2.pdf>.
31. Consolidated versions available at: http://eur-lex.europa.eu/JOHtml.do?uri=OJ:C:2012:326:SOM:EN:HTML.
32. Council Directive 85/374/EEC on the approximation of the laws, regulations and administrative provisions of the Member States concerning liability for defective products of 25 Jul. 1985, OJ L 210, 7.8.85, P. 29–33.
33. Act of 28 Jul. 1990, Dz.U. of 1990, No. 55, item 321.

Code.[34] The Tribunal held that the general clauses of the socio-economic aim of a right and of principles of community life, while introduced during the socialist period, can and should be interpreted in the changing socio-economic reality.[35]

How relevant are these clauses at present? The socio-economic aim of a right, when introduced in 1964, was primarily meant to deal with property rights which were quite unique under socialism. The Civil Code at the time differentiated between forms of property (social property, private property), ascribing to them different socio-economic aims. At present, the Code no longer strictly specifies socio-economic aims of rights, and thus many voices in favour of abandoning this general clause and replacing it with another (for instance the principle of honesty in trading[36]) appeared. Some scholars emphasize that in the new political and economic system the law ought not to regulate aims of rights. They claim that social market economy, based on freedom of economic activity and respect of private property (Article 20 of the Constitution of 1997) should entail that the essence of a right is a personal choice of the person who is entrusted with the right. However, the majority view is still in favour of maintaining the clause, especially that similar clauses are used in other legal systems: for instance in France or Switzerland.[37] It is seen as a valuable tool to determine the manner in which a particular right ought to be used.

The principles of community life lost their political burden and in spite of some calls for their elimination feature strongly in some provisions of the Civil Code and in jurisprudence. They are present in a number of crucial provisions of the Code, for instance: Article 5 on abuse of rights (mentioned above), Article 56 concerning legal acts (*czynnosci prawne*) and their effects (specifying that consequences of legal acts are determined by these acts, but also by law, by custom and by principles of community life) and Article 58 on circumstances entailing that a legal act is void (when it is contrary to law or to principles of community life). More importantly, principles of equity form an exceptional, subsidiary basis of tort liability in the following three cases: Article 417^2 (public authority liability), Article 428 (liability for minors and incapacitated persons), Article 431 §2 (liability for animals).

At present, the legislator when revising the existing Code rules refers to 'principles of equity/fairness' (*zasady sluszności*) instead of 'the principles of community life'. It also appears that the practical application and interpretation of the existing provisions containing the principles becomes more and more in line with other general clauses, especially the one which can be translated as 'proper conduct' or 'good faith'(*dobre obyczaje*), widely used in Polish civil law during the Second Republic (1918–1939). They are grounded in the provisions of the Constitution, and especially Article 20, but also in moral values which transcend borders and have a more universal application.[38] They are seen as generally accepted moral standards of conduct in society.

---

34. Decision of 17 Oct. 2000, SK 5/99, published in Orzeczenia Trybunału Konstytucyjnego (OTK) 2000, No. 7, item 254..
35. Decision of 17 Oct. 2000, at p. 1214.
36. *See* T. Justynski *Naduzycie prawa w polskim prawie cywilnym* (Kraków, 2000), 117.
37. *See* M. Pyziak-Szafnicka *Prawo podmiotowe,* in M. Safjan (ed.) *System Prawa Prywatnego. Tom I. Część Ogólna,* 2nd Edition (CH Beck, Instytut Nauk Prawnych PAN, 2012), 902–903.
38. *See* Z. Radwański & M. Zielinski, *Normy i przepisy prawa cywilnego,* In Marek Safjan (ed.) *System*

In practice the application of 'proper conduct' is very close to the interpretation of principles of community life. Proper conduct also refers to moral values accepted generally in society, drawing inspiration from the provisions of the Constitution. Proper conduct is also close to understanding and interpreting the notion of 'good faith', albeit only when the latter is understood objectively (as an external assessment of someone's conduct, not an inquiry into his intentions and knowledge). Polish legislation and its commentators prefer the notion of proper conduct to good faith, mostly for reasons of historical continuity, coherence and clarity.

§3. Function of the Law of Torts (Indemnification; Prevention; Sanction)

23. The development of mature, stable market economies and democracies grounded in the ideas of welfare state, free market and fair competition entailed the recognition of complexity of functions of tort liability in Western Europe, and earlier in the US. Poland is now also heading towards these models. The contemporary developments challenge the traditional polarity of views between those who advocated the role of tort as a compensation mechanism and those who argued that its main role was deterrence and prevention. Traditionally throughout Europe and beyond one could observe a dichotomy between civil law states on the one hand, and common law jurisdictions on the other. While civil law countries such as Poland or France approached tort law as a compensatory mechanism (prioritizing the distributive justice postulate), English and, more generally, common law saw it much more as a behaviour modification measure (corrective justice). At present, the approach to the functions of tort has become more intricate.

While the debate between the economic theories of efficient incentives and costs reduction and the traditional tort theories of compensation still continues, a strong tendency to reconcile them can be noticed in the current academic thought across Europe and beyond. A more multidimensional, multidisciplinary, multilevel approach transpires from contemporary writings in the US and in Western Europe. On the one hand, functions of tort law are expanded to cover, in addition to compensation of losses and prevention, also 'punishment, vindication, redress of the social order, implementation of legal rules, protection of citizens' rights, recognition and creation of new rights and interests, appeasement of the victim (…), loss spreading, loss shifting, allocation of losses (…), prevention, precaution, reduction of accident costs, justice (compensatory justice, retributive justice, corrective justice)'.[39] On the other hand, tort law finds itself a part of an increasingly complex system of laws, regulations and practices aimed at fulfilling the same functions (such as public regulatory systems, private insurance products, social insurance and other welfare state mechanisms). This complexity and interdependence are only

Prawa Prywatnego. Tom I. Część Ogolna 2nd Edition (C.H. Beck, Instytut Nauk Prawnych PAN, 2012), 96.

39. H. Cousy, *Tort Liability and Liability Insurance: A Difficult Relationship* in *European Tort Law 2001*, 18–55, 23 (H. Koziol & B. Steininger eds, Vienna, New York: Springer, 2002).

starting to appear in Poland, followed or inspired by scholarly writings on tort systems. The reason for the delay was that during socialism tort law played an entirely different role and its application led to different outcomes than in Western European systems.

24. At the time when in the 'West' the welfare state policies played a very significant part in developing the approach to tort, in the 'East' the socialist political ideals and centrally planned market philosophy were overwhelmingly influential. Socialist systems saw compensation as well as market regulation to be best ensured by state-controlled mechanisms placed outside of the realm of private law, and thus the role of tort was very limited indeed. At some level tort law was acceptable because it furthered the state's aim of deterrence and prevention of accidents, especially with regard to private market actors who never entirely disappeared from the market. Scholars emphasized the preventive aspect of damages, and one could even find emphasis on the role of vengeance in tort writings at the time.[40] In particular, A. Szpunar observed the educational role of the provisions on torts, which give guidelines of social behaviour. However, the preventive aspects of tort law were mitigated by the developments of insurance.[41] Further, compensating accidents often took part outside the scope of tort systems – through social measures which included state-provided health care, or through statutory insurance (for instance motor insurance). This compensation was comprehensive and almost universally available. The types of damage which were in fact recoverable in tort were much more limited than what one could expect from an ordinary tort system. If damage occurred as a result of a tort, socialist law focused rather on specific performance than on damages. It was generally agreed that pecuniary incentives were incapable of compensating torts. They reduced the income of undertakings – hence the investment fund and the participation fund of the employees, and central planning did not often allow for purchase of substitutes with the money deriving from damages. Even if compensation was awarded, it was very low indeed, at least in comparison with awards for similar types of damage in Western Europe.

The policy shift away from strict socialism and towards a more market-driven approach took place in Poland in early 1980s. The outcome of the reforms was a blend of market philosophy, limited consumerism and a peculiar approach to welfare policies, as well as the remaining elements of socialist central planning. Market measures were increasingly trusted to control market behaviour. Thus, the trust in administrative mechanisms, and legal measures such as tort liability, to fulfil the functions of deterrence decreased. The role of the law of obligations was growing. Courts started building new forms of tort liability based on the general civil liability provisions of the civil codes, reflecting the market-focused transformations (such as product liability). The language of courts and legal scholars became focused on compensating injuries and damages.

25. The regulatory and institutional rebalancing which started before the demise of socialism was reinforced in the early 1990s. The importance of tort grew together

40. W. Warkallo, *Odpowiedzialnosc odszkodowawcza*, 13.
41. A. Szpunar, *Czyny niedozwolone w kodeksie cywilnym*, Studia Cywilistyczne 31/1970, 36.

with the importance of private law in general. The authorities attempt to efficiently control markets and their participants in the face of the reinforced need for protection of private property, greater protection of individual health, safety, privacy and dignity and a greater emphasis on the monetary satisfaction of wrongs (especially in the light of relaxation of the systems of social insurance which were very prominent during socialism). Consequently, it is the compensatory role of tort which is increasingly emphasized. Continuing the tendency which occurred during the period of socialist market-focused reforms, liability standards are becoming more objective or even strict, the scope of recoverable damage is being extended, and the policy aims of compensation are increasingly applied when assessing causation. These developments have been occurring in the legislative sphere as well as in the judicial decisions. Compensation awards are growing in significance, scope and numbers. Compensation extends upon pecuniary as well as non-pecuniary losses. The latter were somewhat controversial under socialism. Judicial decisions emphasize the compensatory aim of both, even though non-pecuniary losses are difficult to quantify or attribute a sum of money to. The Civil Code prescribes the possibility of claiming compensation for non-pecuniary losses in specified cases (Articles 24, 445, 446 §4, 446^2 and 448). It also offers an option of asking for a sum of money to be paid to a social cause chosen by the victim. The role of the latter remedy is also seen as compensatory, as it fulfils the victim's sense of justice.[42]

New political and economic systems often require a new approach to tort. This is increasingly recognized in Polish doctrinal writings. At the same time as civil liability rules are being reconsidered and reformed, they are becoming surrounded by a plethora of other legal mechanisms aimed at providing compensation, deterring undesirable market behaviour[43] or insuring risks and liability.[44] Poland is gradually adjusting its insurance law to the law of Western European states, also by implementing various pieces of EU legislation in this area. Crucial Polish laws concerning insurance are: a series of Acts of 22 May 2003 – on insurance business, on compulsory insurance, the Insurance Guarantee Fund Polish Bureau of Traffic Insurers, on the control of insurance and of retirement funds, and on the Insurance Ombudsman and on insurance brokerage.[45] While the role of the law of obligations in shaping behaviour and compensating losses is becoming more grounded, the next step for Poland is the recognition of the complexity of market economies and interrelationships between the law of obligations and other mechanisms fulfilling similar

42. M. Pazdan, *Dobra osobiste i ich ochrona*, in Marek Safjan (ed.) *System Prawa Prywatnego. Tom I. Część Ogólna*, 2nd Edition (C.H. Beck, Instytut Nauk Prawnych PAN, 2012), 1286.
43. For instance – a very comprehensive product safety regime is being adopted – implementing the European Union product safety laws (http://ec.europa.eu/consumers/safety/prod_legis/index_en.htm).
44. N. Perram, *The Law of Torts in Eastern Europe and the Vital Role of Liability Insurance in an Emerging Market Economy*, 18 Rev. of C. & E. Eur. L. 253 (1992).
45. Dz.U. of 2003 No. 124 at p. 1151.

roles. The multidimensional approach to civil liability aims (mentioned above) only very recently started featuring in academic and policy papers.[46]

In the recent years the doctrinal views have rightly pointed out that although the main function of civil liability in Polish law is still compensation for damage, the other functions, i.e., punishment and deterrence, are particularly important in compensating for infringement of personal rights.[47] The admission of the idea that compensation for harm can serve a punitive and/or deterrent function was usually made in connection with a claim for a money payment to a social cause. Under Article 448 KC, in cases of a violation of personal rights, victims have a choice between filing a claim for damages for themselves or for a social purpose. According to a minority view, the latter claim, despite its satisfactory character, aims at penalizing the perpetrator as well as at prevention and deterrence. A fresh look at the functions of tort law was taken in a recent SN judgment of 21 February 2020.[48] The court held that civil law sanctions must be proportionate (in light of the constitutional standard) and do not aim at punishing the tortfeasor. In the facts of the case, the circumstances were typical for a violation of personal rights by media; the aim of the defendant's news magazine was solely to gain profits and to increase the number of copies of the magazine sold. The court underlined that punitive and deterrent functions are 'derivative' of the compensatory function. The punitive function of tort law is fulfilled when a tortfeasor is liable for fault or at least for unlawful conduct. The degree of fault may affect the extent of the damage and – as a result – the amount of compensation. The Supreme Court referred to the decision of 27 March 2019 (V CSK 77/18) in which it was stated that the retributive nature of compensation manifests itself in the fact that the sanction should be appropriate to the act committed. When considering the punitive function, a court should take into account the financial situation and the behaviour of the tortfeasor after inflicting the harm, as well as whether the latter has taken steps to remedy the consequences of their wrongful actions. In order to determine the amount of compensation for a violation of personal rights, the aim of the wrongful conduct should be taken into consideration (in particular, the aim such as to increase readership and gain financial or other benefits). The discussed functions are intertwined. Neither the punitive, nor the deterrent, function is fulfilled if a compensation award is too low in relation to the financial benefits gained by the tortfeasor. The amount of damages should be such as to be financially significant for the person liable for the violation. As far as the press publisher is concerned, a sufficiently high award fulfils a punitive function, which in turn also increases deterrence. The degree to which compensation for non-pecuniary loss should also serve to deter and punish the wrongdoer depends on several factors. Crucial are the seriousness of the infringement of personal rights, intentional fault, poor motives, an awareness of the unlawfulness of the conduct or a desire to achieve financial benefits. Moreover, a deterrent effect of compensation

46. M. Kalinski, *Odpowiedzialnosc odszkodowawcza,* 68–75; Joanna Kuźmicka – Sulikowska, *Zasady Odpowiedzialności Deliktowej w Świetle Nowych Tendencji w Ustawodawstwie Polskim* (Wolters Kluwers Polska, 2011), and L. Nowakowski '*Ubezpieczenia odpowiedzialności cywilnej*' (civil liability insurance) (Poltext, 2004).
47. A. Śmieja, in: A. Olejniczak (ed.), *System Prawa Prywatnego*, vol. 6 (2018) 741 ff.
48. I CSK 565/18, OSNC 2020/12, item 105, reported by E. Bagińska/P. Wyszyńska-Ślufińska, *Poland*, in: E. Karner/B.C. Steininger (eds), *European Tort Law 2020* (2021) 475, Nos 2–13.

should be considered if the risk of further infringements is high, such as in the case when personal rights can be infringed within the framework of a business activity and in order to increase profits. In conclusion, the court held that, in the case of a grave violation of personal rights, a compensatory award which is too low in relation to the financial gains sought or gained by the tortfeasor cannot be regarded as fulfilling punitive, deterrent and compensatory functions of compensation for non-pecuniary harm.

If we read the judgment to say that the compensation must be sufficiently high to deter the tortfeasor, otherwise the protection of personal rights would be illusory, it deserves full approval. It should be borne in mind – as the court emphasized – that the amount of compensation should not exclusively serve punitive and deterrent functions and should not be 'disconnected' from the type of infringed rights and the extent of damage. The punitive function does not prevail over the compensatory function of civil law sanctions, although it is now certainly gaining importance. Many decisions of common courts indicate that if personal rights were infringed as a result of the publication of press materials, compensation must provide a perceptible sanction to the tortfeasor. On a general note, the directive of taking account of the profits gained or sought by the tortfeasor as well as his intentional fault recalls the idea embedded in a claim for aggravated damages in *common law* or in the French concept of *faute lucrative*. The judgment of the Supreme Court presented above certainly marks the beginning of a new and bold approach of the Supreme Court to media misconduct cases.

§4. Relationship Between Torts and Criminal Law

26. In general, both criminal law and tort law protect individual rights and interests. Because of the common aim Polish tort law writings emphasize that basic concepts, such as fault, causation, should not be marked by any essential differences. Nevertheless, the scope of protection of individual interests is different in each of the branches of law. This is justified by the fact that they fulfil varying functions (*see supra* nos 23–25 for elaboration of functions of tort liability).[49] The protection granted by civil law is broader than that afforded by criminal law. As a rule, however, the amount of damages may not exceed the scope of damage or enrich the injured party.

Obviously, not all torts are penalized by criminal law sanctions. Also, not every offence is at the same time a civil wrongfulness (tort). However, if a tort constitutes an offence, criminal punishment does not pre-empt civil claims.

The deterrence function of the law of torts is much stronger in types of liability based on fault. However, criminal liability may only be imposed when the actor committed a fault; there may be no criminal liability based on risk (strict liability) or on equity principles. Finally, tort law does not aim at penalizing the wrongdoer.

---

49. A. Szpunar, *Czyny niedozwolone w kodeksie cywilnym*, 37.

This notwithstanding, a clear convergence of the meaning of 'fault', so-called normative, objective definition of fault, needs to be noted here, albeit the criteria that determine fault may vary in tort cases and criminal cases.[50]

As a rule, civil proceedings are most appropriate for filing a claim for damages. However, if the tort that gives rise to damage is simultaneously a criminal offence, the victim may use an alternative way to seek compensation in the criminal proceedings. Namely, the penal code (*kodeks karny*, KK) allows the court to apply an additional criminal sanction which takes a form of an obligation to repair pecuniary damage directly arising from the criminal conduct (with the exception of a rent) and compensation for non-pecuniary loss (Article 46 §1 KK). The court can order full or partial compensation. Adhesion procedure is not available under the present law on criminal proceedings.

27. The penal code provides for various measures against the perpetrators, including penalties and so-called additional punishments. There are two additional punishments of a compensatory nature that may be ordered by a criminal court:

(1) obligation to redress damage, including compensation for non-pecuniary harm (Article 46 §1 KK), but excluding any annuities;
(2) punitive monetary satisfaction for non-pecuniary damage (*nawiązka*) – capped at PLN 200,000 (Articles 46 §2 and 48 KK).

The obligation to redress damage (fully or partially) requires proof of actual damage. If it is too burdensome to provide such a proof, a criminal court may instead award the punitive monetary satisfaction in the amount of up to PLN 200,000 to the wronged party, and in the event of his/her death as a result of the offence committed by the convicted person – a payment in favour of the closest person, whose life situation has significantly deteriorated due to the death of the wronged party. In the case when more than one such person has been identified, the compensation shall be ordered in favour of each of them. The duty to redress damage is a criminal sanction that may be imposed in addition to other penalties or in the place of such penalties. However, it may never be imposed once the damage has already been redressed, be it by the victim herself or by the insurer. On the contrary, should the scope of damage exceed the award made by the criminal court, the victim may still bring additional claims before a civil court (Article 46 §3 KK). This possibility is important if the victim claims an annuity, as the latter is excluded from the jurisdiction of criminal courts.

Until 2010, Article 46 §1 KK referred to a claim for 'reparation of damage' with respect to limited offences only, and in addition provided for a punitive monetary sanction on the basis of Article 46 §2 KK.

A problem arose with respect to a particular category of cases, namely road traffic accidents and the third-party insurance coverage of perpetrators who were sentenced for traffic offences and additionally punished by the criminal court in one of the two ways mentioned above.

---

50. J. Dąbrowa, *Wina jako przesłanka odpowiedzialnosci cywilnej* (Wrocław, 1968), s. 155.

With respect to punitive/exemplary damages (*nawiązka*) the Supreme Court in the judgment of 21 December 2006[51] ruled that the insurer's liability did not cover potential criminal liability of the insured and thus the insurer was not liable to repay the insured the sums paid by him as a criminal sanction (*nawiązka*) to the relatives of the victim killed in a car accident. The court correctly emphasized the differences between the functions and structure of the sanctions. These differences are the following:

– The normative scope of the guarantee liability of the insurer in traffic accident liability insurance contracts is limited to civil liability of any person who, while driving a car during the period envisaged in the contract, caused damage to anyone. While the damages are paid within the limits of civil liability of the insured, the criminal sanctions may go beyond the limits of full compensation, thus beyond the limit of the insurer's liability.
– The availability of sanctions of a compensatory nature in criminal proceedings gives no ground for alleging convergence of civil and criminal liability. The legal basis of compensatory sanctions is in the provisions of the Penal Code, and the subsidiary use of the provisions of the Civil Code considers solely the notion of damage, its scope and the manner of its redress. Moreover, criminal proceedings are not the 'court proceedings in which the recovery for damage is sought' in the meaning of insurance law; in fact, unlike in a civil suit, the insurer may not intervene in a criminal suit.
– Sanctions imposed by a criminal court, despite their compensatory character, constitute a specific penal reaction. They aim at penalizing the perpetrator, as well as at prevention and deterrence. A criminal court may refrain from application of the principle of full compensation and hence reduce or increase the compensatory sanctions according to the sentencing guidelines and in consideration of facts such as the perpetrator's financial standing. Hence, the said sanctions are quite different from sanctions that may be imposed on a tortfeasor by a civil court.

With reference to the obligation to redress damage imposed by a criminal court, the Supreme Court in the judgment of 13 July 2011[52] ruled that a tortfeasor responsible for a car accident, sentenced to pay damages on the basis of Articles 46 §1 and 39 (5) KK has a claim for reimbursement from his/her traffic liability insurer. According to the court a liability insurer is contractually liable to repay the insured the sums paid as compensation. The punitive function of this 'additional punishment' does not prevail over its compensatory function. The court emphasized that the normative scope of the insurer's liability under traffic accident liability insurance is dependent upon and limited to the amount of the civil liability of the insured. Furthermore, the victim may sue the insurer directly (*actio directa* –), but may not recover twice (e.g., where the insurer pays before the criminal court imposes the duty to redress the damage, typically after a lengthy trial). No exclusion or limitation to the insurer's liability may be inferred from Article 822 KC and Article 34 of

51. III CZP 129/06, OSN 10/2007, item 151.
52. III CZP 31/11, OSP 4/2012, item 43.

the Law on Compulsory Insurance of 2003 merely because the duty to repair damage has been imposed by a criminal court. Hence, it is irrelevant whether compensation is paid voluntarily or enforced through a judgment of a civil or a criminal court; otherwise it would be totally in the hands of the victim whether the tortfeasor or his insurer bears the burden of compensation.

On 8 June 2010 a new version of Article 46 KK came into force, pursuant to which a criminal court may award a victim of any offence compensation for non-pecuniary loss (*nawiązka*).[53] The award is mandatory if the victim or the next of kin demanded compensation, and discretionary if no such claim was filed. For the sake of avoiding the aggregate of monetary sanctions and damages for moral harm that might be adjudicated by a criminal court either for the benefit of the victim or for a social cause, *nawiązka* may only be granted to the victim (Article 46 §2, Article 57a §2 KK), and if he is unknown – to the Assistance for Crime Victims and Post-penitentiary Help Fund. If the perpetrator is convicted of an intentional offence against life or health or another intentional offence resulting in the death of a human being, serious bodily injury, violation of bodily organ functions or health disorder, the court may order a sum of money to be paid to the Fund for Victims' Aid and Post-Penitentiary Aid (Article 47 § 1 KK).

Until the amendment of the criminal law regulations in 2015,[54] this institution of *nawiązka* was included in the category of penal measures, and it consequently fulfilled various functions, not only the function of compensation but also of deterrence and repression. Currently, the main emphasis in the doctrine has been placed on its compensatory function. In order for it to be applied, it is required that all prerequisites for imposing the obligation to redress damage are met. *Nawiązka* is useful in cases where the court is not able to estimate even an approximate amount of damage or harm caused. In principle, the only difference between *nawiązka* and the obligation to compensate for damage is that its amount is not statutorily determined by the extent of damage caused by the offence. They both fulfil, although to a different degree, compensatory function. Nevertheless, the payment of compensation is ancillary to the obligation to make reparation, since the latter is intended to fully satisfy the interests of the injured party and is therefore of superior importance to the payment of *nawiązka*. A joint application of *nawiązka* and the obligation to compensate for damage is unacceptable.[55]

The changes which the legislator has recently introduced in the area of standardization of measures for compensation of pecuniary and non-pecuniary damage on the grounds of criminal law have resulted in the fact that the wronged party may, in the majority of cases, successfully avoid a separate civil lawsuit and more quickly obtain satisfaction of his/her claims through a criminal lawsuit. In the light of the amendments also the removal from the Code of Criminal Procedure of provisions

53. The Act of 5 Nov. 2009 on the Revision of the Penal Code and other Acts, Dz.U. of 2009, No. 206, item 1589.
54. The Act of 20 Feb. 2015 amending the Act – Criminal Code and certain other acts (Journal of Laws of 2015, item 396).
55. P. Bróżek, Obowiązek naprawienia szkody lub zadośćuczynienie za doznaną krzywdę – główna czy jedyna forma kompensacji szkody na rzecz pokrzywdzonego na gruncie prawa karnego? [Obligation to redress pecuniary damage or compensation for non-pecuniary damage: main or sole form of compensation to an injured party under criminal law?], Prokuratura I prawo 9/2021, 126 ff.

regulating the so-called adhesion claim, as well as the provision which authorized the court to award compensation ex officio is of significant importance. However, it can be considered that the evolution of solutions in the discussed respect has not yet been fully completed.[56]

28. In the case of parallel proceedings brought by the victim of a tort, the civil court may suspend its proceedings on its own motion if it finds that the outcome of the suit may depend on the finding in the criminal suit (Article 177 §1 section 4 KPC). Should a criminal court establish liability first and the victim file a separate action in a civil court, the conviction will be binding on the civil court. According to Article 11 KPC a civil court in a subsequent civil action must abide by the convicting sentence of a criminal court as to the commission of an offence. Hence, if criminal fault has been established, the civil court may not decide otherwise. A person who was not indicted, however, may rely on a civil suit in any circumstance that would limit or exclude her civil liability. The civil court decides on its own as to the consequences of the criminal act and the scope of compensation; it hears evidence and assesses the evidence de novo.

§5. Relationship Between Contractual and Tortious Responsibility

29. Polish law does not know the *non cumul* principle. Thus, according to Article 443 KC, a tort claim is possible even if the conduct in question was a breach of an existing contract between the parties (unless the contract specifies otherwise). This approach was advocated by Polish scholars and was followed by the judiciary even before the enactment of the 1964 Civil Code. In the decision of 26 October 1956 the Supreme Court confirmed that in cases of breaches of contracts, claimants may use tortious or contractual liability as a legal basis of their claims.[57]

Contractual and tortious liability are clearly separated, both in written law and in scholarly writings. These two liability regimes are in many respects independent and distinct from one another, and yet they remain subject to some common rules and principles applicable to the law of obligations in general. They are contained in Book Three of the Civil Code ('Law of Obligations'), but placed in two different Titles: Title III – 'General rules on contractual obligations', and Title VI – 'Illicit Acts' (*czyny niedozwolone*). Title I which regulates general matters within the area of obligations applies to both. It contains provisions concerning determination of extent of liability and compensation, through defining causation (Article 361 §1), the principle of full compensation (Article 361 §2), contributory negligence (Article 362) and acceptable forms of compensating damage (Article 363), all of which are examined in further parts of this study.

30. The key differences between contractual and tortious liability pertain to the following issues:

---

56. *Ibid.*, 135 ff.
57. Judgment of the Civil Chamber of the SN of 26 Oct. 1956, OSN 1958, item 1.

- burden of proof of fault (which in tortious liability rests upon the claimant, and in contractual liability which uses presumption of fault it is to be disproved by the defendant);
- scope of recoverable damage (with non-pecuniary damage only recoverable under tort law); and
- limitation periods.

It is important to point out here that while the Code allows contractual parties to circumvent the choice of liability (Article 443 applies 'unless the contract between the parties stipulates otherwise'), such contractual clauses must comply with the law and with the principles of community life.[58] Polish law respects the principle of freedom of contract, provided that the contents and aims of the contract do not contravene the very nature of the contract, the law, or the principles of community life (Article 353 §1 KC). In consumer contracts they would also now be under scrutiny of the provisions of the Unfair Contract Terms Directive.[59] The Directive was implemented into the Civil Code by the Act on Protection of Certain Consumer Rights and Liability for Dangerous Products.[60]

Courts have established that inflicting bodily injury upon a person always constitutes a tort. If this is caused by a failure to perform or an improper performance of an existing obligation, the wrongdoer may be liable either *ex contractu* or *ex delicto*.

31. The practical implications of this approach to the relationship between tortious and contractual liability are significant in some areas of law. For example, liability of a privately contracted physician is contractual (Article 471 KC) in conjunction with tortious liability (Article 415 KC). The victim has a choice between the contractual or the delictual basis of her claim. Hence, the source of civil liability of a physician may be either a tort or a contract between the former and the patient, or a contract between a patient and a medical care establishment. Product liability law is also a good example. Some of the first product liability cases, involving defective cars, were brought by buyers against sellers. Yet, courts found that a tortious claim was possible even if providing a defective car was a breach of a contract of sale.[61] Following these decisions courts moved to using tort law in product liability cases.

32. The concept of *culpa in contrahendo* (pre-contractual liability) has undergone a very significant change in Poland recently. Until the Act of 14 February 2003[62] *culpa in contrahendo* was not regulated by the Civil Code in general. There were provisions concerning specific conditions where such liability would be possible: for instance in case a party knew of the impossibility of performance at the

---

58. W. Czachórski, *Zobowiązania. Zarys Wykładu*, 8th ed., 273 (Lexis Nexis, 2002).
59. Council Directive 93/13/EEC on 5 Apr. 1993 on unfair terms in consumer contracts, OJ L 0/95, 21.04.1993, P. 0029–0034.
60. Act of 2 Mar. 2000, published in Dz.U. of 2000, No. 22, item 271.
61. For a detailed analysis *see*: M. Tulibacka, *Product Liability Law in Transition. A Central European Perspective*, 178, 189, and 199–201 (Ashgate Publishing, 2009).
62. Act of 14 Feb. 2003, Dz.U. of 2003, No. 48, item 408. In force since 25 Sep. 2003.

time of concluding the contract (Article 387 §2 KC), or if a party whose profession it is to accept commissions to perform tasks does not wish to perform a certain task and yet makes a different impression (Article 736). More generally, *culpa in contrahendo* was seen by a majority of scholars as a type of tortious liability.[63] As such, it was based on the general tortious liability provision of Article 415 which requires proof of fault of the defendant.

Since the new Article 72 §2 KC came into force in 2003, fault is no longer the necessary requirement of liability of those whose conduct during contractual negotiations caused losses to the other party. Article 72 §2 specifies that a party, who commenced or proceeded with negotiations against the principle of proper conduct, especially when there was no intention to conclude a contract, 'is liable to the other party for losses sustained because the latter expected that the contract would be concluded'. It appears that the liability lost its tortious nature. The provision is not placed in the Title of the Code concerning tort liability, or in Book Three: 'Obligations'. Indeed, Article 72 can be found in Book One: 'General Provisions'. This emphasizes its distinct character. Further, it is not fault liability, nor is it strict liability. It is dependent upon a party negotiating against the rules of proper conduct.

The scope of recoverable compensation is limited to what scholars refer to as the 'negative interest of the contract'. Thus, a person who was under the impression that the contract would be concluded can recover costs incurred during negotiations, for instance, costs of telephone calls, travel, preparation of contractual documents, legal assistance and translation and any official charges incurred in the preparation of the transaction. While the 'positive interest of the contract' includes everything the victim would have obtained if the contract was performed properly, the negative interest focuses on the fact that the contract was not concluded at all, and thus it is considered that compensation of the latter is not always very high. There is no consensus among scholars and the judiciary whether the compensation ought also to cover the potential profits and other benefits which would follow a contract potentially concluded with someone else. However, if there is sufficient proof that another contract would have been concluded (such as an offer from another potential contracting party) there seem to exist no obstacles for compensating profits and benefits which would thus have been obtained.[64]

§6. Protected Interests

33. The Civil Code follows the French *Code Civile* with its approach to tort liability based on a general fault-based clause, and not the Germanic concept of 'protected interests'. No list of legally protected interests similar to the German BGB is to be found in the Civil Code. The Code contains a general tort provision (*infra* no. 38) which specifies that those who cause damage to others should repair

63. W. Czachorski, *Zobowiązania. Zarys Wykładu* (*Obligations. A textbook*), 8th ed. (Lexis Nexis, 2002), 169.

64. M. Kalinski *Odpowiedzialnosc odszkodowawcza* in A. Olejniczak (ed.) *System Prawa Prywatnego: Prawo Zobowiązań. Część Ogólna*, Vol. 6, [Warszawa: Wydawnictwo C.H. Beck, Instytut Nauk Prawnych PAN, Warszawa, 2009), 109.

it. The scope of liability as well as damages do not depend in any way on the basis of the actor's liability, nor on the type or degree of the actor's fault (intent/negligence). In the Civil Code, the scope of liability is determined by Articles 361–363 KC (property damage) and Articles 444–449 KC (with respect to personal injury). Material (pecuniary) loss is to be compensated in every case, while non-pecuniary loss is compensable when law permits it. Pure economic loss is compensated when it falls within the category of lost profits.

34. In Polish law there is no legal definition of damage. Traditionally, damage is considered to be wrong upon any interest or value protected by law, be it property or personal interests,[65] suffered by a person against her will. Hence, the notion of 'damage' used in general terms (as in 'liability for damage') refers both to pecuniary and non-pecuniary loss. From the general principle of full compensation it follows that all kinds of damage must be compensated. According to Article 361 §2 KC, the scope of damages comprises *damnum emergens* and *lucrum cessans*. They must be established in accordance with the theory of differentiation. Moreover, the adequate causation test (Article 361 §1 KC) relates to both types of damage. Traditionally, there are three heads of compensable damage: damage to person, damage to property and damage to the environment (subject to special rules of Environmental Protection Law).

Although a hierarchy of interests may not be known in written law, certain types of interests are emphasized as deserving special protection in judicial decisions. The Supreme Court held that the level of care required from physicians is higher than ordinary because the subject of their professional activities is a human being and because the effects of wrong treatment are often irreversible.[66] Jurisprudence is also firm on the question of contractual limitation or the exclusion of the actor's liability for personal injury. Any clause that aims at the exclusion or the reduction of liability for personal injury violates the principles of fairness (Article 58 §2 KC) and/or is deemed unfair in a consumer contract (Article 385 §1 KC). Further, written law to some extent emphasizes certain types of interests as especially protected. Personal interests have a particular place in the Polish legal system, therefore any question regarding the scope of protection of personal interests should favour the actual or future victim (such as in the case of contractual clauses aiming at the reduction of liability).[67]

In recent years the problem of the scope of protected interests has risen in connection with family law relations. First of all, the Supreme Court held that strong family bonds should be considered to be a personal right and are protected by the rules of the Civil Code (Articles 24, 448 KC); however, this applies only in exceptional cases when these bonds are broken as a result of the death of the closest member of a family or a serious and permanent injury (*see infra* Part VI, Chapter 4, §1).

65. *See* A. Szpunar, *Ustalenie odszkodowania w prawie cywilnym* (Warszawa, 1975) 36, and A. Szpunar, *Odszkodowanie za szkodę majątkową* (Warszawa, 1998), 22–24.
66. The Court of Appeals in Cracow of 9 Mar. 2001, IACa 124/01, PS 10/2002.
67. *See* A. Smieja, *Umowna modyfikacja deliktowego stosunku odszkodowawczego,* A. Olejniczak (ed.) *System Prawa Prywatnego: Prawo Zobowiązań. Część Ogólna,* Vol. 6, [Warszawa: C.H. Beck, Instytut Nauk Prawnych PAN, Warszawa, 2009); 616.

35. The above tendency has been tested outside of personal injury cases. In 2018 the Supreme Court held that a long-term adultery, resulting in a divorce and the subsequent discovery that all four children were in fact fathered by the mother's *paramour*, is not a violation of personal rights of the husband (loss of reputation and of family bonds).[68] According to the judgment relationships between spouses and children are governed by family law provisions and it is only possible to demand protection of these relationships to the extent that family law so provides. There are no such regulations in the Family and Guardianship Code. Thus, the behaviour of the defendants could only have effects envisaged by family law (a spouse may be found at fault for a marriage breakdown and financial sanctions, such as an obligation to pay maintenance might be imposed). Moreover, the court ruled that there was no infringement of the plaintiff's personal rights, i.e., his reputation, as the defendants' conduct was not aimed at the plaintiff's reputation. Regardless of the assessment of the defendants' behaviour in the light of moral norms, it is necessary to stress that the mere infringement of loyalty and the establishment of intimate relations with other persons cannot constitute the basis for the protection of the plaintiff's personal rights. The court's reasoning was aimed at preventing unjustified complaints by betrayed spouses. According to the court, if the provisions on the protection of personal rights were applicable to adultery, it would lead to unacceptable consequences. The policy argument was decisive and is to a certain extent plausible. Nevertheless, the other arguments raise serious doubts. It should be pointed out that, although relations between spouses and children are regulated in the Family and Guardianship Code, compensation issues in relation to violations of personal interests are governed by the Civil Code. It cannot be approved that the lack of a specific reference to the application of the Civil Code excludes the possibility of compensation for damage if the conditions of civil liability are met. While the violation of the duty of marital fidelity by a wife has consequences resulting from family law, it is hard to find any rules in family law dealing with remedies for lost parental status due to the fault of another.

It is also worth noting a precedent decision of the District Court in Krakow of 7 September 2017 (II Ca 1111/17, unpublished) in which the court awarded compensation for non-pecuniary loss stemming from the death of a dog which had been attacked by another dog. The court held that the emotional bond between the owner and the dog was worthy of protection by tort law and the violation of that bond is an infringement of a personal interest.

68. SN 11 Dec. 2018, IV CNP 31/17, OSNC 2019/9 item 95, OSP 2019/10 item 94.

Part I. Liability for One's Own Acts

Chapter 1. General Principles

§1. Unlawfulness and Fault

36. As mentioned above (no. 34) Polish tort law represents the 'general clause model', not the German 'protected interests model' or the common law-style casuistic approach to torts. The general clause establishes tortious liability based upon fault. It is supplemented by a number of separate provisions located in the Civil Code and in other pieces of legislation which regulate tortious liability in specific situations. While some of them are also based on fault, others are examples of strict liability, absolute liability or liability based on equity.

37. Indeed there are two very similar general clauses in the Civil Code: one for tortious liability of physical (scil. anyone) persons (Article 415) and one for legal persons (Article 416). The latter concerns liability of legal persons for damage caused due to the fault of their 'organs' (*organy* – literal translation). In practice this means that legal persons are liable for actions or omissions of physical persons representing their organs. This liability is limited, however, to the conduct of persons who have been duly appointed as representing the organs of a legal person, and only to those actions or omissions which remain within the persons' authority. Subject to these conditions all the remarks below, although referred directly to physical persons only, are also relevant for liability of legal persons. In fact, Article 415 KC has been more often applied to the liability of legal persons than Article 416 KC. The prerequisite of the legal persons' liability pursuant to Article 415 KC is typically their 'organizational' fault or negligent omission. Some distinct features of liability of legal persons are presented in a further part of the study (Part II, Chapter 1, §3).

Article 415 of the Civil Code, and before it Article 134 of the Code of Obligations of 1933 with exactly the same wording, followed the French Code Civil's Article 1382.[69] By virtue of Article 415:

> Whoever by his fault caused damage to another, is obliged to repair it.

Scholars drafting both the Civil Code and the Code of Obligations discussed the wording of the clause in detail. In particular, the point of some contention was whether the provisions should in fact mention both fault and unlawfulness. The final

69. *'Tout fait quelconque de l'homme, qui cause à autrui un dommage, oblige celui par la faute duquel il est arrive à le réparer'.*

decision was to follow the French example and simply state that a person must be 'at fault'.[70] Yet, scholars and the judiciary agree that two necessary elements (in addition to damage and causation) are needed for liability to be established: the objective element – unlawfulness (wrongfulness – *bezprawnosc*)[71] and the subjective element – fault (*wina*).

38. Until today there has remained lack of consensus as to whether unlawfulness and fault are simply components of a wider notion of fault, or whether fault is a distinct, subjective and narrower notion and unlawfulness is an independent prerequisite of liability. The contemporary tendency is rather to follow the latter approach. However, while some scholars see the two as independent elements of tortious liability,[72] others focus on their common function and their relationship to one another. They point out that unlawfulness is a necessary prerequisite of fault.[73] It appears that this view, emphasizing the relationship between unlawfulness and fault, is the correct one. Only upon satisfactory determination that a person's conduct was unlawful (objectively wrong) can the analysis proceed to determine the person's attitude towards the conduct and its consequences – thus towards establishing whether the conduct was also subjectively wrong.

39. The objective element – unlawfulness – is linked to legally established norms of behaviour. These norms can be generally binding laws, or, also generally binding, other norms of a moral or ethical nature. As far as the former are concerned, in Poland such generally binding laws are: the Constitution, an act of Parliament, a ratified international treaty, a piece of EU law, a regulation, or an act of local law (Article 87 of the Constitution) (*see* no. 13 for further explanation of sources of Polish law). They can be placed within any area of law and are not limited to civil law. With regard to the norms of a moral or ethical nature mentioned above, the most important are the general clauses of proper conduct and the principles of community life (explained in more detail *supra* no. 22). While in most cases the general clauses constitute the basis for determination of unlawfulness when they are part of a specific legal provision, at times they also establish general standards of conduct independent of any legal provision. An example of the latter position is the decision of the Supreme Court of 2 December 2003, where the court dealt with liability of restaurant owners for injuries caused to customers. The court held that the obligation to ensure protection of health and life of customers does not only arise from legislation, but also from principles of community life. The latter indicates that a reasonable person would not take unnecessary risks and would take positive steps to ensure health and safety.[74]

70. R. Longchamps de Berier, *Zobowiązania* (Poznań, 1948), §34.
71. The Polish legal writers are divided as to whether one should refer to one notion of wrongfulness (unlawfulness) in the law or a plurality of its many types (e.g., criminal wrongfulness, civil wrongfulness, public illegality, etc.).
72. A. Szpunar, *Czyny Niedozwolone w Kodeksie Cywilnym*, 49.
73. J. Kuźmicka-Sulikowska, *Zasady Odpowiedzialności Deliktowej w Řwietle Nowych Tendencji w Ustawodawstwie Polskim*, 85.
74. III CK 430/03, OSNC 2005, No. 1, pp. 60 and 64.

40. Polish tort law assesses unlawfulness of conduct solely by reference to that conduct. In this context the result of the conduct – damage or injury – is not taken into consideration. Thus, it is not the damage or the injury but the manner in which they were caused which is the basis for determination of unlawfulness.[75]

41. There is some disagreement among scholars concerning the relationship between the content of norms the breach of which can lead to tortious liability in a particular case and the conduct itself. This concerns the notion of 'relative unlawfulness' (*bezprawnosc wzgledna*), which also exists in other legal systems: for instance in Austria (the 'doctrine of protective goal of a provision').[76] The majority of scholars are of the opinion that unlawfulness in the context of tortious liability is only possible if the legal norm breached by the potential tortfeasor established rights for the group of persons to which the victim belongs.[77] In other words, the obligation to repair damage only arises if the norm breached was aimed at protection against the type of damage actually caused, and only if the victim belongs to the group of persons whom the norm was aimed to protect. Further, even those scholars who do not agree with the concept attempt to narrow down the scope of liability in other ways: in particular by using causation and the limits of what 'adequate consequences of the particular unlawful conduct can be.[78] It appears that whether the concept of unlawfulness is limited to relative unlawfulness or not is not a pertinent issue in many typical tortious liability situations, such as personal injuries or damage to property. These are protected by norms establishing unconditional rights (*prawa podmiotowe bezwzgledne*). In these situations a breach of a right is automatically unlawful, unless one of the conditions excluding unlawfulness is present.[79] Nevertheless, the concept of relativity of unlawfulness plays an important part in tort law scholarship and is increasingly present in judicial decisions.[80] It is now an accepted practice in cases involving liability of the state for actions of public authorities).[81] However, the concept remains dogmatically controversial in strict liability cases (*see* section 6), because when liability is based on the principle of

75. J. Kuźmicka-Sulikowska, 123.
76. *See* Willibald Posch, *Austria,* International Encyclopaedia of Laws Series, 45 (Kluwer Law, 2004).
77. For instance: E. Bagińska, *Odpowiedzialnosc odszkodowawcza za wykonywanie wladzy publicznej* (Warszawa, 2006), 397–401; and G. Bieniek, *Odpowiedzialnosc Skarbu Panstwa za szkody wyrzadzone przez funkcjonariuszy po wyroku Trybunału Konstytucyjnego z dnia 4 grudnia 2001 r.*, PS 4/2002, 16.
78. The views are examined by P. Machnikowski, *Odpowiedzialnosc za wlasne czyny*, in A. Olejniczak (ed.) *System Prawa Prywatnego: Prawo Zobowiazan. Część Ogolna,* Vol. 6 (Warszawa: C.H. Beck, Instytut Nauk Prawnych PAN, 2009), 379. Examples of scholars who do not agree with the concept: T. Pajor, *Pure Economic Loss. Polish report, in RAPPORTS POLONAIS PRÉSENTÉS AU XVIIE CONGRES INTERNATIONAL DE DROIT COMPARÉ,* Utrecht, 16–22 juillet 2006, Łodz 2006, s. 41; M. Safjan, *Problematyka tzw. bezprawności względnej oraz związku przyczynowego na tle odpowiedzialności za niezgodne z prawem akty normatywne, [w:] Księga pamiątkowa Profesora Maksymiliana Pazdana* (Kraków, 2005), 1326–1327; and M. Owczarek, *Problem bezprawności wzglednej w systemie odpowiedzialności deliktowej,* Palestra 5–6/(2004), 72.
79. Machnikowski, Odpowiedzialnosc za wlasne czyny, 403.
80. SN of 27 Apr. 2001, III CZP 5/01, OSNC 2001, No. 11, item 161, SN of 14 Jan. 2005, III CKN 193/04, OSP 2006, 7–8, item 89.
81. Judgment of the Supreme Court of 24 Sep. 2008, II CSK 177/08, unpublished. Quoted by Machnikowski, *Odpowiedzialnosc za własne czyny,* 380.

risk, it is severed from the unlawfulness of the tortfeasor's conduct. Even in those cases, however, the courts sometimes employ the language of 'protective purpose of a provision' to ensure that the liability of the tortfeasor is consistent with the scope and aim of the norm which is deemed to be infringed.

The concept of unlawful conduct covers actions as well as omissions. It must be pointed out, however, that an omission can only be unlawful in the face of an obligation to act established by law or by the general clauses mentioned above.

42. While the notion of unlawfulness covers potentially a wide array of norms, including written law and moral or ethical rules of behaviour, according to the dominant opinion it does not include a general obligation not to harm others. Indeed, it is debatable whether Polish civil law accepts such a general obligation which can be referred to as the duty of care. This issue is further examined below (no. 49).

§2. The Concept of Fault

43. Fault was defined as a subjective, improper nature of a person's conduct, improperness of behaviour concerning foreseeability and will.[82] It can thus be said that it is an unacceptable attitude of a person who causes damage towards the specific conduct which damages interests protected by law. Similarly with the notion of unlawfulness, it is not the result (damage) but the conduct only which is taken into account in determination of fault. The defendant is held to be 'at fault' because in the particular circumstances he failed to behave in a way he should have, and could have, behaved.

With regard to assessing the tortfeasor's attitude, two theories appeared: a psychological theory and a normative theory. The psychological theory suggests that conduct should be evaluated using the person's mental attitude towards it or towards its consequences. The normative theory, which prevails in Polish legal thought and in judicial decisions, emphasizes the manner in which the mental attitude can be judged by an outside observer.

Polish civil law in many respects follows the manner in which criminal law deals with fault (*supra* no. 26). According to civil law, fault can be either intentional or unintentional. However, while criminal law sees unintentional fault as either negligence or recklessness, civil law contains the entire concept of unintentional fault in negligence. Neither intentional fault nor negligence has been defined by the Civil Code, and thus the interpretation of the terms was left to scholars and jurisprudence. Intentional fault is described identically with the same notion in criminal law: as a situation when the perpetrator foresees the possibility of a negative outcome of his or her conduct (damage) and either directly wishes for this outcome (*dolus directus*) or simply accepts that it may occur (*dolus eventualis*). [83] Negligence is understood as not exercising the appropriate level of care (*należyta starannosc*). Thus the person in question either does not wish for the outcome but is

---

82. W. Czachórski, *Zobowiązania. Zarys Wykładu*, 2002, 203.
83. J. Kuźmicka-Sulikowska, 121.

aware of its possibility, or is not aware of such possibility while he should and can be. The departure from the required standard of care does not need to be egregious in order for liability to be imposed. Any degree of departure, even *culpa levissima*, is enough for liability to be found.[84]

44. What is the required level of care and how is it assessed in individual cases? Article 355 of the Civil Code (placed in Book Three *Obligations,* Title One *General Provisions)* provides that a debtor in an obligation relationship has a duty to exert the level of care generally required in relations of the particular type. It follows in §2 that if the conduct under scrutiny took place within the course of business of the debtor, the appropriate level of care is assessed taking into consideration the professional nature of the conduct. Further, it is normally not the highest possible level of care or the average level of care which is sought in individual cases, but rather an optimum level of care in a particular situation. Of course, in contrast to a contractual relationship where it is much clearer what is required of the parties, tortious liability demands a much more contextual and objective analysis. Thus, what is generally required in relations of a particular type depends upon a whole array of factors including the type of relation in question, the position and profession of both parties, as well as some external factors such as the time and place, weather conditions, availability of specialist equipment.

45. It is important to note that, while the discussion here concerns a subjective element of liability – fault – the construct of appropriate level of care is a relatively objective one. In other words, an abstract model of appropriate care is constructed, not based on a particular person in question but rather on a category of people to which he or she belongs. A construct of a 'good ... lawyer, doctor, driver', etc., is used to establish what should be done in a situation, and subsequently the position is juxtaposed with the specific individual in question: could/should he or she have behaved in the required manner? As regards the latter, fault will not be attributed to a person who while theoretically capable of the appropriate level of care could not have acted in a required fashion because of the specific position he or she was in at the time, including information available to them and any circumstances limiting their free decision-making. If the person in question performs an activity in the course of a business, the standard of conduct should reflect this. Specifically, if the person is a member of a profession: a lawyer, a doctor or an architect, rules concerning these professions contained in ethical rules and codes of conduct or guidelines will be taken into account. There is a strong tendency to see duties of such professionals as significantly higher than those of a layperson. For instance, what can be referred to as a very high level of care is often required of physicians, both in jurisprudence and in doctrinal writings (*see infra* nos 58–64, especially 61). The Court of Appeal of Krakow held in the judgment of 9 March 2001 that a higher than average standard of care exists for doctors because of the serious potential consequences of their activities (*see also supra* nos 34–36 on protected interests).[85] A

84. SN of 10 Oct. 1975, ICR 656/75.
85. I ACa 124/01, published in Przegląd Sądowy (PS) 2002, No. 10, item 130.

commentator of this judgment added that doctors are required to continuously broaden their knowledge and be aware of the latest developments within their field.[86]

46. In most cases it will not be material for the existence of tortious liability whether the tortfeasor's fault was intentional or not. The general clauses (Articles 415 and 416), and most provisions establishing specific types of liability do not distinguish between the two. However, in some provisions the distinction is relevant. This is for instance in Article 422, where the Code regulates liability of those who did not directly cause damage but who enticed or aided the direct tortfeasor or who consciously took advantage of the damage. Here in most cases only intentional fault is relevant.[87] Further, Article 441 which regulates joint and several liability of a number of people for the same damage provides that the person who compensated the victim should be reimbursed by the others. The amount of reimbursement depends on the circumstances, but in particular on the level of fault of a particular person and their contribution to the damage.

47. In addition to the general conceptual approach to fault described above, specific types of tortious liability add their own characteristic features to the debate. Product liability is a very good example. Before the implementation of the Product Liability Directive it was fault-based liability, albeit with some evidential and procedural mechanisms developed by courts which made the proof of fault much easier for victims of defective products. Through the use of *res ipsa loquitur* courts could attribute liability even in cases where the source and exact nature of the defect were not clear: thus implying the existence of fault as well as of defect. In this fault-based system, defect, risk and foreseeability of an accident became the integral part of the considerations of 'fault'..

§3. Duty of Care

48. Polish civil law does not use the notion of duty of care. There is no positive general obligation to prevent damage or injury to others. However, it must be said that in the light of the wide scope of the concept of unlawfulness a distinct concept of duty of care is not necessary. Legal norms and moral and ethical rules contained in general clauses such as the principles of community life establish a wide catalogue of duties. This catalogue is a true counterpart to the general concept of duty of care. If duty of care did in fact exist, it may lead to elimination of the need to consider unlawfulness as a requisite of liability. Every conduct would be assessed focusing also on its results (which is not done at present), and thus it may always

86. M. Nesterowicz *Glosa do wyroku Sądu Apelacyjnego w Krakowie z dnia 9 marca 2001 r.*, PS 2002, No. 10, item 132.
87. SN of 27 Feb. 2013, IV CSK 443/12, OSNC ZD D/2013, item 78.

be presumed unlawful if it led to damage or injury.[88] In the judgment of 2 December 2003[89] the Supreme Court held that an owner of a club (and similarly: of a discotheque or a restaurant) had a duty to undertake all the necessary means to prevent the risk of damage to people's life and health. Particular obligations do not need to be envisaged in legal provisions. They can stem from life experience, common sense and the professional nature of the defendants' activity. In the court's view the general duty not to cause damage to anyone (the so-called *neminem laedere* rule) requires that all necessary action be taken in order to avoid damage to persons or things. Failure to do so can be wrongful, depending on the circumstances.

§4. Capacity (Infants, Minors)

I. Minors below the Age of 13

49. Polish law requires a certain level of awareness of the nature of one's conduct and its consequences in order to attribute fault to a particular person. One way in which such capacity to bear fault is determined is using the age of the perpetrator.

50. The Civil Code describes anyone below the age of 13 as 'not liable for damage caused' (Article 426). The liability thus appears to have been transferred upon their guardians, who can be their parents, other carers, or institutions. Article 427 regulates liability of persons who are obliged to have in their care, or who exercise care over someone without being obliged to do it by law or by contract, those who cannot be at fault because of age, or mental or physical state. These issues are examined in detail in a further part of this study (Part II, Chapter 2. §1). However, upon a more systemic look at the manner in which the Code regulates minors, doctrinal writings on the subject observe a more complex position. First of all, Article 428 of the Code specifies a situation where a minor can indeed be liable for damage caused by his own conduct. This is possible if the victim cannot be compensated because there is no one obliged to have the person in his care, or there is such a person but it is impossible to obtain compensation from him or her. The article allows the victim in this position to claim compensation from the wrongdoer if the circumstances (especially a comparison between the respective financial positions) indicate that a compensation award would comply with the principles of community life (principles of justice).[90] It would seem, therefore, that minors below the age of 13 can be liable in tort where their liability is based on the principle of equity. Indeed, doctrinal writings go even further in this respect. The majority of scholars are of the view that Article 426 only relieves minors below the age of 13 of fault liability, but

88. P. Machnikowski *Odpowiedzialnosc za własne czyny,* 386.
89. III CK 430/03, OSP 2/2005, item 21.
90. The same article applies when a person is not liable because of incapacity caused by his/her mental or physical state.

not of strict liability or liability based on equity.[91] In a very influential treatise on Polish private law, Smieja wrote that Article 426 was 'wrongly formulated' and ought to be interpreted very narrowly.[92] Systemic interpretation of the entirety of the Civil Code provisions concerning minors indicates that this is the correct approach. The interpretation also complies with the functions of tort liability realized and emphasized by various liability principles. The compensatory aim features much stronger in these other principles than in fault liability. Thus attributing such liability to minors remains in line with the main function of strict or equity liability provisions. Fault liability rather emphasizes a behaviour modification and retribution functions, which cannot be realized effectively in cases where the perpetrator is unable to assess the consequences of his or her conduct.

51. Having concluded that minors below the age of 13 are not capable of being at fault, one must also point out an important implication of this position. Their conduct should not be an exonerating factor in the types of cases where strict liability provisions stipulate that the wrongdoer is not liable if the damage was caused entirely by fault of the victim or of a third person.[93] Such provisions are: liability for damage caused by something spilled, thrown out or fallen from a dwelling (Article 433 KC), liability for damage or injury caused by the operation of an undertaking set in motion by the forces of nature (for instance gas or electricity – Article 435), and liability for damage or injury caused by a mechanical vehicle (Article 436). However, conduct of a minor may be deemed to have contributed to the occurrence or increase of damage and thus lead to limitation of the amount of compensation in respect of the damage (*see* Part IV. Chapter 3 for further explanation of the principle of contributory negligence).

52. The somewhat arbitrary dividing line set at the age of 13 has been the subject of some controversy. It certainly does not leave any scope for discretion in individual cases where it is clear that a minor, whilst not yet 13, understood the consequences of his actions. There are also suggestions that the age limit ought to be lowered. It may seem that children are more aware and simply grow up faster nowadays.[94] The greatest doubts have been expressed with regard to children between the ages of 10 and 13.[95] However, a comparison with the position before the enactment of the Civil Code suggests that there may well be more advantages

91. J. Kuźmicka-Sulikowska, Zasady odpowiedzialności deliktowej ..., 155; Z. Banaszczyk, *O odpowiedzialności deliktowej osoby małoletniej za czyn własny na zasadzie winy*, in M. Pyziak-Szafnicka (ed.) *Odpowiedzialnosc cywilna. Księga pamiątkowa ku czci Profesora Adama Szpunara* (Kraków, 2004), 103.

92. A. Smieja, *Czyny niedozwolone*, A. Olejniczak (ed.) *System Prawa Prywatnego: Prawo Zobowiązań. Część Ogólna*, Vol. 6 (Warszawa: C.H. Beck, Instytut Nauk Prawnych PAN, 2009), 341.

93. P. Machnikowski, *Odpowiedzialnosc za własne czyny*, 405.

94. J. Kuźmicka-Sulikowska, *Zasady odpowiedzialności deliktowej ...*, 157; A. Smieja, *Wiek sprawcy szkody jako przesłanka odpowiedzialności cywilnej z tytułu czynów niedozwolonych*, Państwo i Prawo (1979), 126.

95. J. Kuźmicka-Sulikowska, *Zasady odpowiedzialności deliktowej ...*, 157.

than disadvantages to the current rules. The Code of Obligations of 1933 established no age limit, and thus it was courts which had to determine whether a particular minor was sufficiently mature and aware to attribute fault to him in each individual case. While this certainly allowed judicial determination of each case individually, it also created significant evidential burdens, additional costs and uncertainty for victims.[96]

II. Children Between the Ages of 13 and 18

53. Minors who are 13 or older are obviously beyond the scope of application of Article 426 of the Civil Code. This does not entail, however, their full liability in tort as if they were adults. The prevailing opinion of scholars and the judiciary is that Article 425 §1 applies to them. This provision reads:

> A person who for whatever reason is in a state precluding him from making a conscious and free decision and from expressing his will is not liable for damage caused while in this state.

It is widely agreed that children between the ages of 13 and 18 may be unable to consciously and freely make decisions and determine the implications of their actions, however this is a matter for the court to determine in each particular case. While the latter does not mean the courts have a duty to examine the position in each case, courts certainly may ex officio examine the issue if they deem it justified.[97] Further, the burden of proof of lack of such decisional capacity of a minor is on the latter.

54. The same provision also applies to people who for one of a number of other reasons are unable to freely and consciously make decisions. Common examples of causes of this inability are: mental retardation, mental illness, dementia and some temporary states such as being under the influence of alcohol or narcotics,[98] or high fever.[99]

---

96. *Ibid.*, 156.
97. P. Machnikowski *Odpowiedzialnosc za własne czyny*, 411.
98. With regard to the use of narcotics or alcohol, however, liability is still possible unless the state of unconsciousness or lack of awareness occurred with no fault of the person concerned (Art. 425 §2 KC).
99. P. Machnikowski, *ibid.*, 408.

Chapter 2. Specific Cases of Liability

§1. Liability of Professionals

I. In General: Higher Statutory Standard of Care for 'Experts'

55. As mentioned above in the section concerning fault, in Polish law the standard of care is addressed in Article 355 KC and it is common to contractual and tortious liability:

- a person is obliged to exert the level of care generally required in relations of a given type; and
- the appropriate level of care of the debtor within the scope of his business activity shall be assessed with consideration to the professional nature of that activity.

Pursuant to the above provision, the level of care required of a person engaged in a business, such as a physician, a banker or a broker, is higher than what is required of an ordinary person outside the profession.[100] The standard against which a professional tortfeasor's conduct is measured is mostly objective. The comparison is with the conduct that would be expected of a professional of the given type, and only to a small extent with the conduct that would be expected of the individual tortfeasor himself.

56. Particular obligations of professionals do not need to be envisaged in legal provisions. They can also stem from life experience and common sense, as well as from deontological norms (professional standards, usually incorporated in codes of ethics). The latter are typically included in the analysis of unlawfulness. It is, however, debatable whether professional diligence should be treated as part of unlawfulness or as part of subjective fault. The Supreme Court adopted the widest possible approach to unlawfulness. Both objective standard of care (Article 355 §1 KC) and the professional character of a given activity (Article 355 §2 KC) allow the conclusion that negligence of a professional is established through the sole breach of his duty.[101]

II. Medical Practitioners

57. The basis of civil liability of a physician may be either a contract entered into between a physician having a private practice and his/her patient, or a tort.

In the first case, it is typically a contract for the provision of medical services (Article 750 KC) to which the corresponding provisions on the contract of mandate (Article 734 KC) apply. The physician is obliged to treat the patient pursuant to the

100. SN of 20 May 1986, CRN III 82/86, OSN 8/1987, item 125.
101. SN of 1 Dec. 2006, I CSK 315/06, OSN 11/2007, item 169.

terms defined in the contract. She/he is also subject to the general professional obligations applicable to all physicians. A physician's failure to perform or improper performance of his/her obligations results in contractual liability (Article 471 KC).

The tort basis of liability covers first of all services financed from public sources and provided to the patients entitled by law or insured in the universal health insurance scheme. Causing harm without a pre-contractual relationship results in tortious liability (Article 415 KC). The tort regime also applies when a failure to perform or improper performance by the physician of his/her existing obligation is at the same time a tort. According to judicial decisions, inflicting personal injury or disturbance of health is always a tort.

58. A medical care institution employing medical staff is liable for any damage caused by its staff on the basis of risk arising from liability for assistants or subcontractors (Article 474 KC – *ex contractu*) or for a subordinate (Article 430 of KC – *ex delicto*). In the former case the negligence of a member of staff is presumed, and in the latter it must be proven by the victim. However, Polish case law accepts the concept of 'anonymous fault' of an unidentified worker or a public servant, which assists the plaintiff. It has been developed and applied regularly in medical malpractice cases.[102] Hence, it is irrelevant who among the physicians or nurses caused the damage as long as the damage is causally linked with a breach of professional duties and has occurred in the course of the performance of a healthcare service.

In Poland, an increasing number of physicians are employed as independent contractors pursuant to a contract for services. The Supreme Court has held that even a physician who is a registered entrepreneur may be considered as an auxiliary in the light of all circumstances of a given case.[103] This means that a medical institution will not exempt itself easily from the strict liability for auxiliaries governed by Article 430 KC (vicarious liability). However, in the discussed situations a physician will not be able to invoke its immunity as an employee (*see* below for an explanation), and hence he will face the hospital's claim for a full recourse.

59. A physician is liable for fault (Article 415 KC). Fault denotes a transgression of professional duties by the physician. In court practice, the duties are understood broadly and comprise both those stipulated by law and those rooted in the essence of the medical profession. If there is a contract with the patient, the duties may also arise from the contract.[104]

Fault is different from medical error. Fault usually consists of negligence, i.e., failure to act with due diligence while treating a patient.[105] A medical error is an objective notion and means conduct contrary to commonly recognized principles of medical science and practice. The physician's error results in civil liability provided

102. *See* M. Sośniak, *Cywilna odpowiedzialnosc lekarza* (2nd ed. 1977), 143. E.g., Court of Appeal in Łódź, judgment 8 Jul. 2015, I ACa 63/15, OSP 11/2016 item 109.
103. SN of 26 Jan. 2011, IV CSK 308/10, OSP 11/2011, item 112.
104. *See* M. Nesterowicz, *Prawo medyczne* (10th ed. 2013), 87–89.
105. *See* K Bączyk-Rozwadowska, *Medical Malpractice and Compensation in Poland*, 1233.

that the subjective element of the physician's fault is also established.[106] The existence of an error is independent of a given person or concrete circumstances, both of which are important to establish the subjective element of the physician's fault.

60. The Law on the Professions of Physicians and Dentists[107] defines the rights and duties pertaining to the practice of physicians, the rules of professional conduct as well as detailed rules regarding the recognition of qualifications, the practice of medicine, admissibility and conditions for medical experiments and criminal sanctions imposed for the provision of health services without the necessary skills. Binding rules of professional ethics are also contained in the *Code of Medical Ethics*, proclaimed by the National Medical Congress (1993). The Code defines the physician's conduct towards the patient, the rules of proper medical practice, the duties of the physician towards the public, mutual relations between physicians, as well as the principles of scientific research and medical experiments.

The duty of competence (skill) and the duty to inform a patient are of vital importance. A physician has a duty to maintain his/her competence in medicine, which means continually improving his/her knowledge and following scientific developments (Article 18 of the Law on the Professions of Physicians and Dentists and Article 55 of the *Code of Medical Ethics* [108]). The knowledge and personal skills have to be genuine, not merely formally certified.

61. The standard of care required of a physician is based on objective criteria, such as: personal qualifications (specializations, academic degrees), general professional experience and specific experience relating to given medical procedures, the nature and scope of continuing education, the education in new methods of treatment. In many cases courts referred to the highest professional diligence required of physicians.[109]

The professional requirements must be particularly high because of the potentially far-reaching consequences of the physician's acts and omissions.[110] The high standard of care, however, cannot lead to a situation where physicians are attributed duties that are practically impossible to fulfil. This approach would turn their liability into strict liability.[111] Especially in cases of frequent serious risks, even if all available precautions have been used, the possibility of inflicting harm cannot be excluded. The risk that is an inevitable element of such practices is not to be attributed to anybody's fault.

Fault of a doctor may consist not only in lack of sufficient knowledge and practical skills required by professional medical standards, but also in carelessness or

---

106. SNof 1 Apr. 1955, IV CR 39/54, OSN 1957, item 7.
107. The Act of 5 Dec. 1996, Dz.U. 2002, No. 21, item 204.
108. SN of 13 Oct. 2005, IV CK 161/05, OSP 6/2006, item 71.
109. For instance: SN of 29 Oct. 2003, III CK 34/02, OSP 4/2005, item 54, and judgment of the Court of Appeals in Krakow of 12 Oct. 2007, I ACa 920/07, PiM 1/2010 151, with the commentary of M. Nesterowicz.
110. SN of 7 Jan. 1966, I CR 396/65, OSPiKA 1966/item 278.
111. The Appeal Court in Warsaw judgment of 3 Mar. 1998, I ACA 14/98, Wokanda 10/1998.

unskilful performance of a procedure.[112] If a general practitioner undertakes procedures for which only specialists have been trained, he/she should be evaluated in accordance with the standard of a specialist.

62. Courts have held that the following types of conduct constitute negligent actions:

– applying an obsolete method of treatment, leading to an injury or to the aggravation of an existing injury;[113]
– applying wrong treatment in contradiction to the indications of medical knowledge, coupled with ignorance of alternative courses of medical treatment and delay of counselling with a specialist;[114]
– performing an obviously unnecessary treatment or surgery;[115]
– operating on a wrong limb or body part of the patient, even if the operation was performed correctly.[116]

63. Examples of negligent omissions include:

– failure to carry out adequate initial tests;
– failure to inform the patient about his/her health condition, or the diagnosis, or the necessity to have proper tests or treatment, or the consequences of delayed treatment;
– failure to obtain informed consent;
– failure to ensure post-operational care in a healthcare institution.[117]

III. Legal Practitioners

A. Attorneys

64. Recent judicial decisions reflect the increased focus on liability for legal services.[118] Such liability for damage caused by unprofessional conduct of lawyers was not very popular in Poland until the 1990s. Presently, all legal professionals (except for judges and prosecutors) must have compulsory civil liability insurance in order to carry out legal services.

112. SN of 10 Feb. 2010, V CSK 287/09, OSP 2012, item 95.
113. Regional Court in Katowice, judgment of 17 Dec. 2003, II C 844/01/5.
114. Regional Court in Radom, judgment of 15 Jul. 2003, I C 955/98, PiM 2/2007.
115. SN of 12 Apr. 1976, IV CR 83/76, OSPiKA 11/1978, item 199; Regional Court in Bydgoszcz, judgment of 19 Jul. 1999, I C 1150/981, OSP 2002, item 59.
116. Case involving operation on a wrong hip – Regional Court in Lublin judgment of 1 Feb. 2006, I C 213/04, PiM 4/2008.
117. *See* Nesterowicz, Bagińska, den Exter, *Medical Law*, No. 81.
118. *See* SN of 2 Dec. 2004 r., V CSK 297/04, M. Prawn. 2005, No. 1, 9, also SN of 5 Jun. 2007 r., I CSK 86/07, unpublished, and SN of 18 Apr. 2002, II CKN 1216/00, OSNC 4/2003, item 58.

65. One of the leading cases involving liability of an attorney was decided by the Supreme Court on 18 April 2002.[119] The Supreme Court stated that the plaintiff's failure to file a separate claim for interest on a money claim was in an adequate causal connection with the attorney's earlier omission to seek the interest together with the main debt, if the attorney was still contractually retained to represent a client and to seek the outstanding interest in court. The damage suffered by the client comprised the costs of the new suit and the loss suffered because the client did not have use of the money he would have received if the interest had been awarded together with the main debt in the first proceedings.

Compensation granted by courts typically includes the reimbursement of costs and expenses that the lawyer's client paid in connection with a lawsuit (such as court fees, court expert fees.) as well as the remuneration for the defective services. In one case the Supreme Court held that an error in indicating a proper defendant justified liability for the costs and expenses incurred in the lost lawsuit.[120]

66. Polish courts have not yet tackled the problem of loss of chance in the context of professional negligence. In the judgment of 15 March 2010 the Supreme Court declared full recovery for the plaintiff whose attorney included wrong information on an *in blanco* draft and consequently failed to secure a money judgment on its basis. When the original claim was dismissed, the client sued his attorney for the full amount that should have appeared on the draft. The court emphasized that a defective completion of the draft justified full liability for damage,[121] regardless of the chances to win in the first suit (the defendant questioned the possibility of success for other reasons). The court thus applied the 'all or nothing' approach, instead of the proportional recovery dependent on the chances to win the first suit.[122]

67. The emerging standard of care for attorneys indicates that they are not liable for failure to win a case if the court interpreted the law differently than expected, or when it used other legal concepts to adjudicate the claim, or when the line of case law changed during the proceedings and as a result the representing attorney relied on an incorrect legal doctrine. However, an attorney is obliged to acquire proper knowledge of the law and to demonstrate adequate care in safeguarding the interests of the client. The level of care fails to meet this standard only when a legal opinion or the manner of managing the legal case is patently contrary to the relevant legal rules, or to the universally accepted doctrinal views, or to an established line of reasoning in judicial decisions before taking legal action.[123] Hence, the present standard of professional diligence is rather lenient.

119. II CKN 1216/00, OSN 4/2003, item 58.
120. *See* R. Horbaczewski, Rzeczpospolita of 30.07.2007, III C upr 78/07.
121. I CSK 330/11, OSP 2012, No. 12, item 123 with the commentary by J. Jastrzebski.
122. *Ibid.*
123. SN of 15 Mar. 2010, I CSK 330/11, OSP 2012, No. 12, item 123.

68. Moreover, a great number of professional malpractice lawsuits fail on the grounds that adequate causation between the damage and the professional negligence was missing.[124] The courts require the plaintiff to prove that if not for the misconduct of the attorney he would have obtained a better result in the given legal proceedings.[125] Adequate causation is thus an instrument used by courts to deal, albeit in a manner which is difficult to explain, with the problem of standard of proof. The court hearing the case should rather evaluate the attorney's actions or failures independently; otherwise it does not adjudicate on the essence of the legal conflict.

B. Public Notaries

69. Polish law makes a sharp distinction between the legal status of a notary and of other professions rendering legal services on a professional basis, i.e., attorneys, legal counsels or bailiffs.[126] The Public Notaries Act[127] (1991) governs the functioning of the notaries in Poland. Prior to the privatization of notaries' services in 1989, it had been assumed that the State Treasury was liable for damage caused by notaries acting in their capacity of state officials, which, *inter alia*, had its justification in their strong relationship with the judiciary (former Articles 417–419 KC). In the contemporary Notaries Act, Article 49 provides:

> A notary is liable for damage inflicted when performing notarial activities based on principles specified in the Civil Code, taking into account the level of care a notary is obliged to observe when performing such activities.

The provision does not determine whether a notary bears contractual or tortious liability. As a consequence, a controversy arose in legal writings and in judicial decisions as to the appropriate regime of a notary's liability. A very wide array of views are offered by legal scholarship and court practice. This notwithstanding, a notary's liability is certainly a type of professional liability with many distinctive features. We share the viewpoint that a notary is liable in tort, because the duties of a notary arise from law and are binding towards all persons (both parties to a notarial activity and third parties). Moreover, a notary's liability is strongly connected with public tasks (functions). According to Article 80 §2 of the Notaries Act a notary is obliged to duly safeguard the rights and just interests of parties and other persons in relation to whom his notarial activity may have legal effects. The liability of notaries towards clients and third parties is thus based on fault (Article 415 KC). In addition to typical requirements of tort liability, the victim must prove a connection between the tort of a notary and the infringement of his professional

124. *See*, e.g., SN 19 Dec. 2012, II CSK 219/12, OSNC 7–8/2013, item 91.
125. SN of 21 Dec. 2010 r., IV CSK 461/10, unpublished; Court of Appeals in Warsaw judgment of 2 Dec. 2010, VI ACa 844/10, unpublished.
126. *See also* the judgment of the Constitutional Court of 26 Mar. 2008 r., K 4/07, OTK ZU 2008, No. 2, item 28.
127. The Act of 14 Feb. 1991 (*Prawo o notariacie*), Dz.U. of 2008, No. 189, item 1158 with amendments.

(statutory) obligations. He should also prove that the violation took place 'when performing the notarial activity' (cited Article 49 of the Notaries Act). A notary is also vicariously liable for his auxiliaries. The tort law basis of claims towards notaries is relatively well established in legal scholarships and judicial decisions.[128]

The views in favour of contractual liability of notaries (Articles 471 et seq. KC), or arguments that there is a concurrence of contractual and tort liability (Article 443 KC)[129] are less convincing. Contractual liability of a notary may, of course, arise in situations where a notary undertakes activities which he is not obliged to perform by law (e.g., taking safety deposits, opening a bank account).

70. The detailed contents of the duties and rights of a notary are shaped by the provisions of the Notaries Act and deontological norms (the code of notaries' rules of ethics). A notary is obliged to perform notarial activities in person, to ensure general safety and stability for the parties during the performance of notarial activities, and to keep professional secrecy. Unlike attorneys and legal counsels, when performing an activity a notary is obliged to take into account legal certainty of both parties to a notarial activity and of third parties. In the case of the latter, the obligation encompasses persons against whom the activity takes effects as well as these who, in a longer term, should have confidence in the public value of the notarial deed. The obligation to provide explanation and advice results from the latter.

71. Judicial decisions indicate a rather broad interpretation of the notary's statutory obligations. The standard of care of a notary (Article 49 of the Notaries Act in connection with Article 355 KC) has been increased in the last two decades. 'Professional torts' of notaries may take several forms. The reported court decisions most often concerned violations of the duty to protect the rights and interests of parties (Article 80 section 2 of the Notaries Act), the duty to inform (Article 80 section 3 and Article 82 of the Notaries Act) and the duty to refuse to perform a notarial activity which is contrary to law (Article 81 of the Notaries Act).[130]

In the judgment of the Supreme Court of 8 December 2004[131] the court held that failure to fulfil the duty to provide information concerning all the consequences of statements made by the clients is a violation of a general obligation of a notary envisaged in Article 80 section 3 of the Notaries Act, and constitutes a professional tort of the notary. The court emphasized that a notary is obliged to perform his duties with enhanced degree of care, especially when drawing up notarial deeds resulting in the transfer of ownership, perpetual usufruct (public ground lease) and

---

128. *See* B. Lewaszkiewicz-Petrykowska, *Uwagi o zasadach rzadzacych cywilna odpowiedzialnoscia notariusza*, PS No. 2/1995, p. 29 ff. For jurisprudence *see* decisions of the Supreme Court: SN of 30 May 2000, IV CKN 36/00, OSNC 2000, No. 12, item 223; SN of 12 Jun. 2002, III CKN 694/00, OSN 2003, No. 9, item 124; SN of 9 May 2008, III CSK 366/07, unpublished; SN of 15 Apr. 2010, II CSK 544/09, OSN ZD, no D/2010, item 113.

129. *See* M. Kolasinski, *Odpowiedzialnosc cywilna notariusza* (Toruń, 2005), 164 and following.

130. *See* M. Bączyk, *Liability of a Notary under Polish Law According to the Latest Judicature of the Supreme Court of the Republic of Poland,* in Civil Liability of a Notary and Its Insurance in Poland and Other Selected Member States of the European Union, 49–82 (M. Kolasiński ed., Toruń, 2012), A. Oleszko, *Starannosc zawodowa notariusza jako przeslanka odpowiedzialnosci za szkodę wyrządzoną przy wykonywaniu czynności notarialnej*, Rejent 1999, No. 11.

131. I CK 303/04, unpublished.

of limited property rights, which have major significance for the subjective rights of the parties to the notarial act and for the legal certainty of real estate transactions.

However, the Supreme Court has explained in another judgment[132] that the duty to inform does not include actions of an advisory nature, and it is not reasonable to expect it to cover all possible future actions undertaken by the party to the deed. The scope of the duty is limited to a specific action performed before a notary public. The plaintiff wrongfully equated the functions of a notary with a 'private advisor, tax advisor or investment advisor'. Such a position finds no legal basis and the claim was dismissed.

Failure to observe the relevant provisions regarding effective creation of a specific property right in real estate causes defectiveness of the notarial deed. This failure is not only an unlawful notarial act, but also a negligent act proving the notary's ignorance of legal regulations fundamental for his professional activity.[133] The same may be said about a defective, hence negligent, transfer of a property right in real estate.[134]

In the decision of 15 April 2010[135] the Supreme Court confirmed that, by failing to file for the entry of the deed in the land registry within the prescribed time of seven days from the execution of the deed, the public notary negligently breached her professional duties. A required causal connection (both the *sine qua non* and the legal causation) exists between the breach and the encumbrance upon the plaintiff's property (which constituted the damage in this case).

As regards the duty to verify the authenticity of documents submitted by parties, a notary is required to observe due care, without the need for his own expert knowledge or the need to refer to any expert examination. In a judgment of 5 April 2002[136] the Court of Appeals in Poznan found that a notary who acted on the basis of a power of attorney should have verified (e.g., by phone) whether the power of attorney had indeed been granted.

IV. Builders and Architects

72. There are no special rules concerning liability of builders and architects in Polish law. Thus, they are liable under general contractual and tortious liability rules.

73. The position is different with regard to construction companies, which are strictly liable for damage on the basis of Article 435 KC. Anyone who runs his own enterprise or business set into operation by natural forces is liable for any damage to persons and property caused by the operation of the enterprise or business. This

132. SN of 28 Jun. 2019, IV CSK 224/18, OSNC – ZD 2020/C, item 50.
133. SN of 23 Jan. 2008, V CSK 373/07.
134. SN of 7 Jun. 1997, II CKN 420/97, OSNC 1998, No. 5, item 76.
135. II CSK 544/09, OSNC-ZD, no D/2010, item 113.
136. I ACa 1317/01.

liability is strict which means that as soon as it is established that the alleged damage is linked to the operation of the defendant's enterprise, the latter is liable regardless of whether he has complied with regulations, professional standards and the requirements of the highest care and prudence. There are only three exonerations from this liability: (1) force majeure, (2) the exclusive fault of the injured and (3) the exclusive fault of a third person for whom the defendant is not liable. Hence, for instance, the defence that an investor had provided a contractor with defective building documentation is not relevant. According to established court practice, a construction company is not absolved from strict liability if heavy work carried out under the ground and in the vicinity of water supplies, albeit performed in accordance with the architectural documentation and the building contract, were based on defective documentation regarding the means of securing the neighbouring real estate. The fact that the constructor performed his duties with professional diligence and in compliance with the law is not an exonerating fact. A modern construction company must autonomously assess the risk of carrying out works in the conditions that do not guarantee full safety even when observing highest prudence and care. The inflicted damage falls within the scope of the building risk and the construction company is liable to compensate third parties regardless of the potential negligence on the part of the investor.[137]

V. Specific Cases Others

A. Financial Services (Banks, Auditors)

74. General duties of banking institutions are stipulated in the provisions of Banking Law (1997),[138] and – as regards dealing in publicly traded securities – in the Law on Public Trade in Securities of 1997.[139] The general duty of care is independent of the specific obligations arising from a particular type of contracts concluded by banks.

75. Banks have a general duty of care towards depositors to ensure safety of money deposits. This duty was initially developed by courts and is currently envisaged in statutory norms (Article 50 section 2 of Banking Law). In practice, the scope of this duty goes beyond contractual obligations and banking laws. A breach of the duty constitutes the bank's own fault leading to its liability (Article 415 KC).[140] According to court practice and legal scholarship, the duty exists both in the pre-contractual and post-contractual phase of a legal relationship with the client.

In the Supreme Court case of 20 May 2005[141] the bank was held negligent in tort and in contract because 'it tolerated the practice of accepting by its employee (a

137. SN of 28 Nov. 2007, V CSK 282/07, OSNC-ZD 2/2008 item 54.
138. The Act of 29 Aug. 1997, consolidated text Dz.U. of 2012, item 1376, with amendments.
139. Act of 21 Aug. 1997, Dz.U. of 1997, No. 118, item 754, with amendments.
140. SN of 20 May 2005, III CK 661/04, Prawo Bankowe 10/2005, 11; SN of 19 Nov. 2009, IV CSK 257/09, OSP 7–8/2010, item 79.
141. III CK 661/04, OSNC 2006, No. 4, item 73.

securities broker) money orders signed by a client in blanco'. Any losses resulting from fraudulent transfers of money imply a breach of a banking account contract. The breach is negligent when the bank fails to act either with the special degree of care in respect of safety of deposited money, which is required by banking law, or with the 'ordinary' (professional) due diligence required by the Civil Code (Article 355 §2 KC). With regard to the tort basis, however, the application of *respondeat superior* principle in this case was arguable because of the criminal nature of the employee's conduct. The court ruled that the bank's conduct led to liability arising from Article 415 KC. Defective functioning of the banking services that facilitates or allows criminal conduct of a bank employee constitutes the bank's own tort.[142]

76. Professional auditors and accountants have a statutory duty to draft opinions conforming to facts and legal rules. Their liability for professional fault is typically based on a breach of the contract for services. The Act of 29 September 1994 on Accountancy[143] only provides for criminal sanctions for unprofessional conduct, even if committed unintentionally. However, if the negligent conduct violates the accountant's (auditor's) duties independent of any contractual relation, courts may establish tortious liability. An auditor should foresee that publication of his opinion, sometimes required by law, could be a basis for economic decisions of third persons (e.g., investors). However, no such case can be found in Polish tort law practice.

In the case of 1 December 2006[144] the Supreme Court ruled that an auditing company was liable for losses sustained due to a negligent breach of professional standards for chartered accountants and a breach of the rules of proper auditing. The parties had a contract, but the contractual claims were time-barred (two years) and hence the plaintiff based the claim on tort law. The contract stipulated that the audit would be performed according to the requirements of the accounting law and the standards set by the National Council of Chartered Accountants. Thus, the standard of care was both part of the contract and envisaged in the provisions of law. The Supreme Court held that a breach of contractual obligations did not per se constitute a tort. However, a breach of professional standards envisaged in the statutes and deontological rules may under the given circumstances create a tort and justify a claim *ex delicto*. A chartered accountant is entrusted with a public function. His conduct, albeit within a contractual relation, may amount to a tort. This is notwithstanding the fact that the rules of accounting law are addressed to accountants and not to the public, thus they are not to be considered to be generally binding legal standards of proper and careful conduct.

77. In the financial services sector the type of damage typically sought is pure economic loss. Due to the fact that such loss must be proven with high probability

142. *See also* SN of 16 Jan. 2008, IV CSK 380/07, OSNC ZD, no D/2008, item 102; and SN of 19 Nov. 2009, IV CSK 257/09, OSP 7–8/2010, item 79 - OSNC 5/2010, item 81.
143. Consolidated text Dz.U. of 2013, item 330.
144. I CSK 315/06, OSN 11/2007, item 169.

and it must be causally linked to the professional tort, the successful claims typically embrace the reimbursement of the fee for the defective service when the parties were bound contractually. As for third-party claimants, no court decisions may be reported yet. So far, the recognition of liability of auditors or banks for pure economic loss derives from tortious consequences of the breach of an existing contract. Putting the limits to the reparable loss requires an analysis of the duties violated by the professional. The liability is likely to be established if the duties were general and binding on the actor regardless of any contractual bond, and where the actor was aware that the breach of such duties will likely cause damage to certain third persons.[145]

B. *Sport Activities*

78. In the judgment of 25 April 1973[146] the Supreme Court considered duties of a coach towards an athlete involved in a particularly risky sport. It held that if a boxer who was to participate in training exercises informed his coach that he was physically unfit and unable to do so, the coach should have released him from training. This was the duty of the coach if he had no possibility to ask for a doctor's opinion or failed to ask for one. Refusal of such a release always constitutes negligence on the part of the coach who should be aware of the potential consequences of his professional decisions. Hence, he is liable jointly and severally with the sports club for injuries suffered at the training session. Boxing is a particularly dangerous sport that brings a risk of injuries also during training. Therefore, not only the rules of fair play must be obeyed, but a coach (a club) also has a duty of care towards the athlete concerning his physical and mental health. The risk assumed by a boxer cannot embrace damage inflicted due to the fault of another (a coach, a doctor, or a club).

79. There is no special provision in Polish civil law concerning duties of organizers of sports activities or events. Scholars argue that the duty of care required of a person professionally engaged in organizing sports events should be higher than the duty required of an ordinary person outside the profession. Tomasz Pajor suggested that judiciary and scholars should develop the archetypes of a 'good organizer' and a 'careful sportsman'.[147] He emphasized the role of a sports organizer as a central actor whose influence on the safety of an event is most significant. The liability of sports organizers for damage arising from a sport event caused to its spectators, players and other persons most often arises from a contract, albeit the tort basis (Article 415 KC) is far more favourable to the victim (availability of redress of non-pecuniary loss). Where the organizer is a legal person (a club or a

145. *See also* T. Pajor, *Poland*, [in:] V.V. Palmer & M. Bussani, *Pure economic loss. New horizons in comparative law*, 272–273 (London/New York), B. Lewaszkiewicz-Petrykowska, *Nowe tendencje w zakresie cywilnej odpowiedzialności zawodowej*, in *Rozprawy z polskiego i europejskiego prawa prywatnego. Księga pamiątkowa ofiarowana Profesorowi Jozefowi Skapskiemu* (Kraków, 1994), 186 ff.

146. I CR 306/73, OSN 2/1974, item 34.

147. *See* T. Pajor, *Odpowiedzialnosc cywilna organizatora imprezy sportowej*, PS 10 (2002), 37–52.

federation), it is generally easier to prove its fault. The scope of the duty to ensure safety (duty of care) is specified in the Polish sports law and relevant European standards. Deviations from the imposed standards of safety entail unlawfulness, and this is sufficient to establish the liability of the legal person. Under the general principle of Article 471 KC (contractual liability), the burden of proof of lack of negligence is on the defendant.

C. *Selling Practices*

80. An enterprise distributing goods through authorized dealers has a duty of care towards buyers to examine the dealers' reliability and to monitor his commercial activity. Such an enterprise commits professional negligence if it maintains the contractual relationship with its dealer although it is aware of the latter financial difficulties or of its improper marketing practices in violation of the dealership agreement. The negligence is further confirmed if the relationship is maintained despite the high economic risk of dealing with the distributor, and despite complaints from the dealer's clients or several months' delays in payments (to the defendant, the banks and the state). In the judgment of 17 July 2003[148] the Supreme Court emphasized that a wholesaler (producer) benefits from authorizing a dealer (distributor). The buyers rely on the trademark in their choices. Therefore, the defendant may not ignore the interests of the dealer's customers. Failure to sufficiently monitor the diligence and the honesty of the dealer is against the principle of proper conduct and hence negligent. A client has a right to expect little transactional risk when buying from an authorized dealer of a large, well-known company. Hence, the wholesaler should be responsible for the dealer's practices.[149] The wholesaler's liability may only be in tort (Article 415 KC or 416 KC – liability for one's own conduct), since no privity of contract exists between him and the buyers. The wholesaler's own negligent omissions and negligent monitoring of unfair commercial practices of the buyer undoubtedly constitute a tort.

§2. Liability of Public Authorities

81. The new constitutional model of state liability was introduced in 1997 by Article 77 of the Constitution.[150] Article 77(1) stipulates:

> Everyone shall have the right to compensation for any harm done to him by any action of an organ of public authority contrary to law.

148. III CKN 29/01, OSP 5/2005, item 59.
149. *See* M. Nesterowicz, Casenote, OSP 2/2005, 246.
150. About the constitutional model *see* E. Bagińska, *Poland*, in: *European Tort Law 2001*, 382 (H. Koziol & B.C. Steininger eds, 2002); E. Bagińska, *Liability of Public Authorities for Damage to Individuals: Is Article 77 of the Polish Constitution a Model Solution?*, in *The Emerging Constitutional Law of the European Union – German and Polish Perspectives*, Beiträge zum ausländischen öffentlichen Recht und Völkerrecht 163 (A. Bodnar, M. Kowalski, K. Raible, F. Schorkopf eds, 2003), 185, 188–206, E. Bagińska, *The Liability of Public Authorities in Poland*, w: *The Liability of Public Authorities in Comparative Perspective* (K. Oliphant ed.Intersentia 2016), 351.

By virtue of this provision the principle of strict liability of public authorities was introduced into Polish law. In the seminal judgment of 4 December 2001[151] the Constitutional Tribunal held that Article 77 of the Constitution, by creating a subjective right, gave individuals a mechanism for protection of their personal rights and freedoms. The Constitutional Tribunal also emphasized that the constitutionalization of the right to compensation of damage caused by illegal exercise of public authority is a guarantee of legality of state actions. Statutory provisions may not exclude or limit the constitutionally guaranteed claim for damages. The latter may only be restricted under the same conditions as applicable to the restrictions of any other constitutional right; hence the fundamental requirements of proportionality and 'justification in the democratic society' must be met.

82. The amendment to the Civil Code in 2004[152] was the most significant change in tort rules since the enactment of the Code in 1964. It introduced liability for legislative wrongs and liability for omissions to issue jurisdictional acts (i.e., a court judgment or an administrative decision) or legislative acts. The amendment was meant to adjust the Code to the constitutional model of state liability. It also repealed the relevant provisions of the Code of Administrative Procedure (KPA), and thus ensured that almost all cases of public liability are embraced by the rules contained in the Civil Code. The revision came into force on 1 September 2004 and applies to the facts and situations occurring after this date. The rules on liability for unlawful judgments were again revised by two Acts: the Act of 22 July 2010 on *the Revision of the Civil Code, the Code of Civil Procedure and the Bankruptcy Law*[153] and the Act of 12 February 2010 *on the Revision of the Administrative Court Procedure.*[154]

83. Poland adopted a model where a public authority (a legal person) is directly responsible for the damage caused by the exercise of public authority. On the constitutional and statutory levels the liability rests on the institution (structure), not its agents (functionaries). Although the formal link between a direct tortfeasor and an organ of public authority is less relevant, the establishment of such relation facilitates the proof of the fact that damage arose from the exercise of public authority. Public authority liability is not considered a form of vicarious liability. It is the state's (or other body's) own tort that gives rise to compensatory claims.

Article 417 §1 KC in its new version provides a general rule of liability for damage resulting from an unlawful exercise of public authority. Article 417 KC states that the liability for damage caused by illegal action or omission in the course of the exercise of public authority rests with the State Treasury, a local authority, or another legal person who exercises authority conferred upon it by law. If the exercise of tasks falling within the scope of public authority was delegated to a local authority or other legal person by way of an arrangement, both the performer of the task and the State Treasury or the local authority who delegated the tasks are liable

151. The judgment of 4 Dec. 2001 (SK 18/00), available at http://trybunal.gov.pl/ (in Polish).
152. The Law on the Revision of the Civil Code of 17 Jun. 2004, Dz.U. 2004, No. 162, at 1692.
153. Dz.U. of 2010, No. 155, item 1037.
154. Dz.U. of 2010, No. 36, item 196.

and their liability is joint and several. A natural person cannot be liable in this regime, but only in recourse towards the public authority (*see* Part I, Chapter 2, §2).

84. Hence, all legal entities exercising public authority are subject to strict liability for the damaging consequences of their conduct. No distinction is made between acts and omissions or between public or private nature of the entity. The character of the act (whether it is governmental or proprietary) is the sole factor that determines the application of the strict liability regime. Consequently, 'regular' torts of public bodies that do not involve an exercise of public authority are governed by the general rules (Articles 427, 430, 435, 436 et seq. KC). On the one hand, the legislator put all legal persons that exercise public prerogatives on an equal footing, irrespective of the public/private ownership, and on the other hand it subjected them to the same rules with regard to acts of a private character.

85. Public authority liability is connected with exercise of public authority – exercise of prerogatives and official powers. This notion refers to all kinds of activities (*imperium, actes de pouvoir*), which usually, but not always mean the ability to affect the rights, liberties or interests of individuals. The prevailing views in judicial decisions and legal writing support the functional interpretation of 'exercise of public authority', derived from Council of Europe Recommendation 84.[155] Examples of activities which have been held to belong to the sphere of imperium include:[156] refusal of treatment or the right to legally abort that is financed from public resources, injuries suffered by soldiers during training exercises, issuing certificates by public registries and activities of disciplinary commissions in higher education institutions, although this liability does not exclude individual liability of a commission member for fault (Article 415 KC).[157]

In the present shape public authority liability rests on the institution, hence it is important whether the statutory duty was imposed on the state (or a state entity). Duties of agents or employees are of secondary importance. However, the duty must be sufficiently precise in order to establish an omission.

86. The principal rule is that the obligation to repair damage arises when the act causing the damage is unlawful (literally 'contrary to law'– *niezgodne z prawem*). This includes any illegal action or omission, including physical acts, administrative acts (decisions, orders and decrees), as well as normative acts. The words 'contrary to law' caused some doubts as to their relation to the private law notion of unlawfulness. The Constitutional Tribunal (SK 18/00) held that only acts in breach of the constitutional sources of law (Article 87) may be considered unlawful within the meaning of Article 77 of the Constitution. Nevertheless, this narrow definition does not prevent the legislator or courts from establishing the traditional meaning of unlawfulness at the Civil Code level.

155. The Council of Europe Recommendation no R (84) 15 of the Committee of Ministers to Member States relating to public liability adopted on 18 Sep. 1984.
156. E. Bagińska, 'The Liability of Public Authorities in Poland, in K. Oliphant (ed.) *The Liability of Public Authorities in Comparative Perspective*, Intersentia 2016, No. 78.
157. SN of 27 Sep. 2012, III CZP 48/12, OSNC 3/2013, item 31.

Generally speaking, unlawfulness of a public authority's conduct is to be understood broadly and traditionally.[158] This definition includes conduct that violates both the law and established customs, and rules of conduct established by general clauses such as the principles of community life (*see* no. 40). In the case of 6 February 2002, the Supreme Court construed unlawfulness under Article 77 of the Constitution as incompatibility of the public organ's conduct with its powers, its prescribed course of action and a model decision appropriate in the circumstances.[159]

87. For some sources of damage a prior procedure determining the unlawfulness of a public act or omission is a precondition for filing a compensatory claim. This is based on the assumption that public liability should solely arise when damage arose from the final administrative decisions that were reversed in the renewed administrative proceedings or otherwise invalidated.[160] The same holds true in respect of court judgments. If damage resulted from the rendering of a valid judgment or a final decision, compensation may be demanded only after the illegality of the respective judgment or decision has been declared in proper proceedings, unless special rules provide otherwise (Article 417^1§2 KC). The same applies to a case where a valid judgment or a final decision have been rendered on the basis of a legislative act not conforming with the Constitution, an international agreement or a statute (Article 417^1§2 KC).

88. According to the Code of Administrative Procedure (KPA) a final administrative decision may be declared void because it had no legal grounds or it was made in violation of the law (Article 156 KPA). Both a nullifying decision and a decision that reopens proceedings are the first step to claiming compensation. Accordingly, a nullification of a decision, a declaration of its illegality or reopening of the proceedings by an administrative court judgment opens a way to the reparation of losses.

89. As to final court judgments, the Supreme Court is solely competent to render a valid final judgment unlawful for the purpose of seeking compensation from the state. A special 'action for rendering a valid judgment unlawful', governed by Article 424^1§1 and §2 KPC, can be commenced provided that the following three conditions have been met:

(1) when a final decision issued by a second instance court is concerned, or in exceptional cases when a first instance final judicial decision the unlawfulness of which stems from the breach of fundamental legal rules or of constitutional rights and freedoms is concerned;
(2) the rendering of the judgment caused damage to the party; and

158. *See* E. Bagińska, *Odpowiedzialnosc odszkodowawcza za wykonywanie władzy publicznej* (Warszawa, 2006), 320–334.
159. V CKN 1248/00,OSP 9/2002, item 128.
160. SN of 19 Nov. 2004, V CK 250/04, OSP 7–8/2005, item 98.

(3) the change or reversal of the decision could not and still cannot be obtained by other means (or if the violation of fundamental rights is at stake – when the party did not make use of other means of reviewing the judgment – Article 424^1§2 KPC).

The claim must be filed within five years from the issuance of the judgment in question.

Since 2010[161] a claim for damage arising from judicial act that cannot be subject to an 'action for rendering a valid judgment unlawful' may be brought before a district court without prior determination of illegality (Article 424^{1b}§1 KPC). This exception concerns non-final judgments, as well as acts rendered in the execution of judgments and in bankruptcy proceedings. There are no special proceedings with regard to establishing the unlawfulness of such acts.

The Act of 12 February 2010 introduced the 'action for rendering a valid judgment unlawful' into the administrative court procedure (Articles 285^a–285^l of the Act). It is based on the model used in the system of civil procedure. An important substantive difference is that the law on administrative courts procedure provides for an explicit basis of liability for a judgment of the Supreme Administrative Court which was issued in clear breach of the EU law (Article 285^a§3).

90. No procedure has been designed as regards judgments issued by the Supreme Court. This leads the majority of scholars to the conclusion on the state's immunity concerning the Supreme Court decisions. However, one should note that the conclusion is incompatible with the EU rules on Member States' liability.

91. According to the Supreme Court case law, 'unlawfulness' of a valid judgment is interpreted very restrictively.[162] Thus, a judgment in unlawful when it is unquestionably contrary to principal legal provisions which are not subject to different interpretations, or contrary to the general rules of judicial discretion, or when it was issued as a result of patently erroneous interpretation or application of law. The Supreme Court's interpretation is compatible with ECJ's requirements of Member States liability set out in its case law.[163] The interpretation has been challenged on grounds of unconstitutionality, but the Constitutional Tribunal upheld that restrictive interpretation as conforming to Article 77 of the Constitution, as long as it remains an objective criterion.[164]

92. If damage resulted from an omission to render a judgment or decision, and a provision of law provides for a duty to this effect, compensation may be claimed only after having the illegality of the omission declared in proper proceedings,

161. The Act of 22 Jul. 2010 on the Revision of the Civil Code, the Code of Civil Procedure and the Bankruptcy Law, Dz.U. of 2010, No. 155, item 1037.
162. SN of 22 Jun. 2007, III CNP 37/07, OSP 7–8/2008, item 94, TK 1 Apr. 2008, SK 77/06, OTK 39/3/A/2008.
163. Joined Cases C-6/90 and C-9/90, *Francovich*, [1991] ECR I-5357, C-224/01 *Köbler v. Austria [2003] ECR I-10239,* C-173/03 *Traghetti del Mediterraneo SpA, v. Italy* [2006] ECR I-05177.
164. Judgment TK of 27 Sep.c2012, SK 4/11, OTK 97/8/A/2012, TK of 27 Oct. 2015, SK 9/13 OTK 151/9/A/2015.

unless special rules provide otherwise (Article 417[1]§3 KC). The latter are contained in the Act of 17 June 2004 *on the claim for the violation of the right to judicial proceedings conducted within a reasonable time.* [165] By virtue of the Act, a party to any court proceedings, including enforcement proceedings, may file a claim for the violation of her rights due to an unreasonable delay of the proceedings. This can be done as long as the proceedings have not ended. The court may order the trial court to take necessary measures in a given time framework and may award the plaintiff 'an appropriate sum' of between PLN 2,000 and PLN 20,000. This specific head of damages is paid by the State Treasury or by a court executor. This award notwithstanding, an aggrieved party whose action was successful may institute a separate legal action for the recovery of any damage, including non-pecuniary loss, which ensued from the unreasonable delay in court proceedings. The court hearing the suit for damages is bound by the judgment declaring the delay in the said proceedings. The statutory cause of action does not bar a claim for damages, based on Article 417 KC, filed after the conclusion of the proceedings. The compensation for non-pecuniary loss is awarded in addition to the just satisfaction for the violation of the right of access to justice. The injured party has the burden of proving all necessary prerequisites of state liability applicable in a given case scenario (Articles 417 §1, 445, 448 KC). As explained by the Supreme Court, according to the ECtHR case law, there is a strong presumption of moral harm stemming from the violation of the right to due process. However, the said presumption relates only to remedies embraced by the Act of 17 June 2004 and not by the Civil Code.[166] The court practice relating to the presented rules, in particular the unsatisfactory sizes of 'indemnity sums' generally awarded by courts, has not created the level of protection which is expected by the ECtHR. In the pilot judgment of 7 July 2015 *Rutkowski* et al. *v. Poland* [167] the ECtHR held that Poland violated Articles 6 sections 1 and 13 of the ECHR. Hence, a reform of the legislative model followed in 2017.[168] The amount of special damages remains within the same limits, but the minimum quantum is PLN 500 per year of delay (regardless of the phase of the proceedings) unless the importance of the case to the aggrieved party who has not contributed to the delay justifies a higher sum. The sums awarded with respect to the same case are cumulated.

93. A party whose claim was recognized may institute a separate legal action for the recovery of any damage, including non-pecuniary loss, which ensued from the unreasonable delay in court proceedings. The court hearing the suit for damages is bound by the judgment declaring the delay in the said proceedings. The statutory cause of action does not preclude a claim for damages, based on Article 417 KC, filed after the conclusion of the proceedings.

---

165. Dz.U. No. 179, at 1843.
166. *See* SN of 6 May 2010, II CSK 640/09, OSNZD A/2011, item 4.
167. *Rutkowski et al. v. Poland* No. 72287/10, 13927/11 i 46187/11 – hudoc.echr.coe.int.
168. The Act of 30 Nov. 2016 amending the law on the system of judiciary and some other laws, Dz.U 2016, No. 2103, effective 6 Jan. 2017.

94. A final remark concerns the liability for violations of personal interests by public organs. The Supreme Court has recently separated this special regime (Articles 23, 24 and 448 KC) from the general, 'normal' regime of public authority liability. According to the commonly accepted interpretation, Article 448 KC provides for a claim for compensation of non-pecuniary loss due to the *faulty* infringement of personal rights. Any degree of proven fault suffices. However, in the judgment of the Supreme Court (a panel of seven judges) of 18 October 2011[169] an exception was made to that interpretation for cases where personal interests are infringed by the unlawful exercise of a public authority. Accordingly, Article 448 KC should be interpreted in conjunction with Article 77 of the Constitution and the principle of strict liability of public authorities, both of which dismiss the requirement of proving fault. Hence, unlawfulness is a sufficient condition for a claim for damages for non-pecuniary loss. The above interpretation was followed in a case of 17 September 2014, which concerned a Sikh, who was repeatedly asked to take off his turban during the security checks at Warsaw airport. He usually did so in a separate room and without the presence of any other passengers. After he had refused to do so on one occasion, he was not allowed to continue his journey, fined for not showing his identity card and refusing to leave the security check area. He sued the State Treasury for a violation of his freedom of religion and of conscience, raising a number of non-pecuniary claims as well as demanding damages for non-pecuniary loss.[170]The Supreme Court reiterated that the competence of the public authorities to undertake acts which can interfere with personal rights and freedoms does not mean that the public acts cannot be considered as unlawful. However, when compared to the general system of public authorities' liability, the burden of proof of unlawfulness in the case of a violation of personal rights by a public authority is shifted to the defendant. In the absence of the jurisdiction of administrative courts, a civil court should examine whether there was a disproportionate interference with the exercise of the plaintiff's right to freedom of religion. The Supreme Court upheld the opinion of the Court of Appeal that public safety in civil aviation is a highly protected interest. The value of this common interest is objectively higher than the value of an individual legal interest. The measures applied to protect public safety were effective, necessary and – consequently – proportional. Thus, disproportionate interference established by constitutional and conventional standards, would have been considered unlawful and justified compensatory remedies.

§3. Legislative Wrongs

95. If damage was caused through enactment of a legal act, compensation may be demanded only when in proper proceedings the act was declared void on the ground of its unconstitutionality or non-conformity with an international agreement or a statute (Article 417^1§1 KC). Hence, a prior procedure before the Constitutional

169. III CZP 25/11, OSNC 2/2012, item 15 (an overpopulated cell case).
170. SN of 17 Sep. 2014, I CSK 439/13, OSNC 7–8/2015, item 93, reported in E. Bagińska & I. Adrych-Brzezińska, *European Tort Law 2013*, Nos 19–27 (2014).

Tribunal or before the Supreme Administrative Court (depending on whether the act in question was passed on the general or the local level) is required.

96. If the damage resulted from an omission to issue a legal act, where there is a legal duty to issue such act, the court hearing the claims for compensation determines the illegality of the omission (Article 417^1 §4). The jurisdiction of a common court in this situation is justified by the fact that the Polish Constitutional Tribunal may not hear cases of normative omissions. In the case of 6 July 2006[171] the Supreme Court held that liability for a normative omission could arise only in a situation where there is a legal duty to issue a normative act. Such duty, and not the mere possibility of action by the Parliament, must be imposed in an unequivocal manner. It may not be inferred through interpretation of a statute by a court. Courts should not interfere with the competence of the legislator through the construction of statutes.

97. The Supreme Court has limited the scope of this liability. Thus, liability of the state for losses caused by legislative omissions arises solely when the rights of individuals granted unconditionally and unambiguously by the legislator cannot be enforced due to the failure to pass a relevant legal act.[172] This approach is compatible with the rules developed by the ECJ which permeate the principle of Member States' liability for breach of EU law. The ECJ maintains that the rule infringed must be 'for the protection of individuals' (Article 288 EC) or 'confer rights on individuals' (*Francovich*).[173] Although Article 77 of the Constitution does not introduce such a constraint, Polish courts have exploited it in the sphere of legislative wrongs.[174]

98. So far most of the cases involving legislative wrongs were linked to complex social and historical problems.[175] The key issue is whether a claim for reparation of damage caused by a legislative omission before 1 September 2004 could be brought against the state. The Supreme Court came to the conclusion that after World War II and prior to the entry into force of the Constitution of 1997 (17 October 1997), the state enjoyed immunity. This was supported by the Constitution of 1952. Hence, there were no legal grounds for holding the state liable for legislative wrongs. In 1997 Article 77 section 1 of the Constitution modified the position of potential victims, but the principle of *lex retro non agit* prevents the application of this provision in an action for damages where the event triggering the damage

171. III CZP 37/06, OSN 4/2007, item 56.
172. SN of 4 Aug. 2006, III CSK 138/05, OSN 4/2007, item 63, SN 20 Dec. 2012, III CZP 94/12, OSNC 7–8/2013, item 85, SN of 19 Jun. 2013, I CSK 392/12, OSN IC ZD C/2014, item 58, commented by E. Bagińska & K. Krupa-Lipińska, in: *European Tort Law 2014* Nos 24–32 (2015)
173. The latter condition is automatically met whenever the rule is enshrined in a directly applicable provision of Community law.
174. SN of 21 Nov. 2003, I CK 323/02, OSNC 6/2004, item 103.
175. SN (Panel of 7 judges), 19 May 2009, III CZP 139/08, OSNC 11/2009, item 144 and SN of 5 Dec. 2007, I CSK 273/07, OSNC 2/2009, item 28.

occurred before it entered into force. Interestingly, in 2014[176] the court held that a municipality could be liable in damages for unlawful acts, such as those which impose excessive burdens on land owners, lead to uncertainty as to the future designation of their plots of land as well as for the prolonged implementation of local development plans. The liability of the municipality is independent of the state's liability for eventual legislative omission to provide compensation to owners for restrictions on the use or reduction in the value of immovables due to amendments to local development plans (which is a legislative function of municipalities).

99. A claim for damages against the state is treated as a private law (tort) claim, hence it is heard by a court of general jurisdiction. This refers both to an unlawfully caused damage and to cases governed by Article 417^2 KC (a case when a lawful act causes damage to person – *see* below).

100. The first case arising from a breach of EU law reached the Supreme Court Civil Chamber in 2013.[177] Poland had failed to observe its obligations under EU law by failing to implement the MiFID Directives[178] on time and that the Directives intended to confer rights on individuals. The failure by Poland to implement the MiFID II Directive was confirmed by the ECJ judgment.[179] The court concluded that the requirements for state liability under Polish law are not less favourable than the requirements under EU law. In the given case, the plaintiff proved that he belonged to the category of persons who would have benefitted from the normative act which was not implemented on time. However, the extent of differences between the protective rules of the non-implemented Directives and the then existing Polish banking regulations were not considerable, and hence the failure to implement the Directives could not be considered as a factual cause of the plaintiff's damage. The claims were thus dismissed.

§4. Special Rules

101. The above-presented rules are not applicable if liability for damage resulting from the exercise of public authority is subject to special rules (Article 421 KC).

---

176. SN 27 Mar. 2014, III CSK 161/13, OSNC 4/2015, item 45. *See also* E. Bagińska, 'The Liability of Public Authorities in Poland, in K. Oliphant (ed.) *The Liability of Public Authorities in Comparative Perspective*, Intersentia 2016.
177. SN of 19 Jun. 2013, I CSK 392/12, OSN IC ZD C/2014, item 58, commented by E. Bagińska & K. Krupa-Lipińska, in: *European Tort Law 2014* Nos 24–32 (2015).
178. Directive 2004/39/EC of the European Parliament and of the Council of 21 Apr. 2004 on markets in financial instruments amending Council Directives 85/611/EEC and 93/6/EEC and Directive 2000/12/EC of the European Parliament and of the Council and repealing Council Directive 93/22/EEC, OJ L 145, 30.4.2004, p 1–44; Commission Directive 2006/73/EC of 10 Aug. 2006 implementing Directive 2004/39/EC of the European Parliament and of the Council as regards organisational requirements and operating conditions for investment firms and defined terms for the purposes of that Directive (Text with EEA relevance), OJ L 241, 2.9.2006, 26–58.
179. *See* the judgment of the Court (Eighth Chamber) of 19 Mar. 2009 – C-143/08, *Commission v. Republic of Poland*, European Court Reports (ECR) 2009 I-41 (in respect of MiFID II).

One of the key examples of special rules includes the state liability for unjust conviction, arrest or detention based on Articles 552–559 KPK (the Criminal Procedure Code).[180] This regime embraces liability for pecuniary and non-pecuniary damage suffered by a person wrongfully convicted or sentenced to an excessive penalty, or arrested without grounds. The condition of the liability is at least a partial execution of the sentence (or arrest) or establishing of the wrong conviction, sentencing or arresting in reopened proceedings or following cassation. The nature of the claim was subject to debate. At first, Polish legal writers did not see a civil law claim in this situation, but the Supreme Court ruled otherwise in 1958.[181] Reparation includes damages for pecuniary and non-pecuniary losses arising from:

- a total or partial execution of the sentence or the preventive measure that the victim should not have endured; and
- an unjust deprivation of liberty in the course of temporary arrest or detention.

The evidence of a decline in the financial situation of the claimant has no influence on the compensation for non-pecuniary harm,[182] but it may point at the lack of recoverable pecuniary damage. The assessment of non-pecuniary damages should take into account the period of the penalty or the detention, the consequences thereof (such as public infamy), the conditions of the deprivation of freedom, the impact of any financial measures on material situation, actual loss of reputation, etc.

102. Another special regime is included in the Act of 23 February 1991 on Declaring Void the Judgments Rendered against Persons Prosecuted for Activities Performed for the Benefit of the Independent Polish State.[183] Article 8 of the Act entitles the victims or their families who sustained pecuniary and non-pecuniary losses arising from such judgments issued in the period 1944–1956 to claim compensation from the State Treasury. This type of state liability is strict and claims are heard by criminal courts.

103. A specimen rule is envisaged in Article 23 of the Act on Court Bailiffs and Execution.[184] A bailiff is liable for damage caused by his unlawful act or omission. The State Treasury answers jointly and severally for the damage. According to the Supreme Court, the conduct of the executor includes any acts or omissions, i.e., execution acts *sensu stricto* (aiming directly to execute, i.e., receive sums for the creditor) and other acts. The distinction between the two kinds of acts, stemming from Article 2 section 1 of the Act on Court Bailiffs and Execution is irrelevant for the question of tortious liability for damage. A decision regarding execution cost

180. The Act of 6 Jun. 1997, Dz.U. of 1997, No. 89, item 555 with later amendments.
181. *See* W. Wagner, W. Wagner. 'Obligations in Polish Law'. In D. Lasok (ed.), Polish Civil Law. Vol. II. A.W. Sijthoff-Leiden, 1974, 262–263.
182. SN of 24 Apr. 1972, [1972] OSNKW No. 9.
183. Dz.U. No. 34, item 149.
184. Dz.U. of 1997, No. 133, item 882 with later amendments.

certainly belongs to the acts for which a bailiff is liable.[185] Moreover, a bailiff is liable for damage not only when his/her acts are negligent, but also when they are criminal or simply disproportionate to achieving the aim of satisfying the creditors. Disproportionate actions are unlawful, in particular they violate the civil procedure rule (Article 799 KPC), which commands the proportionality of execution measures, and prohibits the harassment of a debtor and the abuse of the execution by a creditor.[186]

104. As mentioned above, lawful activities of public authorities may also trigger tort liability. According to the Civil Code a court may grant compensation for serious personal injury on the basis of equity. This rule was first introduced in 1956, and then incorporated in the former Article 419 KC. In practice it was mostly applied in medical cases, in particular where treatment was carried out for general purposes or experimental methods were used, in cases where the patient's case contributed to the development of new medical procedures or the discovery of new diseases, as well as in cases of a passer-by accidentally wounded by a policeman in pursuit of a criminal.[187] Presently, Article 417^2 KC provides that:

> If a lawful exercise of public authority brings about damage to a person, an aggrieved party may claim full or partial compensation including damages for non-pecuniary loss when the circumstances, and in particular the inability of the injured person to work or a difficult financial situation, show that the considerations of equity (justice) so require.

In 2013 the Supreme Court applied the above rule to the case in which the plaintiff, having joined compulsory military service, was immediately administered a compulsory vaccine against typhoid fever and tetanus. A few days later he was diagnosed with sepsis caused by meningococcal bacteria, which eventually led to the amputation of both of his legs and to other serious injuries. The decrease in the body immunity could have been the result of the vaccine, and the source of the infection was in the military unit.[188]

105. As concerns damage to property caused through legal activities, administrative law covers cases of expropriation and similar situations. Most significant are the Real Estate Management Law of 1997[189] and the Law on Planning and Spatial Order of 2003.[190] When the state lawfully expropriates private property, the liability is always strict, but the catalogue of remedies is provided for in administrative law

185. SN of 30 Oct. 2014, II CSK 60/14, OSNC 10/2015, item 123; SN of 24 Jun. 2015, II CSK 544/14, OSNC No. 6, item 76, commented by E. Bagińska & K. Krupa-Lipińska, in: *European Tort Law* Nos 17–18 (2017).
186. SN of 25 Feb. 2015, IV CSK 302/14, OSNC 2/2016, item 25, commented by E. Bagińska & K. Krupa-Lipińska, in: *European Tort Law 2016* Nos 19–30 (2017).
187. *See* E. Bagińska, *Odpowiedzialnosc odszkodowawcza za wykonywanie władzy publicznej*, 153–154.
188. SN of 7 Mar. 2013, II CSK 364/12, OSP 2/2014, item 16, commented by E. Bagińska & K. Krupa-Lipińska, in: *European Tort Law 2014* Nos 2–13 (2015).
189. Dz.U. of 2004, No. 261, item 2603 as amended.
190. Dz.U. of 2003, No. 80, item 717 as amended.

and depends on a particular situation. A lawful expropriation is conditioned upon just compensation (*see* Article 21 section 2 of the Constitution). Hence, if compensation is unjust or the expropriation is disproportionate, liability ensues from the unlawful conduct.

§5. Recourse Claims

106. Until 2011 public officials, agents and employees were shielded from a lawsuit by labour law rules. In 2011 the Parliament adopted new rules relating to mandatory recourse against functionaries whose acts or omissions led to a manifest violation of law (the Act of 20 January 2011 on the civil liability of public functionaries for a manifest violation of law[191]). A manifest breach of law also embraces conduct undertaken without a legal ground.

Recourse claims will arise under three conditions:

(1) a given public authority paid the compensation determined by a final court judgment or a settlement for damage caused by an act of public authority which manifestly breached the law;
(2) the manifest breach was caused by the negligence of the respondent public functionary; and
(3) the manifest breach was confirmed in accordance with Article 6 of the Act.

The Act equates a manifest breach with certain grounds for invalidation or nullification of acts or decisions in various legal proceedings, all of which are listed in Article 6. At the same time, the Act modifies the respective procedures and imposes on reviewing bodies a duty to declare whether a particular act or a failure to act manifestly breached the law.

The authority employing the official, or its supervisory organ, is obliged to request a special prosecutorial procedure before a district public prosecutor. The prosecutor analyses the case and decides whether to bring a lawsuit against the official in a civil court. The bringing of the lawsuit is mandatory if the official has not voluntarily satisfied the indemnity claims within seven days.

107. Under the Act of 2011, personal liability in recourse is full, but capped at twelve months' salary of the functionary. If several officials contributed to the damage, the extent of their liability depends on the degree of contribution to the manifest breach of law and on the degree of fault. Their liability is pro rata parte if the respective factors may not be established. The cap mentioned above is also applied to the several liabilities. In a case of malice (intentional fault) the cap does not apply, and if several officials acted with malice, their liability is joint and several (Article 9 of the Act). The new law aims to preclude any other grounds for indemnity claims against public officials.

---

191. Dz.U. of 2011, No. 34, item 173.

§6. Others: Liability for Unsafe Condition of Public Roads

108. Some activities performed by legal persons raise the question of qualification to the sphere of imperium or dominium. Proprietary activities are excluded from strict liability of public authorities based on unlawfulness (*see* Article 417 KC). The Polish Supreme Court ruled that all legal persons including the State Treasury are subjected to regular tort rules in actions related to damage stemming from the maintenance of roads (cutting of bushes, cleaning of oil spots).[192] However, in a case decided on 6 June 2014[193] the Supreme Court held that the rules on public authority liability and not regular tort rules should apply to the liability of local authorities for maintenance of roads. The understanding of 'exercise of public authority' should be broad and include all acts of public authorities. Hence, Article 429 KC was not the correct legal basis and Article 417 KC justified liability. This judgment contravenes the earlier line of the case law of the lower courts. We cannot see how maintenance services negligently performed by a contracted service company can lead to the strict liability of a public authority for an exercise of public authority.

§7. Abuse of Rights

109. It is certainly possible in Polish civil law to have a tort claim following abuse of a right (either substantive law right or a procedural right) provided that the conditions of the general clause (Article 415 KC) are met. In order to explore the nature of such a claim it is essential to examine the concept of abuse of rights. The analysis starts with substantive law rights. The concept of abuse exists within the context of what are referred to as *prawa podmiotowe*. The literal translation of the notion is 'subjective rights', but herein for reasons of simplicity the authors use the term 'rights' to denote *prawa podmiotowe*. The concept is not without controversies, and a whole range of definitions was offered by scholars. Some common elements in these definitions are as follows: a right is an ability to behave in a certain way, entrusted to a person by law, and always related to a civil law relationship. The aim of a right is protection of interests of a particular person holding it. It always corresponds with another person's obligation to respect the right, and it gives the person holding the right the capability to enforce it before public authorities (therefore leading to a potential claim before courts).[194]

110. The concept of abuse of rights is seen as essential by Polish legal scholars and by the judiciary. It is deemed to be a sort of safety valve on the exercise of rights. The manner in which it is regulated, through the use of general clauses,

---

192. SN of 26 Mar. 2003, II CKN 1374/00, unpublished, SN of 10 Jun. 2005, II CK 719/04, unpublished.
193. SN of 6 Jun. 2014, III CSK 211/13 OSP 10/2015, item 93, reported in E. Bagińska & I. Adrych-Brzezińska, *European Tort Law 2015*, Nos 47–52 (2016).
194. Current debates concerning *prawa podmiotowe* are presented by M. Pyziak-Szafnicka *Prawo podmiotowe,* in Marek Safjan (ed.) *System Prawa Prywatnego: Prawo Cywilne, Część Ogólna,* Vol. 1, 2nd Edition (C.H. Beck, Instytut Nauk Prawnych PAN, Warszawa, 2012), at pp. 791–804.

allows for ethical and moral arguments to enter the legalistic discourse of rights. In contrast to French law, and in common with German, Swiss or Austrian law, the Polish Civil Code contains a specific provision regulating consequences of abuses.[195] Article 5 of the Civil Code provides:

> One cannot use his right in a manner contrary to its socio-economic aim or to the principles of community life. Such actions or omissions are not deemed to be within the scope of use of the right and are not protected.

The provision expresses the internal theory of abuse. Actions of a person abusing his or her right are not deemed to be within the scope of the concept of 'use of right' and thus do not merit protection which law affords to those who hold rights. The internal theory appeared in the Civil Code of 1964, in contrast to the position in the Code of Obligations of 1933 (Article 135) which applied the external theory of abuse of rights. According to the external theory, abuse of a right remains within the scope of use. The person who abuses his or her right is however required to compensate the damage caused because his conduct constitutes an illicit act (tort).[196]

111. How is abuse of rights interpreted and applied currently in Poland, and what is its relationship with tort liability under the internal theory? Rights are realized through conduct which complies with legal rules delimiting their scope. Conduct which is unlawful because it does not comply with these rules constitutes abuse of a right, as long as some specific requirements are met. These requirements concern the general clauses specified in Article 5 of the Civil Code. As it was mentioned earlier in the study (*supra* no. 22), the clauses of socio-economic aim of a right and of principles of community life, and with them the entire provision, came under the scrutiny of the Constitutional Tribunal recently.[197] It was alleged that the concept of abuse of rights, especially as it is expressed by Article 5 with its use of general clauses ought to be abandoned as unconstitutional. The Tribunal confirmed constitutionality and importance of Article 5. It emphasized that abuse of rights is a legal construct present in most other legal systems. These legal systems also use general clauses, such as aim of a right or good faith.

The general clauses and their application in Polish civil law were elucidated earlier in the study (*supra* no. 22). Here it is important to illustrate how they are used in the context of Article 5 of the Civil Code. In 1997 the Supreme Court, when interpreting Article 5, held that abuse of a right is a contemptible behaviour which is unacceptable from an axiological and teleological point of view.[198] In another decision, the court held that in practice the principles of community life entail referring to such criteria as equity, good faith, honesty and loyalty.[199] It appears that whether

195. A. Stępkowski *Nadużycie prawa a rozwój prawa,* in Hubert Izdebski, Aleksander Stępkowski (eds.) *Nadużycie Prawa: Konferencja Wydziału Prawa i Administracji 1 Marca 2002 roku,* Wydział Prawa i Administracji Uniwersytetu Warszawskiego: Konferencje Naukowe (Liber, Warszawa, 2003), 49–76, at 54.
196. Z. Radwański & A. Olejniczak *Prawo cywilne,* at 105.
197. Judgment of 17 Oct. 2000, SK 5/99, OTK 2000, No. 7, item 254.
198. SN of 24 Apr. 1997, II CNK 118/97, OSN 1998, No. 1, item 3.
199. Judgment of 3 Oct. 2000, I CKN 308/00, Biuletyn Sądu Najwyższego 2001, No. 1, p. 9.

courts refer in specific cases to the principles of community life or the socio-economic aims of rights, the essence always lies in the criteria mentioned by the Supreme Court. However, with regard to the principles of community life the analysis is more complex. It is clear that a comprehensive catalogue of the principles of community life cannot be established. This would drive against the very nature of a general clause: being a dynamic and always an evolving concept. However, the Supreme Court emphasized on a number of occasions that if a court uses the principles in a decision concerning the abuse of rights, it must specify which principle of community life it is using. When it is difficult to precisely spell out a moral rule of conduct which the court used in a particular case, scholars recommend at least specifying what kind of conduct would be desired.[200]

While acknowledging the importance of the concept of abuse of rights in the decision mentioned above, the Constitutional Tribunal stressed that Article 5 is not to replace other legal provisions concerning rights, and is not meant to shape or create rights. Thus it emphasized the need for caution in practical application of this provision by courts. Courts are extremely wary of the need to maintain the rule of law and social trust. Indeed, the Supreme Court emphasized that the use of principles of community life cannot modify or eliminate the application of clear legal rules.[201] There is also a strong suggestion from scholars that in the examination of the circumstances of the case the conduct of the other party, not only the person using the right, must be taken into account.[202] Thus, those who themselves do not respect the principles of community life in a particular situation should not be able to use a breach of the principles by the person holding the right as a valid basis for their claim.

112. Actions of a person abusing his or her right can constitute a tort as long as the requisites of tortious liability (under Article 415 KC) are met. Indeed, cases where abuse of a right is also a tort are the only types of cases where victims of abuses can take an independent action based on Article 5. Otherwise abuse of a right is only used as a defence in a case initiated by the person entrusted with a right. In such independent actions the analysis proceeds as follows: first of all the court determines whether a person in question has been entrusted by law with a right. After confirming this, the analysis proceeds to the possibility of abuse. As mentioned above, it amounts to unlawful conduct, and specifically one that is contrary to the general clauses in Article 5. Having established abuse, and thus unlawfulness of conduct, the court proceeds to find the other requisites of tortious liability as provided by Article 415 KC: fault, damage and the causal link.

It is clear, however, that not all cases of abuses are torts, and indeed the most common forms of remedies for victims of abuses are outside the scope of tort law: such as injunctions requesting specific performance, or rejection of a claim.

113. While the concept of abuse of rights is used throughout the entire system of private law, it does not find application in public law relationships. Thus, actions

200. M. Pyziak-Szafnicka *Prawo Podmiotowe,* 911.
201. SN of 22 Sep. 1987, III CRN 265/87, OSN 1989, No. 5, item 80.
202. Z. Radwański, Adam Olejniczak *Prawo cywilne,* 108.

or omissions of administrative authorities cannot be assessed with the use of criteria for abuse of rights. This view was confirmed both by scholars and by administrative courts in Poland. The Principal Administrative Court of Warsaw held that Article 5 KC cannot be applied to relationships between public authorities and citizens.[203]

114. Article 5 of the Civil Code can also be applied to situations where a procedural activity is involved, thus to possible abuses of procedural rights. This is possible only if procedural rights are closely related to, or are simply an expression of, a substantive right. For instance, a claim for a sum of money due is a realization of a substantive right and yet it is procedural in nature.[204] However, respecting time limits for submissions or for presenting evidence is not seen as conduct realizing a substantive right and thus cannot be examined with the use of Article 5.

§8. Injury to Reputation and Privacy (of Natural and Juristic Persons)

115. Reputation and privacy are within the scope of what Polish civil law refers to as 'personal interests' (*prawa osobiste, dobra osobiste*). Personal interests are protected by provisions of the Civil Code which are separate from the general tortious liability rules. Article 23 of the Code provides:

> A person's personal interests, such as health, liberty, dignity, freedom of conscience, name and pseudonym, image, privacy of correspondence, inviolability of home, artistic, scientific, inventive and creative achievements, are protected by civil law independently of protection provided for in other regulations.

The subsequent provision (Article 24) specifies remedies available in cases where personal interests are threatened or infringed. Those whose personal interests are threatened by another person's conduct may demand that the conduct ceases, unless it is not unlawful. If an infringement was committed, the victims may also 'require the wrongdoer to remove the results of the infringements and in particular to make an appropriate declaration in an appropriate form'. Victims of infringements may also claim, pursuant to the general rules contained in the Civil Code, compensation for non-pecuniary loss or demand that the wrongdoer pay an appropriate sum of money to a specified social cause (Article 448 KC). If an infringement causes pecuniary loss, compensation may be awarded pursuant to the general rules.

Both the scope of protection of reputation and privacy and the remedies prescribed by law received a much more detailed explanation and interpretation in other legal provisions (including the Constitution), in scholarly writings and in judicial decisions. Their review is presented below.

116. It is clear that the catalogue of personal interests in Article 23 KC is a non-exhaustive list. Privacy and reputation are not named expressly in the provision, and

---

203. SN of 5 Mar. 2008, II OSK 113/07, unpublished. Mentioned by M. Pyziak-Szafnicka, *Prawo Podmiotowe,* 885.
204. M. Pyziak-Szafnicka *Prawo Podmiotowe,* 916.

yet they are very firmly within the group of protected personal interests. A large number of cases before the Supreme Court concerned the right to privacy and to intimacy,[205] as well as protection of personal respect (honour), reputation and image.[206]

117. Reputation is seen as part of the wider notion of dignity (*cześć*). The latter is protected by Article 47 of the Constitution, which refers to dignity and good name as well as privacy. Protection of reputation may concern private individuals or those in the public domain, for instance politicians. It can cover press, television, internet and other media, as well as official statements or documents. Reputation may be touched by an explicit statement concerning someone, or by a form or specific focus of an article or a programme, or by specifically selected photos or captions.[207] It is noteworthy that, in contrast with the notion of privacy, protection of someone's reputation does not extend to critical or satirical statements concerning this person, as long as their form and content meet the criteria of professional ethics and honesty, especially by journalists.[208] The Polish Press Law (Article 12)[209] provides that a journalist has a duty to act diligently and honestly in collecting and using of press materials. His duties include in particular ensuring authenticity of the received information or referring to its source. The publication of an untrue story which caused distress constitutes an invasion of personal rights. The Supreme Court held that if a journalist expresses a negative opinion about a person based on false information, he will not be liable for infringing this person's reputation as long as the journalist conducted the fact-finding with an adequate level of care, and most importantly if his conduct was motivated by public interest.[210] The standard of liability established in Article 24 is described below.

118. Privacy is a relatively new concept among the group of personal interests. Specific facets of privacy are mentioned throughout Article 23 of the Civil Code (such as dignity, inviolability of the home, or privacy of correspondence), and yet privacy as such is not mentioned there. While scholars have argued for the need for a legislative footing for the protection of privacy for some time, the express mention came only in the Constitution of 1997. Article 47, mentioned above with regard to reputation, also refers to privacy:

> Everyone has the right to protection of their private and family life, (…), and freedom to decide about their private life.

Further, Article 51 §1 of the Constitution provides that no one can be forced to disclose personal information except for cases provided for by law, and Article 76 concerns duties of public authorities to protect privacy of consumers. No definition

---

205. *See* M. Wałachowska, *Zadoscuczynienie pieniężne za doznana krzywdę* (2007) 152 ff.
206. SN of 10 Sep. 1999, III CKN 939/98.
207. SN of 6 May 2009, I CSK 465/08, quoted by Zbigniew Radwański, Adam Olejniczak *Prawo cywilne*, 116.
208. SN of 20 Jun. 2001, I CNK 1135/98, OSN 2002, No. 2, item 23.
209. The Act of 26 Jan. 1984, Dz.U. of 1984, No. 8, 24 with later amendments.
210. SN of 18 Feb. 2005, III CZP 53/04, OSN 2005, No. 9, item 110.

of privacy is provided by law, but it can be inferred from the provisions of the Constitution quoted here that it entails individual autonomy with regard to personal information, personal life, family and perhaps other relationships. Scholars add information about health, sexual life, someone's past, income and wealth into the scope of privacy.[211] In the judgment of 11 March 1986[212] the Supreme Court declared that each person's intimate life always enjoys the full protection of law. The presumption of unlawfulness when information about someone's personal life was published may not be rebutted by evidence that the facts disclosed in a newspaper publication were (objectively) truthful. In the judgment of 17 November 1995[213] the Appellate Court in Krakow held that information on late payments by a tenant occupying an apartment in a tenant's housing cooperative is confidential. Thus, public disclosure of the information in the building by the Board of the Housing Cooperative constituted an unlawful invasion of privacy.[214] The Supreme Court also held that if a person was detained in overpopulated facilities lacking a separate sanitary area and an individual bed for every inmate, her dignity and right to privacy were violated.[215]

119. The Act of 7 January 1993 on Family Planning, Fetus Protection and Conditions of Permission of Abortion[216] (Article 4c) imposes on persons carrying out activities regulated by it (i.e., physicians performing abortion or giving medical advice to a pregnant woman) a duty to keep secret all information provided in connection with the activities. Negligent breach of confidence entitles a woman to compensation for non-pecuniary loss.[217]

120. While privacy is recognized as a crucial attribute of each individual, its protection differs between private persons and those in public functions. With regard to the latter, the Constitution also provides for a right to information about people who hold public functions, which obviously needs to be balanced against the latter's right to privacy. Thus, provided the information is disclosed in public interest and the facts are material for assessment of their capabilities in such public functions, it will not be deemed as infringing their privacy. The Law of the Press also confirms this position, specifying that no one can publish private information without the person's consent, unless the information is directly related to the person's public function (Article 14.6).[218]

---

211. Z. Radwański & A. Olejniczak *Prawo cywilne,* 167.
212. [1987] OSPiKA, 86.
213. IACr 559/95.
214. *See* E. Bagińska & M. Nesterowicz, *Non-Pecuniary Loss under Polish Law,* in *Damages for Non-Pecuniary Loss in a Comparative Perspective,* 183 (WVH Rogers ed., 2001).
215. SN of 28 Feb. 2007, V CSK 431/06, OSN 1/2008, item 13; SN of 28 Feb. 2007, V CSK 431/06, OSN-ZD C/2008, item 75.
216. Dz.U. No. 17, item 78 with later amendments.
217. SN of 12 Jun. 2008, III CSK 16/08, OSNC 3/2009, item 48.
218. Act of 26 Jan. 1984 *Prawo Prasowe (the Law of the Press),* Dz.U. of 1984, No. 5, item 24, later amended. SN of 11 Apr. 2006, I CSK 159/05, commented by E. Bagińska, M. Nesterowicz, in *Digest of European Tort Law, vol II: Essential Cases on Damage*, National Court Practice and Tort Law series, 646–647 (B. Winiger, H. Koziol, B.A. Koch, R. Zimmermann eds, Berlin, 2011).

121. Special protection is provided in Poland to personal data (*dane osobowe)* consisting of a person's name, address and other data allowing a person's identification (such as the personal identification number – PESEL – which is given to every citizen). The 2018 Act on the Protection of Personal Data[219] regulates cases when such information can be collected, and generally prohibits collecting the information without the consent of the people concerned. To the extent not regulated by Regulation 2016/679, the provisions of the Civil Code shall apply to claims for breach of the provisions on personal data protection referred to in Articles 79 and 82 of that Regulation. In the light of the Law on Data Protection, the telecommunication company remains the administrator of its clients' personal data (which are collected for its own purposes) and a subcontractor who stores the data within the limits of the contract does not become a second administrator. The Supreme Court held that a telecommunication company which is an administrator of personal data is liable for damage caused to its client (a party to the telecommunication services contract) if, acting at fault, it abused its client's trust by outsourcing a part of the services to another company. The Supreme Court held that any client of a telecommunication company should feel confident that the storage and processing of their personal data are safe and that their rights and claims are not automatically transferred from an electronic device of the contractual party to third parties for organizational and efficiency reasons.[220] The liability is based on Article 415 KC (general clause of liability for faulty conduct) and the independent contractor defence (Article 429 KC) cannot be invoked. The court rightly emphasized that, in times of enhancing the consumer protection, the court should not allow telecommunication services companies to outsource their contractual duties to anonymous third businesses coupled with the intention of delegating the duties linked to the protection of personal data of its clients.

122. Protection of privacy and dignity were also invoked in cases concerning wrongful birth. The Supreme Court held that a right to plan a family is protected as a personal interest by the Civil Code (Article 23 KC), and as a personal liberty by the Constitution. If abortion was wrongfully denied to a raped woman and she was compelled to give birth to a child, her right to plan a family was violated, which gives a ground for seeking compensation on the basis of Article 448 KC).[221] A woman's right to privacy and her right to prenatal tests are violated when she has been forced to give birth to a disabled child whereas the pregnancy could have been legally terminated.[222] She is entitled to compensation for non-pecuniary loss beside the pecuniary damages for the costs of the maintenance of a disabled child.

219. Act of 10 May 2018, Dz.U. 2019, item 1781.
220. SN of 1 Jun. 2017, I CSK 597/16 OSNC-ZD D/2017, item 73. The court applied previous law on data protection of 1997, but the holding remains valid under the new law as well.
221. SN of 21 Nov. 2003, V CK 16/03, OSNC 6/2004, item 104, SN of 22 Feb. 2006, III CZP 8/06, OSN 7–8/2006, item 123. *See* E. Bagińska, *The Liability for Wrongful Conception and Wrongful Birth in Polish law*, Lex Medicinae. Revista Portuguesa de Direito da Saude Issue 10, 46 (2009).
222. SN of 13 Oct. 2005, IV CK 161/05, OSP 6/2006, item 71; SN of 6 May 2010 II CSK 580/09, OSP 2/20011, item 13 cmt M. Nesterowicz.

123. Several types of personal interests, including reputation and privacy, are also recognized with respect to legal persons (Article 43 KC).[223] The Supreme Court held that the reputation of a legal person could be infringed by opinions and statements concerning its financial operations, which impute an erroneous conduct capable of causing the loss of confidence and trust necessary for the normal operation of that legal person.[224] The personal rights of a legal person (corporation, local authority) should not be linked exclusively with its organs or with the natural persons creating the legal person. The essence of a legal person lies in its own separate legal existence. Hence, violation of its personal rights relates to all the persons forming the legal entity, not to some of them. A legal person has a right to have its reputation and goodwill protected (Article 43 KC in conjunction with Article 23 KC).

124. Remedies for infringements of personal interests were introduced above. They are regulated by Article 24 §1 KC:

> Whosoever's personal rights are threatened by another person's action may demand that the action ceases, unless it is not unlawful. In the case of infringements already committed, he may also require the wrongdoer to remove the results of the infringements and in particular to make an appropriate declaration in an appropriate form. Pursuant to the rules of this Code, he may also claim compensation for non-pecuniary loss or demand that the wrongdoer pay an appropriate sum of money to a specific social cause.

The remedies available to victims of infringements of personal interests have two main forms: the more immediate remedies of ceasing the conduct and an appropriate statement (such as an apology of a specific form and content published in the press), and compensatory remedies.

125. What transpires from Article 24 is that liability of those who threaten or infringe someone's personal interest is conditional upon unlawful conduct, but fault is not required. Thus, it appears to be an objective type of liability, and the person's intentions, knowledge or approach should not play part in determination of liability. Further, unlawfulness is presumed in such cases, and thus it falls on the person who infringed someone's personal interest to demonstrate that what was done was not unlawful. The notion of unlawfulness was explored above. Conduct is unlawful when it is contrary to legal provisions as well as general clauses of proper conduct and principles of community life (nos 40–41).

There are of course cases where in spite of an ostensible infringement of someone's personal interest the conduct is not unlawful and thus liability will not stand. This is when the person whose interest was at stake consented: for instance someone consenting to publication of his or her photographs or personal information.[225]

223. *See* E. Bagińska & M. Nesterowicz, *Non-Pecuniary Loss under Polish Law*, in *Damages for Non-pecuniary Loss in a Comparative Perspective*, 183–189 (WVH Rogers ed., 2001).
224. SN of 11 Jan. 2007, II CSK 392/06OSP 5/2009, item 55.
225. Zbigniew Radwański, Adam Olejniczak *Prawo cywilne,* at 172.

However, the legal effects of consent are regulated by Article 56 KC which concerns all legal acts. Consent is a legal act and as such will not be valid if it is contrary to law or to principles of community life. Another situation when unlawfulness of conduct is excluded takes place if someone is acting based on a legal provision or is exercising his or her right: for instance publication of a person's photograph on a police search note.

In the context of privacy and reputation there is no complete consistency in judicial decisions with regard to the use of an objective standard of liability. The Supreme Court did emphasize that an accusation based on false information which infringes someone's reputation is always unlawful and will lead to liability even if the author carefully checked the facts and acted in good faith.[226] However, in another decision it did pay some attention to a journalist's motives (*see* the judgment of 18 February 2005[227]). The latter decision concerned a situation where a critical opinion about someone, not an accusation, was published. This is a type of case where it is generally accepted that a person's reputation is not infringed, as critical remarks and satire are allowed.

126. The position with regard to the applicable liability standard becomes more complex when compensatory remedies are involved. While prescribing compensatory relief for infringements of personal interests, Article 24 expressly refers to the general tortious liability provisions concerning compensation for pecuniary and non-pecuniary damage. These are examined in detail in further parts of this study. Pursuant to Article 448 KC, in the case of an infringement of personal interests a court may award an injured person an adequate sum as compensation for non-pecuniary loss or, if the victim so demands, award an appropriate sum for a designated social purpose, irrespective of other means necessary to eliminate the effects of the damage caused. The lack of precision of Article 448 KC gave rise to a dispute about the conditions for compensation. The question was whether the actor's negligence is required or simple wrongfulness of his behaviour suffices (as suggested in Article 24 §1 sentence 1 KC). The dominant view takes into account the fact that Article 448 KC is situated in the title on torts. Since fault is a primary requirement (principle) of tortious liability in the Polish system, Article 448 KC may be applied only in the event of a negligent infringement of personal rights.[228] The same conclusion may be reached with regard to compensation of pecuniary losses which follow from infringements of personal interests. Here general tortious liability provisions, grounded in the general clause based on fault (Article 415), apply.

127. The action based on Article 448 KC may be brought only by an injured person, and on the grounds of Article 7 in conjunction with Article 55 KPC by a public prosecutor when the matter involves the protection of a public interest. Courts must

226. SN of 10 Sep. 1999, III CKN 939/98, OSN 2000, No. 6, item 94.
227. SN of 18 Feb. 2005, III CZP 53/04, OSN 2005, No. 9, item 110.
228. *See* E. Bagińska & M. Nesterowicz, *Non-Pecuniary Loss under Polish Law*, 183.

take account of the type of protected interest, the extent of the non-pecuniary loss, the nature of the results of infringement, the financial situation of the liable person, etc.

It important to note the judgment of the Supreme Court in which it held that the plaintiff seeking compensation for the violation of his person interest by a bank had no standing to assert claims on behalf of other customers of the bank, whose personal rights could also be infringed by the same behaviour of the defendant. Personal interests are strictly individual and the plaintiff only has a right to seek protection of his personal interests, thus the court rejected *actio popularis* for the purpose of protection of personal rights.[229]

§9. Interference by a Third Person with Contractual Relations

128. There is no specific provision in Polish law regulating this matter. Doctrinal views are divided. There are those who consider interference with a contractual relation to always be a tort (against the creditor whose legitimate expectation may not be fulfilled at all or may be fulfilled to a lesser extent).[230] They are, however, in a minority because Polish law rather strictly respects the rule of privity of contract. The majority of scholars critique this approach by pointing out that a creditor-debtor relationship, and all the claims resulting from it, are only relevant between the specific creditor and the debtor. This relationship normally does not entail any obligations *erga omnes*. Further, Polish civil law rarely refers to the general concept of duty of care which would prevent harm caused to anyone. Thus, interference with a contractual relationship is not of itself a tort. Another argument supporting this point of view is that, normally, interference with a contractual relation does not meet the requirement of unlawfulness.[231] As described in an earlier part of this study, unlawfulness means breaching generally binding rules (*supra* nos 39–41), and a contractual relationship does not entail such rules.

129. While the majority of writers agree that interference with a contractual relation is not automatically a tort, they do not exclude the possibility that it may be a tort if certain conditions are present. The person interfering must have had the intention to harm the interests of the creditor, and such an intention to harm is contrary to the principles of community life (thus it is unlawful).[232] Further, taking into account the need for an express intention to harm, the requirement of fault which is generally present in tortious liability must be qualified here: only intentional fault can lead to liability in such cases. It is also argued that the intention to harm the creditor's interests must be the main or the sole purpose of the conduct in question.

229. SN 17 Sep. 2014,I CSK 682/13, OSP 2015, nos 7–8, item 73, reported in E. Bagińska & I. Adrych-Brzezińska, European Tort Law 2015, Nos 19–27.
230. A. Kubas *Rozszerzona skuteczność wierzytelności,* Studia Cywilistyczne (Vol. XIII–XIV, 1969), at 215 et seq.
231. Sometimes, however, it is called 'relative wrongfulness'. The debtor acts wrongfully, if in breach of contract: by violating the creditors' rights under the contract.
232. P. Machnikowski *Odpowiedzialnosc za własne czyny,* 387.

If the main aim was rather to benefit the person interfering, in the context of ordinary market competition, there is no tort.[233]

130. In business relations, the interference with contractual relationships of others is a specific tort of unfair competition (*czyn nieuczciwej konkurencji*). Pursuant to the general clause (under Article 3 of the Act of 1993 on Combating Unfair Competition[234]) a tort of unfair competition is a conduct of a businessperson contrary to law or to the rules of proper conduct (*bonos mores*) if it endangers or violates the interests of another businessperson or the interests of a client. Specific torts of unfair competition are regulated in the subsequent sections of the Act. Article 12 concerns interference with contractual relations. This may take a form of instigating a client or a third person to breach the contract with a competitor or to terminate such a contract, in order to gain benefits (for the instigator or a third person) or to cause loss to the competitor. A tort of unfair competition gives rise to a variety of claims under the Act. The court may rule that the unlawful conduct should be stopped, its effects be removed and that the competitor breaking the law must make a single or multiple declarations with an appropriate form and contents. It may also award an appropriate amount of money to be paid to a social cause relating to Polish culture or protection of national heritage as pecuniary compensation for negligent infringement of fair competition.

§10. Liability for Infringements of Competition Law

131. The Directive 2014/104/EU of the European Parliament and of the Council of 26 November 2014 on certain rules governing actions for damages under national law for infringements of the competition law provisions of the Member States and of the European Union[235] was implemented by the Act of 21 April 2017 on claims for compensation for harm caused by an infringement of competition law,[236] in force since 27 June 2017. The newly established rules strictly follow the provisions of the Directive. Article 3 of the Act establishes that the person who infringed the rules on completion is liable for harm caused to anyone, unless he committed no fault. According to Article 7 it is presumed that the infringement of competition law caused damage. The presumption of negligence combined with the presumption of damage results in the regime of liability which comes very close to strict liability. In matters not regulated in the Act the provisions of the Civil Code on torts apply.

233. *Ibid.*
234. *See* the Act of 1993 on Combating Unfair Competition of 16 Apr. 1993 (Dz.U. of 2003, No. 153, at 1503 with later amendments).
235. O.J. L 349 of 5.12.2014, pp. 1—19.
236. Dz.U. 2017, No. 1132.

Part II. Liability for Acts of Others

Chapter 1. Vicarious Liability

§1. Employer/Employee

132. In Polish law vicarious liability is founded on various bases. The prevailing line of thought formulates vicarious liability in two ways: in the tort regime as strict liability linked with some fault of the direct tortfeasor (e.g., servant) or of the person liable for damage, and in contracts as strict liability requiring no fault of a debtor (subject to exceptions) – Article 474 KC.[237] In some cases vicarious liability is based on fault in supervision *(culpa in custodiendo)*, as in Article 427 KC, or on fault in choosing the contractor (*culpa in eligendo* – Article 429 KC).[238]

133. In accordance with Article 430 KC:

> A person who on his own account entrusts the performance of an act to another person who during the performance of the act is under his control and has a duty to abide by his instructions is liable for any damage caused by that person's fault in the course of performance.

The liability is based on risk, but all the conditions of liability must be met: the fault of the subordinate (employee), the conduct in the course of performance of the entrusted task, subordination and the acting on account of the master.[239] The category of principal/master embraces both natural and legal persons. A 'servant' (subordinate/auxiliary) means a person who acts on behalf of his master and is his subordinate. The subordination means working under someone's leadership and having a duty to abide by the latter's instructions. The source of subordination is a contract of employment, and not a contract for services, for a specific task or an agency relationship.[240] The relation of subordination is interpreted broadly, so as to

237. In contractual liability a debtor is liable for actions and omissions of persons with whose help he performs the obligation, as well as persons to whom he entrusts performance of the obligation, to the same extent as he would be liable for his own conduct (Art. 474 KC). No defence of lack of fault in choice or supervision is available, unless a special provision allows for it.

238. *See* M. Nesterowicz & E Bagińska, *Liability for Damage Caused by others under Polish Law*, in *Unification of Tort law: Liability for damage caused by others*, 185 (J. Spier ed., Kluwer Law International 2003).

239. *Ibid.*, 190.

240. *See* A. Rembielinski, *Odpowiedzialnosc za szkode wyrzadzona przez podwladnego* (The liability for damage caused by a servant) (Wyd. Prawnicze 1971), 67–70.

include organizational dependence and the duty to follow all, even general, orders and instructions. Hence, both the persons performing simple tasks (e.g., a manual worker, clerk, nurse), as well as the persons who are largely independent (e.g., engineer, architect, physician) may be considered subordinates under Article 430 KC. Since the level of professional qualifications and skills among workforce in Poland increases steadily, the instructions of directors are less detailed and the control has become more general. Thus, the test of subordination has been relaxed.[241]

134. A professionally skilled employee may be regarded a servant for the purposes of vicarious liability. Hence, for example a surgeon is independent in performing a medical operation, but this does not influence the relationship of dependency. A physician employed in a hospital is generally considered a servant when he is integrated in the hospital's organization and structure, and subject to the management's control even if he performs medical tasks on the hospital's account as well as in his own interest. In the judgment of 26 January 2011[242] the Supreme court held that even a physician who was a registered entrepreneur could be considered a subordinate in the light of all circumstances of a given case. The source and nature of damage remains the same whether the doctor works in a public hospital or is an individual practitioner because – in the court's words – 'the diagnosis, therapy and surgeries are performed by doctors not by entrepreneurs'. Until this judgment the dominant line in jurisprudence and legal scholarship accepted a contrary solution:[243] physicians who performed treatment in a medical institution pursuant to a civil law contract were not seen as auxiliaries. They were independent contractors who provided services for the benefit of patients of the hospital. The cited judgment reversed this interpretation.

Nevertheless, a physician who only 'rents' an operating theatre from a hospital for a given procedure is personally liable for her conduct and the conduct of her assistants. That said, however, the hospital may still be held liable for the 'organizational' and sanitary part of the service (Article 415 KC).[244]

135. In the light of Article 430 KC, damage must be caused by the servant in the scope of his employment ('entrusted task'). This notion embraces not only instructions as to concrete acts, but also all acts within the scope of the entrusted functions. The purpose of acting for the master is material for determination whether an act is within the course of employment or simply arises from an opportunity presented by the employment. If the employer specified the aim of the task, this naturally implies carrying out the task for him, and the act is to be regarded as within the scope of the employment even if the employee disobeyed orders, instructions and directions. An improper performance of the task is a risk attributable to the employer.[245]

241. M. Nesterowicz & E. Bagińska, *Liability for damage caused by others,* 190.

242. IV CSK 308/10, OSP 11/2011, item 112.

243. *See* E. Bagińska, *Hospital Liability for Self-employed Doctors in Polish Law*, Responsabilità civile e previdenza (Milan), 2012, No. 3, 1042–1045.

244. *See* E. Bagińska, *Medical liability in Poland*, in *Medical Liability in Europe. A Comparison of Selected Jurisdictions*, 411, No. 55 (B.A. Koch ed., de Gruyter, 2011).

245. M. Nesterowicz & E. Bagińska, *Liability for Damage Caused by Others,* 190.

136. In the event that ecclesiastical institutions entrust clerics with official duties, Article 430 KC applies to liability for damage caused by them while performing such duties. In a groundbreaking judgment of 31 March 2020[246] the Supreme Court held that if the tortfeasor acted for personal benefit and the performance of the official act enabled him to cause damage, the superior cannot effectively raise the defence that the subordinate caused damage only on occasion. The behaviour of a subordinate who committed sexual abuse must be qualified as causing damage in the performance of the entrusted activity, which entirely fulfils the premise of acting 'in the performance of the entrusted activity' within the meaning of Article 430 KC. The failure to supervise a subordinate does not release the superior from liability (as the liability is strict). The precedent character of the case was rightly stressed by the Supreme Court itself. Vicarious liability based on Article 430 KC is an instrument to ensure appropriate protection to the injured party, to whom damage is caused by a subordinate of an ecclesiastical institution. The Supreme Court sees the 'entrustment of activities' in the clergy's obligation to provide aid and catechism, which results from membership of a particular order. This can be read to suggest that the damage occurred precisely in the performance of these activities, but this reasoning can be supplemented by other arguments. Legal scholars invoke convincing justifications for the liability of ecclesiastical persons for damage caused by sexual abuse of minors by priests and other members of any church. M. Nesterowicz explains that the rationale for the application of Article 430 KC lies in the fact that priests exert their authority on children; they appear as trustworthy persons, 'as representatives of God on Earth'. The exercise of the functions of a priest makes it possible to meet with minors and in this sense it remains in connection with the performance of the entrusted activities.[247] In turn, E. Łętowska argues that the decisive factor for liability for an act of another person is whether the performance of the entrusted activities was a factor that enabled a typical course of action both as regards its place and time, which resulted in causing damage, in this case the molestation of a minor.[248] Adopting the reasoning presented by the authors clarifies the basis for the liability of ecclesiastical legal persons for the acts of clergy subordinate to them.

137. The fault of the servant is a prerequisite of liability governed by Article 430 KC. Lack of proof of the servant's negligence defeats the claim based on this provision. In principle, the servant must be identified. In order to help the victim, courts utilize the concept of 'anonymous fault' (*la faute anonyme)* of an unidentified worker. Hence, it is irrelevant who exactly among the workers caused the damage if it is causally linked with some breach of professional duties and happened in the course of the performance of the entrusted tasks.[249] This concept is mostly used in

246. II CSK 124/19 OSP 2020/10, item 79.
247. M Nesterowicz, Odpowiedzialność cywilna kościoła katolickiego za molestowanie małoletnich przez księży (prawo USA i prawo polskie), Przegląd Sądowy 1/2014, 16.
248. E Łętowska, Odpowiedzianość Kościoła za szkody wyrządzone przez księży, Państwo i Prawo 3/2015, 18 ff.
249. *Ibid.*, 191.

medical malpractice cases (in particular in the public healthcare system) in which it is often difficult to prove whose negligence (the physician's or the nurse's) caused the patient's harm.[250]

138. The master's liability is strict, independent of his fault (whether it is a fault in choosing, supervising or other). Unless labour law immunity is applied (*see* below), both master and servant may be sued, and their liability is joint and several. Pursuant to the provisions of the Labour Code of 1974 (*Kodeks Pracy*) if an employee causes damage to a third party while performing her duties, the employer solely is obliged to redress the damage (Article 120 §1). This means that labour law rules prevent a person who was injured by the conduct of an employee in the scope of employment from filing a claim in court against the employee. The victim must sue the employer, who is obliged to redress the damage in accordance with the Civil Code rules (in particular Article 430 KC). The rule stipulated in Article 120 abrogates the direct liability of an employee unless one of the following three exceptions applies:

(1) damage was caused by an intentional fault;
(2) the employer is insolvent or underinsured;
(3) the damage was not inflicted in the course of employment, but 'on the occasion' of employment.

139. An employer has the right of recourse against the employee. The recourse in the labour relations is limited to the equivalent of three months' earnings of an employee unless the latter inflicted the damage intentionally, in which case the employer, having paid the damages, has full recourse. Moreover, Article 43 of the Act on Compulsory Insurance provides for the insurer's recourse against a driver without a valid licence (unless he did so in an emergency situation or in a chase after a criminal).[251] This rule prevails over the protection granted to employees by the labour law rules. The Supreme Court held that it is irrelevant whether the fact of not having a driving licence at the time of the accident was causally connected to the occurrence of the damage. The aim of Article 43 is prevention and deterrence. The provision embraces all categories of drivers, hence not excluding professional drivers or those who are protected as employees by Article 120 of the Labour Code.

According to judicial decisions, the limited employee liability does not apply to physicians who are not employed pursuant to an employment contract, but on the basis of a civil law contract (similar to mandate). Such physicians incur full tortious liability for damage inflicted while treating patients (Article 415 KC), which is joint and several with the healthcare institution (Article 441 KC).[252]

---

250. *See* S. Kalus, *Liability for Medical Damages in Polish Law*, in *Tort law in Poland, Germany and Europe*, 51 (B Heiderhoff/G Żmij eds, Sellier 2009). Court of Appeal in Łódź, 8 Jul. 2015, I ACa 63/15, OSP 11/2016 item 109.
251. The Act of 22 May 2003 on Compulsory Insurance, the Insurance Guarantee Fund and Polish Bureau of Traffic Insurers Dz.U. 2003, No. 124, at 1152 with later amendments.
252. *See* E. Bagińska, *Medical liability in Poland*, No. 54.

140. Usually, Polish courts hold that an employer bears the risk of his employee's activity, even if the employee exceeds his competence, unless the conduct in question is criminal. For example, the Supreme Court ruled that an employer is liable for damage when his employee uses the company's car for his private purpose and thereby breaches his authority.[253] In the case of criminal nature of the servant's conduct, the jurisprudence holds the opinion that theft or fraud fall outside of the scope of entrusted tasks in the meaning of Article 430 KC because they fulfil solely personal purposes.[254] However, if such conduct was facilitated by the entrusted function or the latter served as the means to cause damage, the answer may be different. Along this line of argument in some cases courts found a way around the exception to the *respondeat superior* rule. With respect to damage caused by a criminal act of a bank's employee, the bank was held directly liable for its own negligence (Article 415 KC). Defective functioning of the banking services which facilitate or allow criminal conduct of a bank employee constitutes the bank's own tort, because banks have a general duty to organize their operations in such a way as to ensure safety of deposits (*see supra* no. 75).[255]

As concerns recourse towards public officials *see supra* nos 106–107.

§2. Independent Contractors

141. The Civil Code provides in Article 429 that anyone who entrusts another person with the execution of a task is liable for damage caused by that person in carrying out the task, unless the former is free of fault in his choice or he entrusted the execution of the task to a person, enterprise or institution performing such tasks within the scope of their professional activity.

In the tort regime, the possibility of raising the independent contractor defence is conditional upon the determination of whether the case relates to liability for an independent contractor or for a servant (employee). In order to answer this question, one has to look at the scope of power of management and control over this person's activities[256] (*see supra* no. 134). In contrast to employer's liability (Article 430 KC), however, liability governed by Article 429 KC is based on presumed fault in choosing the contractor. The defendant may escape liability if he refutes the presumption in either of the following two ways:

(1) lack of negligence in choosing the contractor; or
(2) the performance of the task was entrusted to a person, enterprise or institution which performs such tasks within the scope of their professional activity.[257]

---

253. SN of 29 Oct. 1960, I Co 20/60, OSPiKA 1961, item 161.
254. SN (Guidelines) 15 Feb. 1971, III CZP 33/70, OSNCP 4/1971, item 59; A. Rembieliński, *Odpowiedzialnosc za szkode wyrzadzona przez podwladnego,* 131.
255. SN of 20 May 2005, III CK 661/04, OSNC 4/2006, item 73, reported in E. Bagińska, *Poland,* in *European Tort Law 2005*, Nos 54–64 (H Koziol/BC Steininger eds, Springer 2006).
256. *See* M. Nesterowicz & E. Bagińska, *Liability for Damage Caused by Others*, 193.
257. *Ibid.*

142. A principal may still be personally liable for any other personal negligence. Should this be the case, both the master and the independent contractor are liable jointly and severally for damage according to Article 441 §1 KC.

143. A specific case of liability for agents is worth mentioning. Under insurance law an insurance company bears liability for damage caused by insurance agents 'in connection with the performance of the agent's tasks' (Article 11(1) of the Act of 22 May 2003.[258]). Article 11 section 1 states that: 'For damage caused by an insurance agent in connection with the performance of an agent's tasks, the insurance company on whose behalf the insurance agent acts, bears liability, with reservation to §2. Article 429 of Civil Code does not apply.'

144. The Supreme Court in a judgment of 13 August 2015[259] ruled that the liability prescribed in Article 11(1) of the Act of 22 May 2003 is strict. An insurance company may not absolve from liability by referring to its fault in appointing the agent, because this is explicitly excluded in the statute. The court correctly observed that in cases of vicarious liability, e.g., in Article 429 KC and Article 430 KC, Polish jurisprudence and doctrine distinguish between 'damage caused in the exercise of a certain act' and 'damage caused on the occasion of exercising a certain act'. In the given case the plaintiff concluded a life insurance contract with an insurance company represented by its agent. Later, an agent suggested the plaintiff invest money in 'investment insurance' on the account connected with the life insurance. The plaintiff agreed and the payment was handed over to the agent upon her assurance of the correctness of this means of payment and the deposit of the amount in the life insurance account. After some time, upon information from clients, the insurance company learned that money paid to the agent had not been not credited to the insurance company's accounts. The company terminated the contract with the agent and reported the crime. The plaintiff brought a suit against the insurance company for the acts of its agent. The Supreme Court held the defendants liable as the damage was caused 'in connection with the performance of an agent's tasks'. The court ruled that it should be interpreted as prescribing a functional connection between causing damage and the exercise of an agent's activities, which means the coexistence of these events.[260]A functional connection should be understood objectively and cover a much broader spectrum of the agent's tasks than it would cover if the liability would refer to 'damage caused in the exercise of a certain act'. The legislator has linked the insurance company's strict liability with every objective connection between damage caused by its agent and the exercise of the agent's activities, and not just for damage caused in the exercise of entrusted activities.

145. The Supreme Court held that a telecommunication company who is an administrator of personal data is liable for damage caused to its client (a party to the telecommunication services contract) if, acting at fault, it abused its client's trust

258. Act of 22 May 2003 on Insurance Agency, Dz.U. 2016, item 2077.
259. SN of 13 Aug. 2015, I CSK 657/14, OSNIC-ZD D/2016, item 77, commented by E. Bagińska & K. Krupa-Lipińska, in *Poland,* in *European Tort Law 2016*, Nos 59–69 (2017).
260. Similarly in a judgment of 30 Sep. 2015, I CSK 702/14, OSNIC 9/2016, item 103.

by outsourcing a part of the services to another company cannot invoke the independent contractor defence).[261] Any client of a telecommunication company should feel confident that the storage and processing of their personal data are safe and that their rights and claims are not automatically transferred from an electronic device of the contractual party to third parties for organizational and efficiency reasons.

§3. Liability of Legal Entities for Acts of Their Organs

146. Polish tort law accepts the concept of the direct personal liability of a corporation ('a legal person is obliged to redress damage caused by the fault of its organ' – Article 416 KC). This relates both to legal persons (incorporated and registered) and to the so-called incomplete legal subjects that do not have legal personality but enjoy legal capacity (Article 33^1 KC). Article 416 KC is also regarded as establishing delictual (tortious) capacity of legal entities.

Polish law follows the doctrine that legal persons act through their organs (Article 39 KC). For instance, if the organ exceeded the scope of authority and caused damage by concluding a contract, the liability attaches only to the natural person acting as an organ.

147. Strict liability for exercise of public authority by a legal entity is governed by Articles 417–421 KC (*see supra* Part I Chapter 2, § 2). This regime includes any legal entity, in particular the State Treasury, a local authority and an association of local authorities. A legal entity must be vested with public authority by law or by an administrative agreement (with the exception of the State Treasury)..

148. The first prerequisite of the liability based on Article 416 KC is that the legal person's organ must act within the scope of its authority entrusted by statutes or other legal provisions. If the conduct under scrutiny exceeds these limits and its purpose is solely private (not linked with the activities of the corporation), liability under Article 416 KC will be excluded. The legal person may, however, be liable for the fault in choosing the performer of the task (Article 429 KC), and the physical persons creating the organ may be liable on the grounds of Article 415 KC, jointly and severally with the legal person (Article 441 KC).

149. The second prerequisite of the liability under Article 416 KC is that the organ must be at fault. The fault of a one-person organ is assessed like a natural person's fault. In the case of a collegiate organ it should be established that some statutory duty was breached or that the act was otherwise wrongful (against the principles of social cooperation[262] or general rules of conduct). No proof of individual fault is required. It suffices to establish subjective fault and wrongfulness of the organ's actions or omissions. The liability attaches to the legal person even if only one member of the organ was at fault (e.g., head of the management board).[263]

261. SN of 1 Jun. 2017, I CSK 597/16 OSNC-ZD D/2017, item 73.
262. SN of 21 Dec. 1970, I CR 517/70, OSPiKA 1/1972, item 4.
263. *See* M. Nesterowicz & E. Bagińska, *Liability for Damage Caused by Others*, 186.

150. Church entities are juristic persons, so they may be held liable in tort for the fault of their organs on the basis of Article 416 KC.[264]

151. Legal entities may also be held liable vicariously (for employees and other auxiliaries under Article 430 KC, for independent contractors – 429 KC, for things and for animals – as well as strictly liable (Articles 433–436, 449^1), not to mention the general clause of liability of Article 415 KC. As a consequence, Article 416 KC has had little practical application.

264. Regional Court in Gdansk, 25 Apr. 2001, Rzeczpospolita 26 Apr. 2001.

Chapter 2. Liability of Parents, Teachers and Instructors

§1. Liability Based on Presumed Fault

152. Persons who are mentally incompetent and minors under 13 are expressly exempt from tort liability based on fault (*see* Articles 425 and 426 KC – *see supra* Part I Chapter 1, §4). However, they may be liable for damages under the regime of strict liability (Articles 433–436 KC) as well as under the principles of equity (Article 428 KC).

Minors above the age of 13 may have full delictual capacity and thus be liable to compensate any damage caused by their conduct. Determination of their liability is conducted in the context of the circumstances of the particular case (*see supra* nos 53–54) and an enquiry whether they acted with sufficient maturity and judgment. This does not preclude the liability of persons supervising them based on the general rule of Article 415 KC, provided that causation is proved between the damage sustained and their personal negligence.[265] In practice most cases concern gross negligence of parents.[266]

153. Pursuant to Article 427 KC:

> A person who, by virtue of a statute or a contract, is obliged to supervise a person who, due to his age or his mental or physical condition, cannot be deemed to be at fault, is obliged to redress damage caused by that person unless he has complied with his duty of supervision, or the damage would have been caused notwithstanding diligent supervision. This provision shall also apply to persons who, without a statutory or contractual obligation, take permanent care of another person who, due to their age or mental or physical condition, cannot be deemed to be at fault.

This provision governs liability for losses caused to anyone by a person under supervision, including any other person remaining under the supervision of the same defendant.[267] It is a fault-based liability. Negligence in supervision (*culpa in custodiendo*) is, however, presumed by Article 427 KC. Causation between the negligent supervision and the damage inflicted by the supervised person is also presumed. The plaintiff's burden is to prove the damage and the causality between the damage and the acts of the wrongdoer.[268]

265. SN of 26 Jun. 1959, I CO 18/59, [1960] OSPiKA, at 194.
266. Appellate Court of Katowice, 25 Jul. 1996, I ACr 377/96, cited by M. Nesterowicz & E. Bagińska, *Liability for Damage Caused by others*, 187.
267. *See* A. Szpunar, *Odpowiedzialnosc osob zobowiazanych do nadzoru* (1978), 652, A. Smieja, *Odpowiedzialnosc odszkodowawcza z tytulu nienalezytego sprawowania nadzoru nad maloletnim* (Wroclaw, 1982), 12.
268. M. Nesterowicz & E. Bagińska, *Liability for Damage Caused by Others*, 187.

154. The position of adults of unsound mind is the same as that of minors, thus on the grounds of Article 427 KC the persons obliged to exercise supervision are liable for *culpa in custodiendo* while the fault is presumed.[269]

The condition of the vicarious liability under Article 427 KC is that the act of the person who cannot be at fault due to age, mental or physical state is nevertheless wrongful.

Article 427 KC does not preclude vicarious liability of persons obliged to exercise supervision for their auxiliaries (e.g., a school for teachers and tutors). Article 430 will be applied in conjunction with Article 427 KC.

155. The statutory duty of supervision is imposed on the following persons and institutions:

- parents, even if they remain de facto separated, unless the parental authority or full exercise thereof is attributed to only one of them, as well as guardians. (The legal position of each parent is considered separately);[270]
- any institution responsible, by virtue of law, for the children entrusted to it (such as schools, kindergartens, orphanages, juvenile detention centres, other child care and socio-educational institutions);
- natural persons, such as teachers, tutors, foster families.

The duty to supervise may arise from a contract, for example a nursing contract, a contract for care with an institution, an organizer of a summer camp or scouts camp, etc. It is irrelevant whether the contract is remunerative. The contract does not exclude liability of persons bound by the statutory duty of supervision (e.g., parents). They will be jointly and severally liable with the contractors, unless they prove lack of fault in choosing the contractors exercising supervision.[271]

Factual care means care exercised without any legal or contractual obligation (e.g., by a family member).[272]

If the child is placed in foster care, foster parents may face liability based on negligent supervision. Article 427 KC will not apply to natural parents in such cases.[273]

156. The duty of supervision is an obligation to exercise the required level of care. A person entrusted with the duty must prove that he/she undertook all possible measures to prevent harm. The scope of the duty depends on the circumstances of the case. The defendant's status, the physical and mental condition of the supervised person, his/her conduct, should all be considered. Particular care should be taken of adults of unsound mind and the disabled. Negligence may take various forms, for example allowing children to play with dangerous objects,[274] failure to

269. *Ibid.*, 189. *See also* SN of 11 Dec. 1965, I CR 326/65, OSN 1966, item 167.
270. *See* M. Habdas, *Tortious Liability in Polish Law for Damage Caused by Minors*, in *Tort Law in Poland, Germany and Europe*, 114 (B Heiderhoff/G Żmij eds, Sellier, 2009).
271. M. Nesterowicz & E. Bagińska, *Liability for Damage Caused by Others,*187.
272. *Ibid.*
273. *See* M. Habdas, *Tortious Liability in Polish Law,* 114.
274. SN of 11 Dec. 1965 I CR 326/65, OSN 1966, item 167.

properly maintain the condition and the safety of a playground,[275] allowing access to and use of explosives on its premises,[276] giving bad behavioural examples, using wrong educational methods and tolerating the child's immoral friends.[277]

157. The Appellate Court in Gdansk in a judgment of 5 May 1995 ruled that the State Treasury had to compensate for the damage caused by a minor inmate while he was on leave (which could not legally be justified) from a juvenile detention centre.[278]

158. The legal duty of supervision over an insane person is imposed upon a guardian, court-appointed custodian or a medical institution (e.g., a psychiatric clinic).

159. Liability of private and public institutions (such as a state psychiatric hospital) for mentally ill persons is subject to the rules described above. The difference may be in the scope of the duty of supervision over a mentally ill patient. In the case of a public institution it is governed by a statute (e.g., the law of 1994 on the protection of mental health), and in the case of a private one, by the contract or both by law and a contract. Article 427 KC does not apply when harm is suffered by the mentally ill person himself (e.g., by a person who jumped out of the window of a psychiatric hospital).[279]

§2. Liability Based on Equity

160. Pursuant to Article 428 KC:

> Where a perpetrator is not liable for damage due to his age or mental or physical condition, and there are no persons responsible for his supervision, or when redress for the damage cannot be obtained from them, the injured person may demand complete or partial redress for the damage from the perpetrator himself if it follows from the circumstances, in particular from a comparison of the financial circumstances of the injured person and those of the other person, that the principles of community life so require.

This subsidiary basis of liability applies to the following situations:

- when the supervisors refute the presumption of *culpa in custodiendo* (Article 427 KC);
- when their assets are not sufficient to pay the damages; and

275. SN of 29 Mar. 1973, OSNC 1974, item 20, SN 16 Jan. 1974, OSNC 1974, item 26.
276. SN of 15 Mar. 1976, OSNCP, 1977, item 12.
277. M. Nesterowicz & E. Bagińska, *Liability for Damage Caused by Others*, 187–188.
278. *Ibid.*, 189. I Acr 117/95.
279. *Ibid.*, Nesterowicz, Bagińska, *Liability for Damage Caused by Others*, 187.

– when there is no one obliged to exercise supervision.[280]

When comparing the financial situation of the parties, the court should take into account their assets, earning capacity, family status and maintenance obligations. It should also consider other circumstances, like the type of harm, the age, mental and physical condition of both the wrongdoer and the victim. The court may award full or partial compensation, depending on the circumstances and on the equity justifications.

161. The liability based on Article 428 KC is meant to supplement the general rule of Article 427 KC, hence it should be narrowly construed. It applies when the direct wrongdoer could have been accountable for faulty conduct, but his liability is excluded by the rules of Article 425 or 426 KC.[281]

280. SN of 9 Mar. 1963, 4 CR 280/62, OSPiKA 1964, item 151. *See ibid.*, Nesterowicz, Bagińska, 189.
281. *See* M. Habdas, *Tortious Liability in Polish Law,* 112.

Chapter 3. Liability for Animals

162. Damages or injuries caused by animals are seen as the responsibility of those who keep or use those animals. Liability for damage caused by animals is regulated by Article 431 KC:

(1) The person who keeps or uses an animal is obliged to redress any damage caused by it, regardless of whether it remains under his supervision or goes astray or runs away, unless neither he nor the person for whom he is liable were at fault.
(2) Even if the person who keeps or uses an animal is not liable under the provisions of the foregoing paragraph, the injured person may demand full or partial reparation of the damage from him if it follows from the circumstances, in particular from the comparison of the financial circumstances of the injured person and those of the other person that the principles of community life so require.

This is a complex provision which does not allow one to determine the principle upon which liability is based until the circumstances of a particular case are fully considered. Liability of those who keep or use animals (the keepers) can be liability for own actions based on fault. It can also be liability for fault in choosing the wrong person to care for the animal (for instance a minor). It can also potentially be liability for actions of another, this time based on risk (although contingent upon fault of the direct wrongdoer). In some cases liability of the keeper may be based on equity (Article 431 §2 KC).[282]

163. The provision includes actions of persons for whom the keeper is liable in the determination of liability. The Civil Code contains several provisions exploring the possibilities of liability for actions of others: those who were entrusted with performing tasks (Articles 429 and 430), minors or other incapacitated persons who are not liable for their own actions (Article 427), or persons who were entrusted with the task of performing an obligation (Article 474). Scholars also add another category: adults sharing the household of the keeper taking care of an animal on his behalf.[283]

164. Whether liability is for own actions of the keeper or for actions of a person for whom he is liable, fault is the necessary requirement. In contrast to the general clause of Article 415, fault is presumed. It is clear, however, that similarly with the general clause of Article 415 both unlawfulness and subjective fault are necessary for liability to be established. As regards unlawfulness, actions of the keeper or the person for whom he is liable must be contrary to generally binding laws or principles of community life. Here the duties of someone keeping or using an animal

282. P. Machnikowski & A. Smieja, '*Odpowiedzialnosc za szkody wyrządzone przez zwierzęta*' in A. Olejniczak (ed.) *System Prawa Prywatnego: Prawo Zobowiązań. Część Ogólna,* Vol. 6 (Warszawa: C.H. Beck, Instytut Nauk Prawnych PAN, 2009), 489.
283. *Ibid.*, 489.

are examined, considering the circumstances of the case: the type of animal involved, the level of risk it poses and where it is kept. With regard to fault itself, the person keeping or using an animal would need to show that he or the person for whom he is liable exercised the required level of care in supervising the animal. The notion of required level of care was explored above, in the part of this study concerning fault (*see* nos 44–48). The Civil Code regulates this issue with regard to all obligation relationships, hence referring to 'care required in obligation relations'. The required level of care depends on the type of relations in question, with the additional point that if a person acts in the course of a business the level of care required will be assessed taking into consideration the professional nature of the conduct (Article 355). With regard to actions of those for whom the keeper is liable, there can be two potential sources of unlawfulness and fault: selecting the wrong person to look after the animal, or direct actions of this person. In the former type of situation, liability of the keeper would be for own action: choosing a person who is unable or unsuitable to supervise the animal. In the latter case, it would be liability based on risk, and yet conditional upon fault of the other person.

165. Not all animals are covered by the provision. Article 431 certainly does not extend upon animals living in the wild, but it does cover any animals which are kept by a person (even if they are indeed wild animals). If an animal living in the wild causes damage, legal effects depend on the type of animal and the type of damage caused by it. Polish law has no single provision or act regulating damage caused by all wild animals. Some animals are covered by the Game Law of 1995,[284] other animals by the Environmental Protection Law of 2004.[285] The Game Law specifies the liability of the administrator or the person who leases a hunting area for damage or injuries caused by hunting animals (game), under certain conditions (including a minimum amount of damage, and the type of damage recoverable).[286] According to the rules contained therein the lessees and the administrators of hunting districts must compensate the damage caused to cultivated lands or crops by wild boars, elks, stags and deer. Their liability is absolute, regardless of fault and conformity of their conduct with law. Other losses caused by game subject to a whole year of protection (e.g., bears, bison, lynx, wolves) are to be compensated by the State Treasury according to the general rules (Articles 415 et seq. KC).[287] The Environmental Protection Law regulates conditions for liability of the State Treasury for certain types of damage caused to certain types of legal and physical persons by specified wild animals, such as bears, wolves or bison. Both laws describe the manner in which the damage is to be assessed and evaluated. They also prescribe procedures for seeking redress, introducing liability independent of fault. In cases not covered by the laws, the State Treasury will still remain liable for damage caused by wild animals. The legal bases for liability will be provisions of the Civil Code: Articles 415, 429 and 430 on entrusting another person with performing a task.

284. Game Law of 13 Oct. 1995, later amended. The amended text published in Dz.U. of 2005, No. 127, item 1066.
285. Environmental Protection Law of 16 Apr. 2004, later amended. The amended text published in Dz.U. of 2013, item 627.
286. The Act of 13 Oct. 1995, Dz.U. No. 147 at 713.
287. M. Nesterowicz & E. Bagińska, *Strict liability in Poland*, 260.

166. As far as a person liable under Article 431 is concerned, the provision covers all those who keep or use an animal, irrespective of whether they own it or not. It is crucial, however, that their custody over the animal must have permanent character and not be purely temporary. Liability extends upon all those actions of the animal which were not directed by a person. Someone who directly influencing the behaviour of the animal causes damage to another is liable under the general clause of Article 415 of the Civil Code, not Article 431.

167. The practical importance and the use of the provision in Poland are not very significant. The number of published judicial decisions is small. Scholars see the following reasons for this situation: very often damage caused by an animal is not extensive, and even if it is, there are certain established customs which mean people tend to prefer resolving such disputes informally.[288] This is particularly true among farmers who are additionally aided by Article 432 KC which gives landowners the statutory lien on an animal who caused the damage on the land.

288. Machnikowski, Smieja *Odpowiedzialnosc za szkody wyrządzone przez zwierzęta,* 490.

Part III. Forms of Strict Liability

168. Explanatory note: in Poland, strict liability is known as 'liability based on risk' (*odpowiedzialnosc na zasadzie ryzyka).* Other notions used to describe it are: objective liability, liability without fault, or liability for result. Polish civil law does not establish a single type of strict liability, but rather approaches the issue on a case-by-case basis. Using slightly different exoneration clauses and thus different levels of stringency, it reflects the argument that various situations call for strict liability for different reasons.

169. In general, strict liability in tort requires a specific norm to this effect. Strict liability attaches to dangerous activities or objects creating a risk of damage, for example premises and constructions, enterprises 'set in motion by natural powers', enterprises creating an aggravated risk of environmental damage, means of transport, dangerous products, nuclear installations.[289]

170. Strict liability has the following justifications: danger created by an activity (activities of an enterprise set into motion by natural forces, driving a car), benefits derived from the activity (*cuius commodum, eius damnum*), and the need to protect victims (particularly in the field of product liability). There is a tendency in Polish law to increase the number of situations where liability for damage is based on risk.[290] In the regime of tort liability the legal norms introducing strict liability have priority over fault rules if both could be applied in given circumstances).

289. M. Nesterowicz & E. Bagińska, *Strict Liability in Poland*, 259–260.
290. *Ibid.*, 261.

Chapter 1. Road and Traffic Accidents

§1. Strict Liability

I. Personal Scope of Liability

171. Under Polish law, liability for damage caused by the movement of a vehicle propelled by natural power is strict and borne by the possessor of the vehicle (Article 436 §1 KC). However, in the case of a collision of means of transport, liability is based on fault (Article 436 §2 KC). Article 436 KC refers to Article 435 which delimits the scope of strict liability by stipulating available defences.[291]

The person liable for damage is first of all the independent possessor of the car, as defined in Article 336 KC (a person who exercises factual dominion over the thing in question as if he was the owner). The law does not differentiate between a possessor in good and in bad faith, hence between situations where the possessor knows or thinks that the right to a vehicle belongs to him or where he knows or should have known that he has no such right (e.g., a thief[292]).[293] Unlawful deprivation of possession transfers liability, but breach of the duty to secure one's own car (such as leaving the key in the ignition or the door unlocked) constitutes the owner's negligence or the negligence of a person for whom he is liable (e.g., a driver). In such cases the owner may still incur liability (Article 415 KC), unless his car was stolen from a guarded parking lot.[294] An employer (the vehicle's owner) bears liability for a driver-employee who uses the car entrusted to him for a private purpose (whether authorized to do so or not), or for other persons who drove the car without a valid driver's licence.[295]

If an independent possessor transferred his car into a dependent possession of someone else, liability for damage falls on the latter. A dependent possessor is a person who holds another person's car on the basis of a contract (rent, lease, usage), having the free will as to the manner, time and place of the use of the car. Thus, a dependent possessor is a user, pledgee, tenant, lessee and a buyer in an instalments sale contract in which the seller reserved the ownership of the car.[296] The possession is not transferred to a dependent possessor in the case of leaving a car in a garage for professional service, during driving lessons, when test driving by a potential buyer, or when leasing the car together with a driver's services.[297]

---

291. *Ibid.*, 259. *See* in general G. Bieniek, *Odpowiedzialnosc cywilna za wypadki drogowe* (2nd Edition, LexisNexis, 2007), and K. Ludwichowska, *Odpowiedzialnosc cywilna i ubezpieczeniowa za wypadki samochodowe* (Dom Organizatora TNOiK, 2008).
292. SN of 26 Nov. 1969, III CZP 79/69, OSN 10/1970, item 170.
293. *See* M. Nesterowicz & E. Bagińska, *Civil Liability for Automobile Accidents in Polish Law*, in: *Essays on Tort, Insurance, Law and Society in Honour of Bill W. Dufwa*, vol. II, 833 (Jure Forlag AB, 2006).
294. *Ibid.*, 833–834.
295. *See supra* para. 140. SN of 11 Aug. 1956, IV CR 258/57, OSN 1/1957, item 28; SN of 29 Oct. 1960, 1 Co 20/60, OSN 1961, item 61; SN of 4 Feb. 1970, II CR 527/69, OSN 11/1970, item 202.
296. M. Nesterowicz & E. Bagińska, *Civil Liability for Automobile Accidents,* 834.
297. SN of 19 Sep. 1967, I PR 288/67, OSPiKA 1968, item 20.

In the case of co-possessors, such as spouses, their liability is joint and several regardless of whether or not the damage was caused jointly. This liability exists independently of the type of legal relations forming the basis of co-possession.[298]

II. Prerequisites of Liability

172. The prerequisite of liability governed by Article 436 KC is 'motion' of a vehicle, which determines whether we classify an accident as a collision (fault liability) or a simple 'running into another car not in motion' (strict liability).

The fact that the Code gives no legal definition of the phrase 'a vehicle in motion' led to discrepancies in judicial decisions and doctrinal writings. There is a general agreement that a car is in motion from the moment of starting the engine to the end of the ride, including entering and alighting from the car, loading and unloading, as well as opening the door.[299] Courts refer to the Law on Road Traffic[300] as well to the linguistic interpretation of the word 'motion' in different contexts. In the pursuit of enhanced protection against risks created by motor vehicles courts took a broad approach to the term 'vehicle in motion'. Thus, in several cases a car was considered to be in motion even though it was not moving in the physical sense and the engine was switched off,[301] when it broke down on route and did not move for a longer while[302] and when the car halted temporarily on the road.[303]

Most legal writers accept the view that the motion of a vehicle is ended when the destination is reached or a planned pause in the travel takes place, as well as when the car is parked in a designated area, such as a parking lot, a public square or a side of a road.[304]

In the decision of 5 February 2002[305] the Supreme Court set 'time limits' to the meaning of 'motion'. The court came to the conclusion that when a taxi, having reached its destination, stopped at the side of a road for more than one minute, and the reasons for the pause were neither attributable to the traffic conditions nor to the regulations, it should not be considered 'in motion' in relation to other moving vehicles. Despite the fact that the stop was temporary, the car's motion came to an end. In this case the cab driver pulled off, switched off the engine, took the key out of the ignition, accepted payment from his client and intended to exit the car to fetch the passenger's luggage from the trunk. At that moment the cab was hit by another

298. Comp. A. Wasiewicz, *Odpowiedzialnosc cywilna za wypadki samochodowe na tle obowiazkowego ubezpieczenia* (1969), 116.
299. M. Nesterowicz & E. Bagińska, *Civil Liability for Automobile Accidents*, 835.
300. The Law on Road Traffic of 20 Jun. 1997, Dz.U. of 1998, item 602 as amended.
301. SN of 4 Mar. 1958, 1 CR 154/56, OSN 1/1960, item 8.
302. SN of 11 Jan. 1974, II CR 703/83, OSPiKA 12/1974, item 261.
303. SN of 30 Dec. 1967, I CR 684/67, OSN 8–9/1968, item 150. *See* M. Nesterowicz & E. Bagińska, *Civil Liability for Automobile Accidents*, 835.
304. A. Rembielinski, *Ruch samochodu jako przesłanka odpowiedzialnosci cywilnej za wypadek*, Palestra 9/1963, 23–24; A. Szpunar, *Wynagrodzenie szkody wynikłej wskutek wypadku komunikacyjnego* (Warszawa, 1976), 114.
305. V CKN 644/00, OSN 12/2002, item 156.

car. According to the Supreme Court the cab had not been in motion, so there was no collision but rather an incidence of one car running into another.[306]

173. The strict liability extends to any victim outside the vehicle (e.g., pedestrians) and inside it (however, in cases of persons transported merely by courtesy liability is based on fault – Article 436 §2 KC), including the driver. The latter's exclusive fault in causing the damage will result in the dismissal of the claim against the possessor.[307]

III. Exonerations to Strict Liability

174. The possessor may avail himself of three possible defences to liability (Article 435 §1 in conjunction with Article 436 §1 KC):

(1) force majeure;
(2) exclusive fault of the injured person; or
(3) exclusive fault on the part of a third person.

175. The legal phenomenon of force majeure and its theoretical framework appear a number of times in this study, especially in parts concerning various types of strict liability. Thus it merits a short explanation. The Civil Code does not formulate the definition of force majeure, even though the concept is found in several provisions, where it operates to preclude liability or to produce other legal effects. The leading *opinio juris* accepts the objective theory of force majeure, but there is some dispute regarding the decisive factors for the establishment of this phenomenon.[308] Judicial decisions, however, are quite consistent in approach. Force majeure is understood to mean an extraneous and an extraordinary event, the effects of which could neither be foreseen nor be prevented. The foreseeability of event should be seen objectively as the ability to forecast a concrete situation and an outcome of force majeure. The anticipation of the phenomenon as such (e.g., the arrival of tornado or flood) does not permit the conclusion of force majeure, unless its consequences could not be foreseen or avoided. Usually force majeure covers phenomena such as a flood, lightning, tornado, avalanche, a sudden unexpected snowstorm or impenetrable fog. In the context of vehicles, some sources of damage, like a defective car mechanism (a brake system, steering system, engine, tyre rupture, or a breakdown of street lights) are not qualified as force majeure. The same is true in a case of such weather conditions as fog or ice which the driver could have foreseen.[309] According to the Supreme Court, the driver's state of health, even if he fainted or died while driving is not considered force majeure. In the judgment of 9

306. *See* E. Bagińska, in *European Tort Law 2002*, 331–332 (H. Koziol, B.C. Steininger eds, Springer, 2003).
307. *See* M. Nesterowicz & E. Bagińska, *Civil Liability for Automobile Accidents*, 836.
308. *See* W. Warkallo, *Odpowiedzialnosc odszkodowawcza*, 288.
309. *Ibid.*

July 1962[310] the court held that an attack of epilepsy suffered by a driver during a journey is not an extraneous event and may not be considered force majeure. This is the case even if the driver's health and current medical tests would not warrant any suspicion that a possible seizure could occur.

176. The fault of the injured person must be the exclusive cause of the damage (e.g., a pedestrian suddenly runs into the street, or a passenger jumps into a moving car). Exclusivity is not present when there are some other circumstances or facts that contributed to the occurrence of damage, whether the possessor may be at fault or not.[311] According to judicial decisions, a driver has a duty to watch both the street and the pavement adjacent to a zebra crossing in order to make sure he is prepared to stop when a pedestrian appears on the car's path. There is no fault on the part of a pedestrian who while crossing the street stepped back, if the reason of this action was fear of other cars. This is the case even though the pedestrian in fact misjudged the traffic situation.[312]

If the victim is a minor below 13 to whom fault may not be attributed due to age (Article 426 KC), the possessor of the car is liable although the compensation may be reduced when the conduct of the injured amounts to contributory negligence (Article 362 KC).[313]

The defence of an exclusive fault of the victim was not admitted in the decision of 22 June 1964,[314] where a driver ran down an intoxicated bicyclist. The latter, while riding on the wrong side of the road, suddenly changed lane and hit the passing car. In the Supreme Court's view the driver should have acted more cautiously after having noticed a cyclist behaving erratically. The proper reaction should have included, in particular, reducing the speed of the car.

The exclusive connection between the faulty conduct and the damage releases the possessor from liability.[315] Poor road conditions (icy road, fog, or bad visibility at night) fall within the risk of the car's possessor. Inadequate road conditions which can be attributed to someone else's negligence are not a defence to the liability of the possessor as long as he should have known about them and should have taken account of them by exercising maximum care.[316]

177. The category of a 'third person' comprises any road user or a person obliged to maintain the safety of the road (state and self-government local authority, a possessor of adjacent real estate, a company carrying out road works). An employee of the car possessor, a driver, a garage where the car is being repaired or a thief are not considered third persons. With respect to the possessor's family members or persons driving on his behalf or with his consent – they are not treated as third persons, either.[317]

---

310. II CR 52/64, OSPiKA 2/1964, item 26.
311. *See* M. Nesterowicz & E. Bagińska, *Civil Liability for Automobile Accidents*, 837.
312. *Ibid.*
313. SN of 20 Sep. 1975, III CZP 8/75, OSN 7–8/1976, at 151.
314. II CR 44/64, OSPiKA 11/1965, item 231.
315. SN of 6 Jul. 1973, II CR 156/73, OSPiKA 5/1974, item 95.
316. *See* M. Nesterowicz & E. Bagińska, *Civil Liability for Automobile Accidents*, 838.
317. *Ibid.*

The possessor cannot avoid liability by pointing to the defects in construction of the vehicle, since the producer is not a third person and the risk of all defects falls on the possessor.[318]

In the judgment of 15 September 1956[319] the Supreme Court held that negligence of a person responsible for road maintenance that had led to an accident did not release a transport company from the duty to repair damage. A company who professionally deals in transportation of passengers and maintains regular courses has a duty to know of the condition of the roads and should give its drivers appropriate instructions.

A strict liability claim against the possessor will not be established if the cause of the damage was both the fault of a third party and of the victim.

§2. Derogation from Strict Liability: Liability for Traffic Accidents Based on Fault

178. Liability for traffic accidents is based on fault as regards two situations:

(1) mutual claims between the possessors of cars which collided; and
(2) gratuitous transport of a person.[320]

The concept of a 'collision' should be understood as a physical contact of at least two vehicles while they stay in motion in relation to each other according to the provisions of the road traffic law.[321] The collision is any contact of cars in motion, regardless of its reason.[322] Recently, the Supreme Court accepted a broad approach to the notion of collision, taking account of the provisions of the Law on Road Traffic of 20 June 1997.[323]

179. In the case of a collision liability falls on the negligent possessor of a vehicle who has a duty to pay full compensation to the other possessor. If both possessors are at fault, each of them is obliged to redress the other's damage. However, when one of the vehicles participating in a collision creates disproportionate risk (e.g., a truck colliding with a motorcycle), it is believed that special scrutiny should be applied to the conduct of the driver whose vehicle creates enhanced danger. In the case where neither party acted negligently, no cause of action arises and each person has to bear her own loss.[324] Injuries resulting from a collision may be suffered by persons other than possessors, for example by persons carried for remuneration or gratuitously (by courtesy), as well as by passers-by. The liability of all

---

318. SN of 4 Oct. 1966, II CR 328/66, OSN 5/1967, item 88.
319. 4 CR 356/56, OSN 1957, item 58.
320. *See* M. Nesterowicz & E. Bagińska, *Civil Liability for Automobile Accidents*, 839–840.
321. SN of 4 Mar. 1958, I CR 154/56, OSPiKA 10/1959, item 257.
322. SN of 2 Jan.1976, III CZP 79/75, OSN 7–8/1976, item 155.
323. Dz.U. of 1998, at 602 as amended. According to the law a driver is obliged to keep a distance sufficient to avoid collision in case of braking or stopping by a preceding car. *See* SN of 5 Feb. 2002, V CKN 644/00, OSN 12/2002, item 156.
324. M. Nesterowicz & E. Bagińska, *Civil Liability for Automobile Accidents*, 839.

possessors towards those victims is joint and several (Article 441 KC).[325] It is based on the principle of risk, except for liability of the possessor who carries a passenger by courtesy, which is based on fault.[326] A driver who does not possess the car is a third party to whom both co-possessors are strictly liable. However, if the accident's cause is solely attributable to the driver, he has no cause of action against the possessors.

180. The second situation of fault-based liability is carriage by courtesy. It is one performed gratuitously, without receiving any benefit, not based on any legal obligation on the part of the person giving a ride and not linked with any financial compensation on the part of the guest passenger (e.g., a ride given to family members, friends, hitch-hikers). In numerous cases the Supreme Court explained the distinction between transport by courtesy and transport for free (without payment at the time the service takes place).[327] In the judgment of 17 April 1970[328] the court held that carriage performed by the possessor of the car with the intent to carry out a contract with the guest passenger to go on a trip and share the cost of travel is not carriage by courtesy. The element of courtesy is also missing in situations where carriage was for the advantage or by order of the possessor (transportation of a mechanic from a service station to the garage or a test ride for a prospective buyer, transportation of employees to or from the work place).[329] A passenger who uses public transportation without buying a ticket is not transported gratuitously.[330]

181. The liability of the possessor towards a guest passenger may be entirely excluded when a very bad technical condition of the car or the fact that the driver was intoxicated indicate that the passenger should have refrained from taking a ride. The awareness of the risk arising for those circumstances justifies the conclusion that the guest passenger assumed the risk of damage.[331]

§3. Liability of the Insurer

182. All possessors of cars are obliged to take out civil liability insurance for damage arising from traffic accidents.[332] In case of an accident the injured person may bring his claim directly to an insurer (*actio directa* [333]) or to the Insurance Guarantee Fund. Civil liability insurance of car possessors covers civil liability of

325. SN of 19 May 1970, II CR 157/70, OSPiKA 5/1971, item 90.
326. M. Nesterowicz & E. Bagińska, *Civil Liability for Automobile Accidents*, 839.
327. *Ibid.*, 840.
328. I CR 73/70, OSN 12/1970, item 233.
329. SN of 11.03.1971, III CKN 524/70, OSPiKA 7–8/1972, item 136.
330. M. Nesterowicz & E. Bagińska, *Civil Liability for Automobile Accidents*, 840.
331. *See* A. Szpunar, *Dzialanie na wlasne ryzyko* (Assumption of risk), RPEiS 3/1968, 225.
332. The law of 22 May 2003 on compulsory insurance, the Insurance Guarantee Fund and Polish Bureau of Traffic Insurers (Dz.U. 2021, item 854). *See* M. Nesterowicz & E. Bagińska, *Civil Liability for Automobile Accidents*, 841.
333. SN of 13 May 1996, II CZP 184/95, OSN 7–8/1996, item 91.

any person who while driving the car during the period envisaged in the contract caused personal injuries to anyone, including a passenger who together with the driver co-possesses the car.[334]

Article 38 section 1 of the Act on Compulsory Insurance excludes the liability of the insurer for damage or loss of property caused by a driver to the possessor of the vehicle. The same applies to the situation where both the damaging and the damaged vehicle are possessed by the same person. On the contrary, the judicature confirmed the civil liability insurance coverage of cases where a negligent driver is not the possessor but the injured passenger is a co-possessor of the car.[335]

183. The insurer who paid the damages may either file a regular (general) recourse action against a person liable for damage (Article 828 KC) or a sui generis recourse action based on Article 43 of the Act on Compulsory Insurance. The second type of recourse is available exclusively in compulsory traffic liability insurance. There are four instances in which the third-party insurer has a recourse claim against the driver of the car. Apart from the lack of a valid licence, those instances include intentional fault of the driver, driving when intoxicated or after the use of illegal drugs or other substances, driving a stolen vehicle and fleeing from the scene of the accident.[336]

334. SN of 7 Feb. 2008, III CZP 115/07, OSN 9/2008, item 96.
335. SN of 19 Jan. 2007, III CZP 146/06, OSN 11/2007, item 161.
336. SN of 10 Sep. 2009, V CSK 85/09, OSNC-ZD B/2010, item 63.

Chapter 2. Product Liability

184. In common with other legal systems, the Polish product liability regime started its evolution from cases based on contract law. Further, also in common with other systems, contract law with its privity limitations and restrictions on recoverable damage did not offer acceptable solutions to the challenges posed by this new legal problem. Thus, judiciary and scholars turned their attention to tort law and at present product liability law is firmly grounded within tortious liability.[337] As in other EU states, product liability in Poland is currently subject to the regime of the Product Liability Directive. Poland implemented the Directive by the Act *on the Protection of Certain Rights of Consumers and Liability for Damage Caused by a Dangerous Product* of 2 March 2000.[338] However, in cases not covered by the latter ordinary tortious liability (as modified by Polish courts for product liability cases) applies. Further, the doctrinal and judicial approach to product liability cases which evolved before the Directive was implemented will no doubt continue to exert influence over the current cases. This phenomenon has been observed in other European jurisdictions as well. Thus, the analysis below contains an elaboration of both: the position before the implementation of the Directive, and the provisions of the Act.

§1. Tortious Liability for Defective Products under the Civil Code

185. Tortious product liability developed based on the general tortious liability clause in the Civil Code (Article 415). Courts applied this provision in the context of cases involving defective products. The elements of liability are:

- defect in the product (which resulted from the defendants' fault);
- damage caused to victim; and
- causal link.

Thus, in theory at least, in addition to furnishing proof of a defect, damage and causal link, a victim would need to demonstrate fault on the part of the defendant. However, in judicial decisions as well as in doctrinal writings on the subject, the concept of fault became much more objective, dependent on expectations of safety rather than focused on the defendant's conduct. Taking into account the fact that defendants in such cases were companies with complex production processes and

337. For a detailed explanation of this evolution, as well as a much more detailed description of Polish product liability law *see*: M. Tulibacka *Product Liability Law in Transition: A Central European Perspective*.

338. Dz.U. No. 22 of 31 Mar. 2000, item 271, later amended. The amended text in Polish can be found on the website of the Polish Parliament: http://isap.sejm.gov.pl/DetailsServlet?id=WDU20000220 271.

organizational structures, courts used the res ipsa loquitur tool to impute the existence of fault when the victim showed that the product caused an accident or damage in the course of normal use. Further, in cases where an accident occurred and yet it was impossible to determine what exactly the cause of it was, the courts also implied the existence of defect.

186. Early jurisprudence on the subject still very much emphasized the need for existence of subjectively wrong conduct as a source of defect, and sought it actively, refusing to uphold liability where such subjectively wrong conduct did not take place. Judgments involving defective cars: Fiat 'Multipla' (1962) and 'P-70' (1963) introduced the idea of sellers being liable in tort to injured buyers.[339] The Supreme Court found that selling a motor vehicle with technical defects capable of causing an accident was not only a breach of contract but also a breach of the duty not to put human life and health in danger.[340] In the 'P-70' case the court explored this issue from a different point of view, holding that supplying a defective product was not only a breach of contract, but could also be a tort provided it constituted a breach of a provision of law or the principles of community life. Both cases failed because no subjective fault of the defendants could be established. On the contrary, in the 'chemical spray' case of 1972 both the seller and the producer of the spray were held liable to the family of the victims for insufficient warnings of the dangerous nature of the product and not supplying protective gas masks.[341] The court analysed the conduct of the defendants in great detail.

187. With time, the focus of courts started shifting away from the defendants' conduct to the very existence of defect (objectively wrong factors). As explained above, two distinct elements must be established for tortious liability to apply: the subjective fault and the objective unlawfulness (*supra* nos 39 and 43). As regards fault, product liability adds its own characteristic features to the debate. Essentially, defect and its exact nature and source become the integral part of the considerations of fault in product liability cases. Reasonability, predictability, avoidability, discoverability and risk-benefit analysis, all play a part in determination of the manner in which the defendant (manufacturer, importer or retailer of a defective product) should have behaved. The objective element – unlawfulness – is linked to duties: those explicitly established by law, or those contained in general clauses such as the principles of community life. The existence of defect in a product which caused damage is linked to a breach of 'objective standards; not fulfilling certain safety requirements and standards of conduct'.[342] Establishing unlawfulness involves complex factual and legal issues concerning the product itself: its construction and design, attached instructions and warnings and protective equipment attached to it. With time unlawfulness became the main if not the only element which was in fact considered. In the evolution of product liability law, courts attempted to gradually

339. 'Fiat Multipla case', II CR 96/62, at pp. 40, 41. P-70 case: SN II CR 540/63, OSN 1965/32.
340. II CR 96/62, at p. 44.
341. SN of 28 Jun. 1972, II CR 218/72, OSN 1972/228.
342. M. Nesterowicz (1979) *Odpowiedzialnosc za szkody wyrządzone wprowadzeniem do obrotu rzeczy niebezpiecznych z wadami*, Palestra, No. 11, 16.

abandon the subjective element (Nesterowicz described this approach as 'objectivization of fault').[343] As mentioned above, through the use of res ipsa loquitur the courts could attribute liability even in cases where the source and exact nature of the defect were not clear: thus implying the existence of fault as well as of defect. Later cases, such as the one involving 'exploding television sets',[344] and in particular the case of 'pin in the cake',[345] illustrate how courts dealt with this issue. In the latter case, the court first of all assumed that the pin must have been inside the cake (it could have been on the plate on which it was served, but this possibility was excluded). No cake should contain a pin, and thus the cake in this case was defective and the producer was liable.

188. Certainly, fault was not entirely absent from judicial decisions. Even though courts were willing to impute fault upon the mere occurrence of an accident which did not comply with the expectations of safety of the product in question, the language of fault was still very much present. This tendency took an interesting turn in the 'airbag case'. Here an airbag opened in a stationary car, seriously injuring a little girl.[346] The reason for the inflation of the airbag was never found, although the manufacturers suspected it had something to do with strong electromagnetic field in a close proximity of the vehicle. It was held that the defendants (Ford Distribution – the Polish importer; and the dealer) were liable for the girl's injuries. First and foremost, the court pointed out that the main function of the airbag was ensuring safety, and it was entirely unpredictable and unnatural for it to inflate while the car was parked. However, the defendants' liability was based on their failure to pass on the information which they held (failure to warn). Apparently, Ford Motor Co. advised its dealers and service stations of the possibility of an inflation of the airbags in certain conditions (for instance strong electromagnetic field), but the consumers were not warned of this possibility. While the result of this case should be applauded, and the court did manage to achieve the outcome which would also be likely to follow under the strict liability regime of the Product Liability Directive,[347] the rationale of the judgment could be questioned.

§2. Product Liability after the Implementation of the Product Liability Directive

189. How did the implementation of the Product Liability Directive change the Polish product liability system? It appears that the transformation, as regards many

343. *Ibid.*
344. SN of 4 Dec. 1981, IV CR 433/81, with the commentary of C. Żuławska, in OSPiKA 1983, book 2, item 55.
345. SN of 6 Aug. 1981, I CR 219/81, OSPiKA 1982, books 7–8.
346. Judgment of the Court of Appeals in Rzeszow of 21 Feb. 2002, I ACa 378/01, OSP 3/2004, item 39, commented by E. Bagińska.
347. This provided the Court confirms the existence of defect. E. Bagińska, in *European Tort Law 2001*, 378–399, at 389 (2002).

aspects of the system, was not very significant. The Act *on the Protection of Certain Rights of Consumers and Liability for Damage Caused by a Dangerous Product* inserted Article 449.1–449.11 into the Book 'Obligations' of the Civil Code. It is in fact a new title (VI.1), separate from the titles on contractual and tortious liability. In spite of this ostensible separation from tortious liability, certain provisions concerning tort, such as those on damages, will be applicable to product liability cases. The Directive does not cover all aspects of these cases, and in matters not regulated by it, of which below, national law applies. However, the Directive is a maximum harmonization measure and as such it cannot be detracted from, for the benefit of consumers or otherwise, by national law.[348] The latter point is material in considering a number of provisions in the Polish implementing legislation which differ from the Directive.

I. Persons Liable

190. According to Article 449.1.1 KC: 'Whoever in the course of his economic activity (producer) produces a dangerous product is liable for damage caused by the product to anyone.'

The Code specifies that producers, own-branders and importers can be liable, and follows the Directive in specifying secondary liability of suppliers (only if the producer or importer or a person higher in the distribution chain are unknown and the seller does not identify them within one month). The notion 'producers' includes those who made the final products and those who made components or materials used in the manufacture of the final products. However, the latter can avoid liability if the defect was due to the manner in which the component or material was incorporated into the final product, especially if the component was further processed by the manufacturer of the final product, or to the final producer's instructions.[349]

The most common example of own-branders (or *quasi-producers)* is that of supermarkets or shopping centres which place their own mark on products made by some anonymous producer. However, there is no agreement among scholars regarding situations where those supermarkets expressly indicate that products were made for them by someone else: 'made by x for y'. While some writers argue that their liability under the provisions of the implemented Directive is thus excluded,[350] the majority are in favour of stricter standards of liability which benefit consumers, and thus see the need for both the supermarket and the actual producer to bear joint and

348. Confirmed in the following ECJ decisions: C-52/00 *Commission of the European Communities v. French Republic,* 25 Apr. 2002, ECR 2002 I-03827; C-402/03 *Skov AEg v. Bilka Lavprisvarehusc A/S and Bilka Lavprisvarehus A/S v. Jette Mikkelsen, Michael Due Nielsen,* 10 Jan. 2006, OJ C 48/4; or C-327/05 *Commission of the European Communities v. Denmark* 5 Jul. 2007, ECR 2007, I-00093.

349. M. Jagielska, *Odpowiedzialnosc za produkt* in A. Olejniczak (ed.) *System Prawa Prywatnego: Prawo Zobowiązań. Część Ogólna,* Vol. 6 (Warszawa: C.H. Beck, Instytut Nauk Prawnych PAN, 2009), 894.

350. J. Rajski, *Odpowiedzialnosc za produkt niebezpieczny w świetle nowych przepisów kodeksu cywilnego,* PPH No. 100 (2001), 24.

several liability, or even for the supermarket to exclusively bear liability.[351] So far there is no response from the judiciary on this point.

191. With regard to importers, Polish law is not entirely consistent with the Directive. While the latter defines an importer as anyone who imports into the EU a product in the course of his business (Article 3.2), the Civil Code limits the definition to those who in the course of their business introduce a foreign product into the national market. It is unclear how this inconsistency affects the practice of product liability cases, for there are no published cases dealing with this issue. Nevertheless, the Polish approach appears to be more advantageous for victims of defective products. While in other EU states they need to seek the person who first imported the product into the EU and who may well be based in another EU state, in Poland they can limit their search to an importer within Poland.

192. The Polish Supreme Court for the first time dealt with the burden of proof in a product liability case involving a seller and an importer.[352] In this case a Chinese defective mobile phone charger, caused electrocution of the plaintiff when she was using the phone when charging the battery. The plaintiff's original charger stopped working so she bought a substitute one from the defendant seller. The producer included warnings against using the phone while charging its battery. The Court of Appeals dismissed the claims because the claimant failed to properly identify the person who sold the product. The Supreme Court interpreted both the Civil Code and Articles 4 and 7 of the Directive in the same manner as did the Court of Appeals. However, it stated that the Directive makes a 'patent distinction' between the importing of the product into the EU territory and the putting of the product into circulation in the EU (Article 3(2) and Article 7(a)). Such a distinction is missing from the Polish provisions and, hence, the latter must be interpreted in conformity with the Directive. In other words, the courts distinguished two elements as regards an importer: the fact of bringing the product into the EU territory and the fact of putting this product into circulation in this territory.[353] The court held that the special rules on the distribution of burden of proof originating in the Directive do not cover the attribution of a concrete product to a concrete producer or an importer. In the light of the Civil Code and Article 3(2) and art 7(a) of the Directive, it is the victim who must identify the producer or the importer into the EU of the unsafe product that caused him or her damage. This burden flows from the general rule of Article 6 KC. On the contrary, the producer or the importer may prove that they did not put the product in question into circulation or that they manufactured/imported the product and/or put it into circulation outside of their business activity. According to the court, the rules should not be interpreted to permit anyone to raise their claims against any manufacturer or importer of a certain line of products, and shift the burden to prove the contrary to the defendant. In order to mitigate the position of the victim, the Supreme Court indicated that the burden of proving attribution of

351. E. Bagińska *'Nowe unormowanie odpowiedzialności cywilnej za produkt'* PS, No. 9 (2000), 47.
352. SN of 02 Oct. 2015, II CSK 816/14, OSNC 9/2016, item 106, commented by E. Bagińska/K. Krupa-Lipińska, in *European Tort Law 2016*, Nos 54–61 (2017).
353. Similarly the Court of Appeal in Poznan of 10.08.2011, I ACa 571/11, unpublished.

the product to the defendant should be facilitated by presumptions of facts, and in particular by prima facie evidence. In particular, a court should consider whether the defendant is the only known producer of a certain kind of products on certain territory or the sole known importer.

193. As far as suppliers' liability is concerned, the Civil Code prescribes that they are obliged to inform the victim (within one month from being notified of the damage sustained) of the identity and the address of the producer, quasi-producer, importer, or a person who supplied the product to them. Only if these other persons cannot be identified can the supplier be liable.

II. Possible Claimants

194. The Civil Code does not expressly limit the scope of persons who can seek compensation under the product liability provisions. For instance, the notion of 'consumer' is not mentioned anywhere with regard to possible claimants. However, it does set one limitation with regard to property damage: the only type of damage recoverable here is the damage to property used for personal purposes only. Further, scholars agree that product liability provisions cannot be used by legal persons, even if they suffered damage as a result of contact with a defective product.[354] In these cases, general tortious liability rules will apply.

III. The Concept of Defect, Strict Liability and Defences

195. Product liability, following the Directive, is strict: all the claimants must prove is that a defective product caused them damage. A defective product (in fact, the Code refers to an 'unsafe product', but the definition follows the Directive)[355] is a product which does not provide safety which can be expected taking into account normal uses for the product. All the circumstances present at the time of introduction of the product into circulation are material in determining safety, and in particular information provided to consumers and the manner in which the product is presented (Article 449^1 §3). There is also a requirement that the defect in question must have been present when the product entered the market (Article 449^3 §2), albeit it is a defence for the manufacturer and other defendants, so it is assumed that the burden of proof falls on these defendants.

196. The Code lists a number of other defences which can be used by producers or other persons liable (these follow the Product Liability Directive, and include the development risk defence). First of all, defendants may show that they did not introduce the product into circulation. This provision is meant to cover situations where

354. M. Jagielska '*Odpowiedzialnosc za produkt*', at 898.

355. This very specific detraction from the phraseology used by the Product Liability Directive has been the subject of some controversy, but its purpose was to distinguish defects in a product liability context from defects in mere warranty situations (Art. 556 §1 of the Civil Code).

the product is used before the producer meant for it to enter the market: including unauthorized uses in the factory, or testing of the product. Further, a person who did not introduce a product into the market in the course of a business will not be liable (Article 449^4 establishes a presumption that a defective product was introduced into the market in the course of a business). The development risk defence, which the Directive introduces as an option, was adopted in Poland. Article 449^3§2 provides that producers will not be liable if it was impossible to determine the unsafe features of the product taking into account the state of science and knowledge at the time of its introduction into the market. There is no published case applying this provision. Scholars agree, however, that the defence has an objective character. What the producer was expected to be able to establish depends on what this type of producer would and should be aware of considering the science and knowledge at the time the product was introduced into circulation. It is therefore not material what the particular producer in question was aware of. The last defence provided by the provisions implementing the Directive is available to producers who demonstrate that the unsafe qualities of the product were due to legally binding laws. However, neither compliance with non-binding codes of conduct and other professional rules concerning products nor compliance with binding general rules on product quality and safety (including the Act on General Product Safety)[356] satisfy the requirements of this defence, unless the compliance with such binding laws was the cause of lack of safety.[357]

197. It may seem at first that the list of exonerating circumstances is exhaustive and no other defences are available. However, scholars add a number of other defences which would apply in product liability cases. First of all, the damage may be due to force majeure, and according to prominent Polish writers this would be a valid defence for producers as long as force majeure was the sole cause of damage (*see supra* no. 175 for an explanation of what force majeure entails in Polish civil law).[358] An exclusive fault of a third person for whom the producer is not liable is another such defence, while if the third person is liable together with the producer, their liability is joint and several (Article 449^6). The latter provision does not comply with the Directive, which expressly provides that liability of producers cannot be reduced if the damage is caused both by a defect in the product and by the action or omission of a third party (Article 8.1). Conduct of the victim is yet another potential defence. The Directive prescribes that producer's liability should be reduced or disallowed if the damage was caused by the defect in the product as well as the fault of the injured party or a person for whom he is responsible (Article 8.2). Polish law is silent on this issue. Scholars agree that if the damage was exclusively caused by the victim's fault, the producer will not be liable because there will be no adequate causal link between the defect and the damage.[359] If the damage was caused by both the defect and the victim's fault, Polish law does not have a precise answer. We

356. Act of 12 Dec. 2003, implementing the General Product Safety Directive. (Dz.U. of 2003, No. 229, item 2275, later amended).
357. Poland does not have a regulatory compliance defence.
358. E. Łętowska '*Ochrona niektórych praw konsumentów. Komentarz*' (Warszawa, 2001), 132.
359. M. Jagielska '*Odpowiedzialnosc za produkt*' at 919.

share the view that the producer will not be exempted from strict liability, but the extent of damages will depend on the level of contribution of each to the occurrence of damage.

IV. Time Limits

198. Time limits for bringing product liability claims are a difficult issue, both with regard to the relationship of the product liability provisions of the Civil Code with the Product Liability Directive, and to their relationship with the general tortious liability provisions. First of all, it must be noted that limitation periods in Polish civil law are not bars to litigation, but merely defences against the claim brought after the period has passed (Article 117 of the Civil Code – *see* Part IV, Chapter 1. for a detailed explanation of limitation periods in Polish tort law). The approach appears to have been transposed into the product liability provisions as well: thus both the three-year limitation period and what the Directive intended as the ten-year long-stop are merely such defences. This runs contrary to the express provision of the Product Liability Directive (Article 11, according to which product liability claims ought to be extinguished ten years after the product was introduced into circulation). Otherwise the product liability provisions of the Civil Code follow the Directive. Article 449^8 KC specifies that claims are limited to three years since the victim learnt, or using an adequate level of care should have learnt, of the damage and the person responsible, and in any case they are limited to ten years since the product was introduced into the market.

199. The latter part of the Article entails some difficulty in assessing the relationship of the product liability provisions to the general tortious liability provisions. The Civil Code, in the general tortious liability part, did until recently contain a very similar approach: tort claims were to be limited to three years since the victim learnt of the damage and the person responsible, but in any case to ten years since the tort occurred. In 2006, the Constitutional Tribunal declared that the situation where some claims may be limited in time before the victim is even aware of the damage was unconstitutional (*see infra* Part IV, Chapter 1 for a more detailed analysis of the Tribunal's judgment).[360] The Code was amended following the decision,[361] and currently Article 442^1 §3 KC provides that in personal injury cases the time limit for claims always expires three years after the victim learnt about the damage and the person responsible, effectively displaying the ten-year limitation period in such cases. It is uncertain what the correct interpretation of the position of the Constitutional Tribunal would be with regard to the provision it declared unconstitutional still existing within the Civil Code (albeit limited to product liability cases). There is no doubt that the provisions of the Code concerning product liability must comply with the Product Liability Directive and thus Article 449^8 KC must remain unchanged. The same approach should be taken with regard to the very

360. Decision of the Constitutional Tribunal of 1 Sep. 2006, SK 14/05, OTK, A- 2006, No. 8, item 97.
361. Act on the amendment of the Civil Code (*Ustawa o zmianie ustawy – Kodeks Cywilny)* of 16 Feb. 2007, Dz.U. of 2007, No. 80, item 538.

nature of limitation periods in Poland. In the context of product liability claims, they should be time-barred after ten years, not merely limited.

V. Scope of Application of the New Product Liability Rules

200. The last point brings the analysis of the provisions of the Civil Code implementing the Product Liability Directive to the scope of their application. Following the Directive, they do not apply to claims which do not exceed EUR 500. They also do not cover damage to the defective product itself and any potential gains from the product which the claimant could have obtained (Article 449^7 KC). Further, as mentioned above, if property damage occurs, producer's liability will only cover property which is usually used for private purposes and which was used for such purposes by the claimant (Article 449^2 KC). What follows from these remarks is that the provisions analysed here will certainly not apply to every situation when injury or damage was caused by a defective product, and thus the regular tortious liability rules (as briefly mentioned above in their application to product liability cases) will continue to apply.

201. Further, the Directive does not comprehensively cover all aspects of liability, and issues such as causation and assessment of damages (especially non-pecuniary damages) will be determined by general tortious liability provisions which are examined in the latter parts of this study.

VI. The Impact of the New Provisions

202. What are the implications of the Directive for product liability cases in Poland? It is very difficult to assess the impact of the new provisions, as the number of cases is very small. It is, however, likely that the following issues arise:

- The position of most product victims is similar in the majority of cases to their position under the old system. There is no need for them to prove fault as long as they show that they suffered injuries or losses as a result of contact with a defective product. Most of the defences, including the development risk defence, contained in the new provisions would also have been relevant under the old system (as they would exclude fault).
- Courts in some Member States of the EU continue to seek the source of the defect, to some extent following the patterns established under fault-based liability systems established before the Directive was enacted. English courts are a good example here.[362] This has never been the case for Polish courts, and the position will no doubt remain so under the new provisions.

362. Decision in the case *Foster v. Biosil* [2000] 59 BMLR 178.

– The provisions implementing the Directive are clearly focused on the business-to-consumer relations, while the old product liability system was wider in scope. For instance, it covered those who obtained products for professional use (albeit the requirements as to their knowledge of potential risks were higher). The old rules will continue to apply in those cases which the Directive does not cover.[363]

363. *See also* E. Bagińska, *Product liability in Poland*, in: *European product liability: an analysis of the state of the art in the era of new technologies* (P. Machnikowski ed., Cambridge; Antwerp; Portland: Intersentia 2016), 377–406.

Chapter 3. Strict Liability of an Enterprise

203. According to Article 435 KC a person conducting on his own account an enterprise or business set into operation by natural forces (steam, gas, electricity, liquid fuel, etc.) is liable for any damage to persons or property caused through the operation of the enterprise or business. Liability will be upheld unless the damage was caused by force majeure, or exclusively by the fault of the injured party, or of a third person for whom the defendant is not liable. This rule applies respectively to enterprises or businesses producing or using explosives (Article 435 §2 KC).

204. Article 435 KC is interpreted broadly. First of all, courts construe a comprehensive definition of an enterprise or business. Further, the Civil Code and other statutory provisions turn away from the criterion of a formal title of the person liable (such as ownership) and give a decisive value to the actual control (usually by a possessor) over the risk.[364] However, farming is considered to fall within the scope of Article 435 KC only when the activities conducted on a farm and their effects directly depend on the use of machines set in operation by natural forces.[365]

The Supreme Court held that modern construction companies must autonomously assess and accommodate the risk of carrying out works in the conditions that do not guarantee full safety even when observing the highest prudence and diligence. Strict liability means that, as soon as it is established that the alleged damage is linked to the operation of the defendant's enterprise, the latter is liable regardless of whether he has complied with regulations, professional standards and the requirements of the highest diligence and prudence. The inflicted damage falls within the scope of the building risk and the company is liable to compensate third parties regardless of the potential negligence on the part of an investor. The contractual relations between the parties to construction contracts, the scope of their duties, as well as compliance with construction law regulations are irrelevant.[366]

205. The word 'operation' is also construed broadly by judicial decisions. Article 435 §1 KC is formulated in a somewhat old-fashioned manner: the emphasis being on the natural powers which must set in operation the whole enterprise, and not on the dangerousness of the activity as such.[367] The natural forces need not be instrumental in causing the harm, as the provision focuses on operation of an enterprise causing risk to the public. For example, a railway company is strictly liable for accidents which happened on its premises, which comprise trains, train stations (inclusive of waiting rooms and restaurants), trackways and office buildings, even if situated outside the train station.[368] Liability of a transport company for road or train accidents is governed by the rule of Article 435 KC and not by Articles 436 §1 and 436 §2 KC (motor vehicles – *see supra* Part II, Chapter 1).

364. M. Nesterowicz & E. Bagińska, *Strict Liability in Poland*, 258–261.
365. SN of 15 Feb. 2008, I CSK 376/07, OSNC – ZD 4/2008, item 117.
366. SN of 28 Nov. 2007, V CSK 282/07, OSNC-ZD 2/2008 item 54.
367. *See* J. Lopuski, *Odpowiedzialnosc za szkody wyrządzone w związku z użyciem sił przyrody (art 152 KZ): jej znaczenie i ewolucja w perspektywie minionego 70-lecia*, KPP 2004, No. 3, 693.
368. M. Nesterowicz & E. Bagińska, *Strict liability in Poland*, 258–259.

206. In cases of harmful emissions produced by an enterprise, earlier court practice took the view that the duty to redress damage arose only in cases where such negative emissions by an industrial plant exceeded the commonly suffered effects of the deterioration of the environment in a given area.[369] The above limitation stemmed from Article 144 KC. According to this provision, the owner of real estate should in exercising his rights refrain from activities which would disturb the utilization of neighbouring real property beyond what could be seen as the average level. What exactly the average level is in a particular case stems from the socio-economic purpose of the real property and the local conditions. This interpretation of Article 435 §1 KC, essentially limiting the notion of risk (hazard) imposed on an enterprise set in operation by natural forces, has no ground in the current law.

The present position was first approved in the Supreme Court judgment of 6 October 1976.[370] In this case, the claimants demanded recovery for personal injuries and damage to their agricultural and farming businesses. The damage stemmed from emission of harmful limestone dust by the adjacent defendant enterprise. In the area where the claimants lived and ran their businesses, various industrial facilities which discharged damaging smoke were operating. The claimants sued only one enterprise, the one they deemed to be the greatest polluter and the cause of the damage. The defendant contested liability claiming that the discharge from their chimneys and from the chimneys of the other facilities was never measured. The Supreme Court held that the causal link between a given disease of the injured party and the operation of an industrial enterprise which emits harmful substances is established as soon as it is proven that the victim was exposed to the damaging pollution, as long as his disease is a normal consequence thereof. In addition, the Supreme Court indicated that even though the damage could arise only in the case of aggravation of harmful substances emitted by different industrial units, strict liability of an enterprise under Article 435 KC was not excluded. Each industrial enterprise can and should be aware of the fact that any additional source of harmful air pollution worsens living conditions in a given area and, as a result of the accumulation of different effluences, it may cause certain harm. This is the case in spite of the fact that the emissions originating in the particular enterprise did not themselves exceed the environmental standards prescribed in the relevant legal provisions. Because the defendant asserted that the density of the limestone dust emitted by him was not measured, the Supreme Court held that the law imposes the obligation to measure the density of polluting gases on the enterprises which emit such gases. It is the defendant enterprise, and not the claimant, who should bear the burden of proving that the harmful dust discharged by the former had no impact on the damage suffered by the latter. This ruling of the Supreme Court was approved by doctrine and since then the Supreme Court has usually held that a defendant enterprise is responsible for the entire damage unless it supplies counter-evidence supporting the conclusion that its activities did not cause the claimant's harm or caused only a small part of it.[371]

369. SN of 7 Apr. 1970, III CZP 17/70, OSPiKA 1971/9, at 169; SN of 3 Jul. 1969, II CR 208/69, OSPiKA 1971/5, at 87.
370. IV CR 380/76, OSN 1977/5–6, item 93.
371. *See* in particular SN of 24 Feb. 1981, IV CR 17/81, OSPiKA 1982/5–6, at 64, cmt. J. Skoczylas.

The case above indicates that strict liability is crucial in relation to any environmental damage caused by any activity. *A fortiori*, liability should be established if the enterprise exceeds the permitted limits of a given activity.[372]

207. The defendants may be exonerated from strict liability only by submitting evidence of one of the exonerating factors which must be the exclusive cause of damage:

- force majeure;
- exclusive fault of the injured person;[373]
- exclusive fault on the part of a third person.

The concept of force majeure was explored above (no. 174).

208. With regard to the fault of the victim, it must be the exclusive cause of damage in order to constitute derogation from liability. In the decision of 24 September 2009[374] the Supreme Court held a power plant liable for injuries suffered by a 14-year old boy. The boy climbed the ladder on a high-voltage post, got electrocuted and fell down from a height of seventeen metres. The post was in a good technical condition and, as it was not surrounded by any fence, an adequate warning was placed on it. The plaintiff suffered severe irreversible injuries and became quadriplegic. The court established that the minor, despite his basic knowledge of electricity, was not entirely aware of the consequences of his conduct. The court also emphasized that 'fault' refers both to a deviation from the required standard of care and to the subjective element. Subjective fault is based on a mental attitude of a person for her own conduct. Persons who are mentally incompetent and minors under 13 are expressly exempt from tort liability (*see* Articles 425 and 426 KC *supra* nos 49–52). In the facts, the plaintiff was not mentally competent because of defects in the mental process and understanding of the consequences of his conduct to a degree sufficient to exclude his fault.

The Supreme Court confirmed the above approach with respect to a third person for whom the entrepreneur is not liable. The judicature emphasizes that the fault of a third person must be the exclusive cause of the damage. Moreover, in the traditional jurisprudence it is accepted that the third party must be identified.[375] The issue of the possibility to escape liability after proving that damage was caused solely by the faulty act of an unidentified third party that the enterprise is not liable for cannot, however, be regarded as settled. In earlier case law, it was accepted that the enterprise can escape liability provided that the third party has been identified. On the other hand, the views of legal scholars in that matter were divergent. In a recent case concerning a railways accident the position of the Supreme Court has been

372. SN of 18 Jun. 2010, V CSK 408/09, OSNZD A/2011, item 11.
373. SN of 3 Aug. 2007, I UK 367/06 OSNP 19–20/2008, item 294.
374. IV CSK 207/09, OSNC 4/2010, item 58, commented by E. Bagińska, in: H. Koziol, B.C. Steininger (eds), *European Tort Law 2010* (2011), 462–464.
375. M. Nesterowicz & E. Bagińska, *Strict liability in Poland*, 262.

modified.[376] The plaintiff – a railway company - sued for damages after one of its railcars was damaged while riding on the defendant's tracks. The plaintiff was authorized to use the defendant's tracks under a contract. The cause of the damage to the railcar was a damaged track, which was caused by an unknown perpetrator. The identity of the perpetrator was not discovered in the course of the police investigation. A damaged railcar was covered by an insurance contract and, on its basis, the insurer compensated the plaintiff and then demanded reimbursement from the owner of the tracks. The Supreme Court noted a high probability of proof that it was the third party who caused the damage and that it was nobody for whom the enterprise was responsible should be considered sufficient to escape liability based on Article 435 KC and provided that fault can be assigned to acts of that person. In the case at hand, it was proved that the damage to the tracks was caused by someone attempting to steal a steel sheet. It was obvious that the perpetrator acted beyond the scope of control of the railway enterprise. At the same time, it was highly probable that the perpetrator was a person to whom fault could be assigned (over the age of 13 and aware of the nature of his acts). The conclusion of the court was that a person who runs an enterprise set in operation by the forces of nature is not liable for damage caused by the movement of that enterprise if there are reasons to believe that the damage was caused by the sole faulty act of a third party for whom the enterprise is not liable, even if that person has not been identified.

209. Views as to who carries the burden of proof of causation and any other intervening event such as force majeure under Article 435 KC are not uniform. According to one view, it is sufficient that the plaintiff proves the causal link in fact (*conditio sine qua non*) between the operation of the enterprise and the damage.[377] Another opinion argues that there is a presumption of a causal connection between the activity of an enterprise and the damage, which can be rebutted by the proof of an exonerating fact.[378] The dominant view is that an event fulfilling the conditions of force majeure exempts the defendant from strict liability and at the same time breaks the causal link between his activity (the operation of the enterprise) and the damage sustained.[379] Courts agree with this approach.[380] Hence, no other causes, whether attributable to any person or not (such as a defect in security systems), that would pass the test of adequate causation may exist in a given situation.

376. SN 26 Jul. 2017, III CZP 30/17, OSNC 6/2018, item 55.
377. *See* M. Safjan in: K. Pietrzykowski (ed.), *Kodeks cywilny. Komentarz* (4th Edition, Beck, 2005), 1233; T. Dybowski, in: Z. Radwański (ed.), *System prawa cywilnego,* vol III, part I (Ossolineum, 1981), 270; M. Nesterowicz, in: J. Winiarz (ed.), *Kodeks cywilny z komentarzem,* vol I (2nd Edition, Wyd. Prawnicze, 1989), 428; Cf. W. Dubis in: E. Gniewek (ed.), *Kodeks cywilny. Komentarz* (3rd Edition, Beck, 2008), 770.
378. *See* B. Lewaszkiewicz-Petrykowska, *Odpowiedzialnosc cywilna prowadzącego przedsiebiorstwo wprawiane w ruch przy pomocy sił przyrody* (art 435 KC) (Wyd. Prawnicze, 1967), 130.
379. *See* M. Nesterowicz, in: J Winiarz (ed.), 1988, 428. Compare W. Dubis, 2008, 770.
380. SN of 27 Jul. 1973, II CR 233/73, OSPiKA 1974/ 9, item 190, cmt. A. Rembieliński, SN of 15 Mar. 1974, I CR 46/74, OSPiKA 9/1976, item 172; SN of 28 Nov. 2007, V CSK 282/07, OSNC-ZD 2/2008 item 54.

Chapter 4. Environmental Liability

210. Environmental liability is governed by the Environmental Protection Law [EPL] of 27 April 2001 (Articles 322–328).[381] The EPL provides that unless a statute stipulates otherwise, the Civil Code provisions apply to damage incurred through influence on the environment. With the exception of the sea, the environment (air, water, soil, forest) is protected by tort provisions of Article 435 KC and Article 415 KC.

211. In accordance with Article 323 section 1 EPL anyone who is exposed to the risk of damage or who incurred damage through another's illegal influence on the environment may demand from the person responsible that he rectifies the position and takes preventive measures, such as installing safety appliances or machines. Where a preventive action is impossible or unreasonably difficult, the claimant may demand that the actor abstain from the infringement. If the exposure to the risk of damage or infringement concerns the environment 'as a common value' the above claims may be brought by the State Treasury, a local authority or an ecological organization (Article 323 section 2 EPL).

212. According to Article 324 EPL, if damage is caused by an enterprise operating with an aggravated or major risk, Article 435 KC applies even if the enterprise is run without the use of natural forces. This rule means that the liability of such an enterprise is strict liability and the category of defendants is broader than in Article 435 KC. The fact that the operation of an enterprise detrimental to the environment has its basis in an administrative decision does not constitute a defence to liability.

213. Pursuant to Article 326 EPL, the person who repaired the damage to the environment has a right of indemnity against the person who caused it. However, recovery is limited to reasonable expenses necessary for the restoration to the state of affairs before the infringement.

214. Redress of environmental damage is also covered by the Act on Prevention and Remedying of Environmental Damage, adopted on 13 April 2007 (PREP, implementing Directive 2004/35 on environmental liability with regard to the prevention and the remedying of environmental damage). It complements the EPL with regard to liability for damage to the environment (*see* Article 7a EPL). PREP does not provide for 'financial defences' exempting the operator from bearing the costs of prevention and remediation ('permit defence' and 'state of the art defence', as provided for by Article 8.4 of the Environmental Liability Directive).

381. Dz.U. 2001, No. 62, item 627 as amended.

215. In the case of mining and geological damage, the Act of 4 February 1994 – Geological and Mining Law[382] applies. The landowner (or other parties endangered by mining plant operations) may not object to the threats caused by the operations if they are carried out in accordance with the rules specified in the Act. They may demand reparation of the damage caused by these operations in accordance with provisions of the Act (Article 91). The damage should be repaired by way of restoration of the former state or by provision of land, constructions, devices, premises, water or other goods of the same kind. Damaged afforested and agricultural lands should be subject to cultivation. If the restoration of the former state of affairs is not feasible or the cost thereof would vastly exceed the loss incurred, pecuniary redress is possible.

216. If the mining operations violated the respective legal rules, the entrepreneur shall be responsible for damage according to the rules specified in the Civil Code (ergo, the claimant has a choice, although not unlimited, between restitution in kind and pecuniary damages). In addition, Article 93 section 1 of the Act regulates liability in cases where the person who caused the damage cannot be identified. Here the corporation holding the right of extracting a mineral substance in the mining area at the time the loss occurred is liable to pay compensation. If the damage was also attributable to causes other than the operation of the mining enterprise, the liability of the enterprise and other persons responsible is joint and several.

382. Dz.U. of 1994, No. 27, at 96 with later amendment.

Chapter 5. Others

§1. Strict Liabilities under the Civil Code

I. Occupier's Liability for Premises

217. Polish civil law acknowledges that certain things and objects can create increased risks for their surroundings, and thus it prescribes special cases of liability for injuries and damages caused by them. These are stricter than the ordinary fault-based tort liability under the general clause of Article 415 KC. Particular emphasis is placed on buildings and premises. It is deemed extremely difficult for those who suffered damage to demonstrate fault when objects, either parts of the building or some other things, fall from a building, or when a building collapses. Thus, the Civil Code provides strict liability in two cases: (1) ejection, emission or a fall of an object from premises, and (2) collapse of a building or falling off of a part of it.

A. *Liability for Damage Caused by Ejection, Emission or Fall of an Object from Premises*

218. Polish law accepted the Roman law action *de eiectis et effusis.* According to Article 433 KC the occupier of premises is liable for any damage caused by the ejection, emission (pouring) or fall of any object therefrom, unless the damage was caused by force majeure or exclusively by the fault of the injured party or the act of a third person for whom the occupier is not liable and whose act he could not have prevented. In jurisprudence 433 KC is interpreted to be applicable in any situations of ejection, effusion or falling of an object from premises outwards.

219. Strict liability as set out in Article 433 KC aims at protecting the party who was accidentally injured. The fact that the legislators chose the occupier, and not the owner, possessor or the person who actually threw something out of the building is likely to make it easier to identify the person liable. Scholars agree that in order to be covered by Article 433 the person must occupy the premises on a rather permanent, not purely temporary basis.[383] Thus, guests or employees of the occupier are not covered. If the premises are occupied by a company, and the damage takes place while one of the company's employees is present, he is not liable under Article 433 (although his actions or omissions may be the basis for the actual occupier to seek exemption from liability). The provision applies irrespective of whether the occupier in fact has any legal title to the premises or not, although a person who occupies premises temporarily in the name of the owner or the possessor is not covered. Article 433 applies to legal as well as physical persons. If there are more than one occupiers, their liability is joint and several.

383. A. Smieja *Odpowiedzialnosc za wyrzucenie, wylanie lub spadnięcie przedmiotu z pomieszczenia* in A. Olejniczak (ed.) *System Prawa Prywatnego: Prawo Zobowiązań. Część Ogólna*, Vol. 6 (Warszawa: C.H. Beck, Instytut Nauk Prawnych PAN, 2009), 507.

220. The scope of cases where the provision is applied is relatively wide. It covers more than the typical examples of something being ejected or thrown out of a building. According to judicial decisions, however, it does not govern the case where an object is thrown out as a result of malice and aggression towards the police attempting to settle down a riot in a juvenile educational institution.[384] Some decisions represent a rather narrow understanding of the provision, and they receive a fair amount of criticism in legal writings.[385] Recent court decisions reiterate that the said provision does not apply to the flooding of an apartment by water coming from the apartment on the floor above.[386] This is in spite of the previous Supreme Court decision which established that Article 433 was applicable to the case of overflow of water from an apartment into the shop beneath, caused by the waterworks breakdown, if in the effect the stored goods were damaged.[387]

221. This is indeed one of the strictest forms of liability among all the tortious liability provisions in the Civil Code. Based on risk, it is independent of fault of the occupier or any person he is liable for. Circumstances excluding liability are exhaustively enumerated in the provision, and are limited to conditions outside of the occupier's sphere of influence: exclusive fault of the victim, or of a third person for whom the occupier is not liable and whose actions he could not have prevented and force majeure. The reasons for such a stringent liability standard lie in the nature of typical situations covered by the provision. Normally it is difficult for the victim to discover what exactly happened, or to identify who, if anyone, threw or spilled something out of a building, especially if the action took place above the victim's head and out of his eyesight. As regards circumstances excluding liability, the exclusive fault of the victim is a rare occurrence, and scholars indeed struggle to offer viable examples of such situations. It may be a burglar who, attempting to get into the premises, causes an object to fall and injure him.[388] Cases where damage was caused by the fault of a third person for whom the occupier is not liable and whose actions he could not have prevented, on the contrary, are relatively common. The clause does not apply to the occupiers' children, spouses and other people who share the premises with him, as well as employees (as long as they are performing their job), or mentally incapacitated persons for whom he is responsible – the occupier is deemed to be liable for their actions. However, the scope of those for whom the occupier is not liable is not agreed upon by the judiciary and scholars. Particular disagreements concern people who enter the premises without the occupier's knowledge or consent (burglars, or the police who are conducting a confidential search). Some prominent scholars argue that because the occupier could never truly have prevented their actions, he should not be liable for them.[389]

384. SN of 7 Feb. 1968, II CR 337/67, OSN 1/1969, item 15.
385. *See* W. Wagner, *Obligations in Polish Law*, in *Polish Civil Law.* Vol. II (D. Lasok ed., A.W. Sijthoff-Leiden, 1974), 230.
386. SN of 19 Feb. 2013, III CZP 63/12, OSNC 7–8/2013, item 81; SN of 5 Mar. 2002, I CKN 1156/99, OSP 1/2003, item 5; SN of 18 Jul. 2012, III CZP 41/12, OSNC 3/2013, item 28.
387. SN of 15 Nov. 1959, 1961 OSPiKA), 159.
388. *Ibid.*, A. Smieja *Odpowiedzialnosc za wyrzucenie, wylanie lub spadnie̜cie przedmiotu z pomieszczenia,* 519.
389. *Ibid.*, 521.

222. Force majeure is an external, unexpected and unusual event, the effects of which cannot be prevented by the occupier exercising the appropriate level of care.[390] Polish scholars and judiciary combine objective and subjective criteria when defining this phenomenon, although the focus is mainly on the objective approach (*see supra* no. 175). The criteria related to the nature of the event itself are much more important than those related to the level of care of persons who faced the event.[391]

B. Liability for Damage Caused by Collapse of a Building or Detachment of a Part Thereof

223. Pursuant to Article 434 KC the independent possessor of a building (construction, structure) is liable for damage caused by the collapse of the building or the detachment of a part thereof, as long as the collapse or the detachment occurred as a consequence of either the absence of proper maintenance of the building or a defect in its construction. The defendant bears the burden of proving that the collapse was due to a reason other than lack of proper maintenance or a defect. The direct cause of the collapse is irrelevant (e.g., a strong wind or human conduct). The provision indicates that only force majeure or a third-party conduct (for instance a terrorist attack) can provide a defence.[392]

224. Here liability is placed on the independent possessor, who is a person using and administering the building as if he were the owner, without necessarily also being the owner (Article 336 KC). Hence, those who lease the building or who administer it in the name of the owner are not liable under this provision. Normally an independent possessor is also the owner, but this is not always the case. Both physical and legal persons can be independent possessors. If there are more than one possessors of the same building, their liability in most cases is joint and several.

225. A building is not defined in the Code. Scholars apply Construction law,[393] which contains a list of objects covered by the notion. The list includes ordinary buildings as well as airports, roads, railway tracks, tunnels, water treatment plants, tombstones, monuments, masts, etc. Writings on the topic contain three criteria for the determination of whether an object is indeed a building within the scope of Article 434. The object must not be a natural structure but must have been built by people, it should be permanently joined with the ground upon which it stands, and its structure must be subject to rules and mandates of construction (thus it is not for example a machine).[394] As far as parts of buildings are concerned, the definition here seems wider than the Code's definition of parts of a thing (Article 47 defines

390. *Ibid.*, 518.
391. J. Kuźmicka-Sulikowska *Zasady odpowiedzialności deliktowej ...* , 177–178.
392. *See* W. Wagner, *Obligations in Polish Law*, 230–231.
393. *Prawo budowlane* of 7 Jul. 1994, Dz.U. of 1994, No. 89, item 414. Later amended.
394. A. Smieja *Odpowiedzialnosc za szkodę wyrządzoną przez zawalenie się budowli*, in A. Olejniczak (ed.) System Prawa Prywatnego: Prawo Zobowiązań. Część Ogólna, Vol. 6 (Warszawa: C.H. Beck, Instytut Nauk Prawnych PAN, 2009), 535.

them as anything that cannot be separated from the main thing without damaging or a crucial alteration of the whole or of the separated part, and anything that is not connected with the main thing only temporarily). While any machinery installed in a building (such as hot water heaters) is covered by Article 434, objects which are connected to the building for decoration or information purposes (such as flower pots or signs) are not covered (although damages or injuries caused by them may be covered by Article 433 – *see supra* nos 217–222). Another key criterion for Article 434 to apply is the fact that the possessor's rights extend upon the part. The Supreme Court has interpreted the 'detachment of a part of a building' rather broadly. It applied Article 434 KC to a situation where a man fell from a balcony after he had leant on the railing of the balcony, which was improperly secured;[395] to the burst of a flue caused by exploding soot which had accumulated in it, consequently causing damage to a the wall in a house,[396] and recently to the breaking of the glass in the front door of the building, which caused its disintegration and personal injury of a minor who had run into it.[397]

226. The possessor's liability is strict (some scholars refer to it as 'pure strict liability'[398]). It is completely independent of any fault of the possessor or any person he is liable for, hence it also does not matter how old the possessor is or whether he has full mental capacity. The scope of liability is however limited in a peculiar fashion. It relates solely to the unsatisfactory state of the building, either through poor maintenance or through defective construction. The provision introduces a presumption that the damage occurred as a result of lack of proper maintenance or defective construction, which can be rebutted by the possessor upon furnishing appropriate evidence. In spite of the laconic form of the provision, scholars and the judiciary constructed the following principle for exclusion of liability: the possessor can avoid liability if he proves that something other than poor maintenance or defective construction caused the damage. Thus, he can demonstrate that the damage was caused entirely by the conduct of the victim or of a third person for whom he is not liable, whether fault on their part existed or not. He can also show that an external event (force majeure) resulted in the collapse of the building or falling off of a part of it. This means that the event caused by the third person or by force majeure must be the only cause of damage, or at least be the only event in 'adequate causal connection' with the damage.[399] For instance: poorly carried out renovations on a building next to the one occupied by the possessor which result in a part of the latter building falling off to injure someone. This situation would exclude the liability of the possessor only if the falling off of the part was not caused in part by the poor maintenance of the possessor's building.[400] Thus, effectively liability under Article

395. SN of 22 Nov. 1985, II CR 378/85.
396. SN of 13 Sep.1988, IV CR 231/88.
397. SN 21 Aug. 2014,IV CSK 673/13, OSNC-ZD 2015, No. 4, item 63, commented by E. Bagińska & I. Adrych-Brzezińska, *European Tort Law 2013*, Nos 40–46 (2014).
398. *Ibid.*, 526.
399. *Seeinfra* paras 269 et seq. for the detailed analysis of causation rules in Poland.
400. In the latter situation, the possessor would remain liable, although he would have a right of partial recourse against the other person at fault. *See* A. Smieja, '*Odpowiedzialnosc za szkodę wyrządzoną przez zawalenie się budowli*', 532.

434 appears less stringent than liability for damage under the scope of Article 433. In order to escape liability the possessor must show that the damage was a result of an occurrence for which he is not responsible.

§2. Other Strict Liabilities for Dangerous Activities

I. Liability of the Organizer of Mass Events

227. The Act of 20 March 2009 on safety of mass events provides for a duty to ensure safety and order with regard to participants in mass events (Article 5).[401] The obligation is imposed on the organizer and to the extent specified in the Act and other regulations it can also be imposed on: a village, town or city mayor, the head of a district (*wojewoda)*, the police, the state fire service and other organizational entities of the fire service, services responsible for safety and public order in railway areas, the national health service and other competent services and authorities. These regulations do not include any reference to the applicable civil liability rules, but the Supreme Court interpreted the law on the safety of mass events in a way that takes account of the aim of the statute. Hence, the organizer of a mass event is solely and strictly responsible for the safety of such an event.

228. According to judicial decisions, the *ratio legis* of the law is to impose on the organizer full liability for safety of mass sport events, concerts and other entertainment events, which often create a serious risk of personal injuries. The duty is not fulfilled by formally contracting it out to other persons or institutions such as security agencies, or by using the help of the police. Breach of this duty results in strict liability of the organizer who has to undertake all available measures to guarantee safety. In consequence, Article 5 of the law on the safety of mass events, by introducing a stricter regime of liability, limits the possibility of exculpation under Article 429 KC (*see supra* no. 141). The Supreme Court held that Article 5 of the law is a *lex specialis* to Article 429 KC.[402]

II. Nuclear Liability

229. According to Title 12 (Articles 100–108) of the Polish Atomic Law (the Act of 29 November 2000), a nuclear operator (for instance an operator of a nuclear reactor) is exclusively liable for nuclear damage caused by a nuclear accident within a nuclear device or caused in connection with a nuclear device, unless the damage resulted directly from acts of war (Article 101 section 1).[403] During the transportation of nuclear material, liability is borne by the operator who dispatched the material, unless the contract with the consignee stipulates otherwise (Article 101 section 2). The reparation of damage is subject to the rules of the Civil Code except

401. Dz.U. 2009, No. 62, at 504, with amendments.
402. SN of 26 Sep. 2003, IV CK 8/02, OSN 11/2004, at 180.
403. Consolidated text Dz.U. of 2012, item 264.

when the Act provides otherwise. Nuclear damage is defined very broadly and includes injury to persons and things, environmental damage and economic loss arising in connection with damage to persons, things or the environment, as well as the costs of taking preventive measures or damage caused by preventive actions.

230. The financial limit to this liability is SDR (Special Drawing Rights) 300 million (since 2011). If claims exceed the limit, a special fund must be created. The establishment and distribution of moneys in such a fund is designed pursuant to the rules of the Maritime Code that relate to the limitation of liability for maritime claims. The fund for nuclear damage is however not limited to damage of a maritime nature. In addition, the state covers compensation for damage to persons above the sum guaranteed in the operator's insurance policy. A nuclear operator has a duty to obtain a civil liability insurance policy.

III. Strict Liability of Air-Carriers

231. According to the Polish Aviation Law (the Act of 3 July 2002[404]) the operator of an aircraft is strictly liable for damage caused to anyone by the operation of an aircraft (Articles 206–207 of Aviation Law). The law refers to the Civil Code's strict liability provision (Article 435), with reservations provided in Article 207 of Aviation Law. This means that all three exonerating grounds mentioned above (*see supra* no. 207) may apply. The said liability concerns damage 'on the ground' caused by the operation of an aircraft.

232. The air carrier is responsible for damage to persons or things caused in connection with the contract of carriage and suffered by passengers involved in air accidents based on the international conventions ratified by Poland (the Warsaw-Montreal system) and the relevant EU laws (Article 208 of Aviation Law). Both the limitations and liability caps provided in the Montreal Convention and the respective EU laws (Regulation (EC) No. 889/2002) apply. In addition, the said restrictions apply to international carriage not falling within the scope of the international conventions but which starts and/or ends in the Polish territory, as well as to domestic carriage by air.[405]

IV. Liability for Genetically Modified Organisms

233. Article 57 of the Law of 22 June 2001 on Genetically Modified Organisms (hereinafter Law on GMOs), addresses civil liability of GMO users.[406] According to Article 57 section 1, a GMO user is liable under civil law for damage to persons, damage to property and damage to the environment caused by the carrying out of a

404. Dz.U. of 2012, item 933 with later amendments.
405. *See* in general A. Konert, *Odpowiedzialnosc cywilna przewoznika lotniczego* (Oficyna/Wolters Kluwer, 2010).
406. Consolidated text Dz.U. of 2007, No. 36, item 233.

contained use of GMOs or a deliberate release of GMOs into the environment, including the placing of GMOs on the market. The liability is strict with three exculpatory grounds: (1) force majeure, (2) exclusive fault of the injured party and (3) exclusive fault of a third person for whom the GMO user is not liable.

The fact that the activity causing damage was carried out on the basis of and within the scope of an administrative decision does not exempt the user from the liability envisaged in Article 57 section 1 of Law on GMOs (Article 57 section 3 of the Law). The same rules of liability apply to the transit of GMO products through the territory of Poland. The losses that are compensable under this special regime include damage to the environment. However, only the State Treasury, a local authority or an ecological organization may bring the claim for compensation in this context (Article 57 section 2 of Law on GMOs).[407]

The regime of civil liability for GMO activities constitutes *lex specialis* with regard to the rules of civil liability for environmental damage envisaged in the EPL (*see supra* nos 210–216). So far, no cases regarding GMOs have been reported and in any case it is difficult to envisage a successful proof of causation.

407. *See* E. Bagińska, *Economic Loss Caused by GMOs in Poland*, in *Economic Loss Caused by Genetically Modified Crops. Liability and Redress for the Adventitious Presence of GMOs in Non-GM Crops*, 337 ff (B.A. Koch ed., Springer, 2008).

Part IV. Defences and Exception Clauses

Chapter 1. Limitation of Action (Suspension and Interruption)

234. In Polish law prescription of claims does not result in the termination of a right. The right (claim) survives the lapse of time, but the debtor, when sued, may raise a defence of limitation of action and the court will thus dismiss the claim (i.e., the claim is time-barred). Should the debtor not raise the defence, the court will enforce the claim, as it has no competence to apply the statute of limitations ex officio.[408] Hence, the duty to perform on the part of the debtor becomes a natural obligation. If it is fulfilled, even accidentally, no restitution is possible (Article 411 point 3 KC). The general rules on prescription (limitation) of claims are contained in the general part of the Civil Code (in Articles 117–123 KC). Article 120 §1 KC stipulates that the period of limitation begins to run on the day the claim accrues. The period may be suspended (Article 121 KC[409]) or interrupted (Article 124 KC[410]), in which case it runs anew once the ground for interruption ceases.

235. The rules on prescription of tort claims placed in the Title on Torts were modified in 2007 by the Act of 16 February 2007 on the Revision of the Civil Code.[411] Before the amendment, Article 442 §1 KC read: 'A claim for redress of

408. *See* W. Wagner, *Obligations in Polish law*, vol. II, 40–41 (Leiden 1974).

409. A limitations period does not start and, if started, is suspended:

(1) for claims by children against parents – for the duration of the parental authority;
(2) for claims by persons who do not have full capacity for legal acts against persons exercising guardianship or curatorship – for the time during which the guardianship or curatorship is exercised;
(3) for claims made by one spouse against the other – for the duration of the marriage;
(4) for any claims if, due to force majeure, the entitled person cannot bring them before a Court or other authority set up to hear cases of a given type – for the duration of the obstacle.

410. Article 123: §1. The running of the limitations period is interrupted:

(1) by any action before a Court or other authority appointed to hear cases or enforce claims of a given type or before an arbitration tribunal taken directly to either assert or establish, or satisfy or secure a claim;
(2) by recognition of a claim by the person against whom the claim is made;
(3) by commencement of mediation.

411. Dz.U. of 2007, No. 80, item 538, reported in E. Bagińska *European Tort Law 2007*, Nos 1–5.

damage caused by a tort is subject to limitation on the expiration of three years from the day on which the injured person learned of the damage and of the person obliged to redress it. In any event, however, the claim is subject to limitation after the passage of ten years from the day on which the event causing the damage occurred.'[412] The reason for the amendment was the Constitutional Tribunal decision of 1 September 2006 (SK 14/05) (mentioned above, *see* no. 194 Product Liability). The decision repealed Article 442 §1 sentence 2 KC because of its unconstitutionality.[413] Dealing with the problem of time-prescribed tort claims in the context of an action involving an injured soldier whose claims were rejected by the state, the Tribunal held that the whole structure of prescription of tort claims in the Civil Code violated constitutional values. The key issue was compensating personal injuries stemming from events that took place earlier than ten years before the occurrence of the damage. Until the decision of the Tribunal, courts had tackled this problem differently: they followed the wording of the Civil Code. In the Resolution of the Full Civil Chamber of 17 February 2006 the Supreme Court[414] held that the maximum ten-year period must always be counted from the day of the tort (*a tempore facti*), and not from the day of the awareness of the damage. It applies equally to future losses and to losses that the victim was unaware of. While construing Article 442 §1 KC, no reference should be made to the notion of 'accrual of claims'.[415] This judgment preceded the ruling of the Constitutional Tribunal, and eventually they both led to the legislative change.

236. The new rules introduced a general rule concerning limitation periods, which is similar to the position before the amendment, but they also established important exemptions to the general rule. Pursuant to the wording of Article 442^1 §1 KC, a claim for redress of damage caused by a tort shall be barred after a period of three years from the date on which the injured person learned about it and about the person obliged to redress it. However, in 2017 this wording was changed again by the Act of 21 April 2017 on claims for compensation for harm caused by an infringement of competition law,[416] in force since 27 June 2017. The wording of §1 of Article 442^1 now reads: 'a claim for redress of damage caused by a tort shall be barred after a period of three years from the date on which the injured person learned or should have learnt about it and about the person obliged to redress it'. The wordings of §2 and §3 have not been changed accordingly. According to established case law the first moment when the injured 'learns about the damage' is the moment when the injured person perceives the negative consequences of an event

412. Article 442 KC originated in the 1933 Code of Obligations, and despite strong criticism has not been changed with the exception of shortening of the prescription period from twenty to ten years in 1950.
413. Reported in E. Bagińska, in: *European Tort Law 2006*, Nos 83–90 (2008).
414. III CZP 84/05, OSN 7–8/2006, item 114.
415. *See* in general on this topic: M.K. Chmielewska, *Przedawnienie roszczen deliktowych o naprawienie tzw. szkody przyszlej*, Rejent 3/2006, 120–137, R. Klimek, *Dyskusyjne problemy przedawnienia roszczen*, Kwartalnik Prawa Prywatnego (KPP) 3/2006, 633–667, A. Jozefiak, *Przedawnienie roszczen o naprawienie szkody wyrzadzonej czynem niedozwolonym w swietle Konstytucji*, KPP 3/2006, 669–697.
416. Dz.U. 2017, No. 1132.

the consequences of which indicate the fact of damage and when she becomes aware of the occurrence of damage.[417] The extent of the damaging consequences is irrelevant in the context of prescription.

237. The general period cannot be longer than ten years from the date on which the event causing the damage occurred (Article 442[1]§1 KC). This means that the three-year period stops running after ten years from the day of the tort. The ten-year period must always be counted from the day of the tort (*a tempore facti*), and not from the day of the awareness of the damage (*a tempore scientiae*).[418] Pursuant to Article 442[1]§2 KC, if damage resulted from a crime or misdemeanour, compensation claims are barred after a period of twenty years from the date when the crime or the misdemeanour was committed, regardless of when the person who suffered the damage learned about it and about the person obliged to redress it. It should be emphasized that a civil court can decide about the criminal nature of the actor's conduct. No criminal court verdict is required.

238. The general rules are suspended in the following cases:

- a personal injury claim cannot expire before the lapse of three years from the day on which the injured person learned about the injury and about the person obliged to redress it (Article 442[1]§3 KC). This means that regardless of the lapse of the time *a tempore facti*, whether ten or twenty years, the claim arising from personal injury will not be time-barred for three years since *tempore scientiae*. Hence, the absolute periods of ten or twenty years are 'suspended' in personal injury cases. Nevertheless, the periods running *a tempore facti* may remain more convenient for the injured party as regards evidentiary burdens;
- the claims of minors for redress of personal injury may not expire earlier than two years from the day when they reached maturity.

239. The new rules on prescription entered into force on 24 May 2007. They did not modify the interpretation of Article 449[8] KC – the special rule on prescription in the product liability regime which must be construed in conformity with Product Liability Directive 85/374/EEC. The 2017 amendment of the general rule applies to claims which arose but were not time-barred before the Act came into force, i.e., before 27 June 2017. However, if the running of the prescription period of three years would have begun before the new law entered into force, that period starts to run on that date.

240. The limitation period for claims of victims *par ricochet* starts on the day on which those persons learned about the loss of the deceased to whom they were related (Article 446 §2 KC) or about a considerable worsening of their material situation (Article 446 §3 KC) and about the person liable. In the judgment of SN of 19

417. SN 18 Sep. 2002 III CKN 597/2000, unpublished, SN of 24 Jun. 2015, II CSK 544/14, OSNC No. 6, item 76, commented by E> Nos 12–18.
418. SN of 17 Feb. 1982, OSNC 1983 item 8.

February 2015, III CSK 167/14, the court held that Article 4421 KC did not differentiate between the kind of claims stemming from the death of the injured and hence the prescription periods contained in the said provision applied equally to all claims listed in Article 446 KC (the cited case considered wrongful death claims). It is sufficient to identify the latter person in the way that a suit against him or her may be filed (*see infra* nos 353 ff for an elaboration of possible claims by such persons).[419]

241. In the judgment of 19 November 2009[420] the Supreme Court held that Article 442 §2 covers a claim raised against a person vicariously liable for a criminal act (such as an offence) of its servant. In the case of vicarious liability, the nature of the event triggering liability of both the servant and the master permits and requires the application of the same prescription period to all claims for redress. As long as the damage arises from an offence it is irrelevant whether the claimant directs his claims against the perpetrator himself or (also) against other persons answerable in tort for the damage.[421] The source of the damage, i.e., a criminal act, is a decisive factor. On the contrary, there are also a number of judgments in which the Supreme Court held that different limitation periods might apply to the same claim brought against different wrongdoers jointly and severally liable for the same damage.[422]

242. As it was mentioned earlier in this section, a civil court decides independently whether the defendant's conduct was criminal in nature, given that no criminal court verdict was rendered. Such a functional interpretation has had impact on two groups of cases.

243. First, on the cases against the Insurance Guarantee Fund (hereinafter IGF) in the circumstances that would have led to the civil liability of the owner (possessor) or the driver of a motor vehicle when their identity had not been established, and the accident was a criminal offence. Article 109a of the Compulsory Insurance Act prescribes that the general rules on limitation periods in torts apply to claims raised against the IGF. The crucial problem relates to which rule should apply to the IFG: the general rule of the three-year limitation *a tempore scientiae* or of twenty years *a tempore facti*. Recently, the judgment of seven judges of the Supreme Court of 29 October 2013 gave a fair answer to this inquiry.[423] The decision pertained, i.e., to the issue of whether an offence should be understood in the same way in criminal law and in civil law (tort law) for prescription purposes, especially in respect of its subjective element (*nullum crimen sine culpa*). The Supreme Court answered in the affirmative, namely that the definition of the offence in criminal law and civil law should be uniform. The offence being the source of damage needs to be established in compliance with the rules of criminal law (an objective

419. M. Nesterowicz & E. Bagińska, *Strict Liability in Poland*, 264–265.
420. IV CSK 257/09, OSP 7–8/2010, item 79.
421. *See* SN of 29 Oct. 1962, 2 CR 1064/61, OSNC 9/1963, item 211; SN of 16 Jan. 2008, IV CSK 380/07, OSNC ZD, D/2008, item 102.
422. SN of 11 Feb. 2003, V CKN 1664/00, OSNC 5/2004, item 75.
423. III CZP 50/13, OSN IC 4/2014, item 35, reported in E Bagińska/K Krupa-Lipińska, *European Tort Law 2014*, Nos 58–64 (2015).

and a subjective element of the offence). However, divergent views are expressed in respect of the subjective element (fault) of the offence committed by an unknown perpetrator. The court correctly rejected the theoretical concept prevailing in criminal law that the subjective element of an offence should always relate to of an individually recognized person. Civil liability and criminal liability play different functions. A victim who seeks damages from the IGF does so precisely because she cannot sue the perpetrator or his insurer because the former has not been identified. Therefore, if an objective element of an offence is established before a civil court, the court may find, by using objective criteria, that the unidentified person was at fault and committed an offence. The court must take into consideration all circumstances of the case and presented evidence. Consequently, compensatory claims against the IGF will be time-barred upon the lapse of twenty years from the commencement of an offence. The Supreme Court rightly emphasized the argument of equal treatment of all victims of traffic accidents, whether caused by identified or unidentified vehicles (owners).

244. The second group of cases involve juvenile offenders who have committed an act similar in contents to a criminal act, which could have been qualified as a crime or an offence was it committed by an adult offender. In Poland, a minor over 15 may be criminally responsible for very serious criminal conduct as if he were mature (18). The Supreme Court has held that a juvenile punishable (criminal) act, for which minor offenders are held responsible in special, juvenile proceedings, can be considered as a criminal act in the meaning of the above rule on prescription.[424]

245. In 1970 the Supreme Court held that an injured person could obtain a declaratory judgment stating a defendant's liability in tort for future damage (*see infra* nos 311–313 for explanation of the position of Polish tort law with regard to future damage).[425] Under the new regime on prescription, the 'suspension' of the period of prescription in personal injury cases (Article 442^1§3 KC) does not preclude obtaining a declaratory judgment that the defendant is liable for any future damage originating from the same event (tort). The Supreme Court in the ruling of 24 February 2009[426] stated that the amendment of the Civil Code had not caused a substantial difference in this respect. Damage caused by injury to persons is dynamic and the consequences of tortious conduct may appear long after the event. The rule stated above performs two functions. First of all it enables the injured person to claim compensation for distant consequences of a tort. The second aim is to facilitate the burden of proving all conditions of liability for those consequences. Therefore, an injured person has, in principle, legal standing to ask for a declaratory judgment if she pursues her interest simultaneously with a claim for actual damages. This conclusion remains valid after the revision of the Civil Code provisions on the prescription of tort claims. If a court holds that the defendant is liable for

424. *See* SN 18 Jan. 2012, I CSK 157/11, OSNC ZD B/2013, item 30, reported in E. Bagińska & I. Adrych-Brzezinska, *European Tort Law 2013*, Nos 37–47 (2014).
425. SN of 17 Apr. 1970, III PZP 34/69 OSNCP 12/1970, item 217.
426. III CZP 2/09, OSNC 12/2009, item 168, reported in E. Bagińska, *European Tort Law 2009* (2010), Nos 34–41.

damage that may occur in the future, the limitation period of three years for the new claims begins to run on the day when the injured person learned of the new damage.[427]

246. A continuous activity usually presupposes that its result is one harm. The Supreme Court in a judgment of 8 May 2014[428] explained that the last day of the continuous conduct/tort is only relevant for the beginning of the long stop of ten years counted from the event triggering the damage and not for the general period of three years calculated from the moment when the plaintiff learned about the damage.

427. SN of 17 Feb. 1972, OSNC 1972 item 149.
428. V CSK 370/13, Legalis database No. 1061026.

Chapter 2. Grounds of Justification

§1. Consent

247. In Polish law consent of the injured person will exclude wrongfulness but not always exclude strict liability. Some authors make a distinction between consent and assumption of risk. The first is said to involve a consent to a certain or at least very highly probable violation of the victim's rights or interests, regardless of the foreseeability of damaging consequences. Assumption of risk, on the contrary, involves putting oneself in a situation where a person contemplates the possibility of danger, and yet the latter seems to be acceptable and no infringement of protected rights necessarily follows (the probability of the expected advantages of the situation at the time the risk is taken is much higher than the possibility of any damage).[429]

248. In general 'acting at one's own risk' is not regulated in Polish law. Such a defence, if at all raised, sometimes overlaps and sometimes runs parallel to the defence of contributory conduct[430] or of the consent of a victim. The dominant approach recognizes that a victim assumes the risk of loss in a situation when he exposes himself to a hazard known to him voluntarily, consciously and for no important reason.[431] According to various theories, the victim is supposed to have accepted the possible occurrence of a hazardous situation that may involve adverse consequences for him.[432] Another approach is to treat the assumption of risk as a variation of a (presumed) consent.

249. Regardless of which theory a court accepts, a successful plea of assumption of risk/consent obliterates the wrongfulness of the tortfeasor's conduct and thus absolves him of liability based on fault. However, consent of the injured person will not always bar recovery in cases of strict liability. According to Article 437 KC the liability defined in Article 435 KC (industrial enterprise's liability) and 436 KC (liability of possessors of vehicles) cannot be excluded or limited in advance. Also in other cases had a person consented to the infliction of personal injury by a wrongful conduct such act would have been invalid (as contrary to public policy – Article 58 §2 KC – *see* below no. 256).[433]

250. In practice, acting at one's own risk is often equated with fault (e.g., accepting a ride from a person who is drunk amounts to an assumption of risk irrespective of whether the passenger was drunk himself) or, conversely, is considered to be free of fault (e.g., where someone participates in a car race). Both scholars and courts

429. *See* W. Wagner, in *Polish Civil Law*, vol. II *Obligations in Polish Law*, 190 (D. Lasok ed., Leiden 1974), E. Bagińska, *A Polish Perspective on the House of Lords Judgment in Corr v. IBC Vehicles LTD*, 18 Eur. Rev. of Priv. L. 3, 671 (2010).
430. *See* A. Szpunar, *O działaniu na własne ryzyko*, *Nowe Prawo* 6/1978, 863.
431. *See* P. Machnikowski, in A. Olejniczak (ed.) System Prawa Prywatnego Vol. 6, 400.
432. E. Bagińska, *A Polish Perspective*, 671.
433. *Ibid.*, E. Bagińska.

require a proof of the victim's general awareness of a risk of a specific nature (everyday risks of life are ignored). Any duress or some unusual motives of his conduct will not justify the defence.

251. Failure to establish the conditions of the assumption of risk (or consent) does not prevent a court from establishing the victim's contribution to the damage.

252. A patient's consent is subject to rules of medical law[434] (*see also supra* nos 60–61).

§2. NECESSITY

253. If damage is caused in a state of necessity or as the consequence of self-defence, the element of wrongfulness of conduct is missing, which excuses the actor from tortious liability.

Article 423 KC stipules that a person who acts in self-defence to resist a direct and an unlawful attack on any of his interests or those of another person shall not be liable for the damage caused to the assailant. The rule covers both personal and proprietary interests.

Self-defence must meet the following requirements in order to be accepted:

- the assault must have been direct and unlawful;
- the counter-action must have been necessary, i.e., the person who acted did not overstep the necessary degree of defence.[435]

§3. SELF-HELP AND SELF-DEFENCE

254. Pursuant to the Civil Code a person who destroys or damages another person's thing or kills or injures another person's animal in order to avert danger directly threatened by the thing or animal to himself or others is not liable for the resulting damage. Liability can be avoided if the person in question did not cause the danger himself, if the danger could not otherwise have been averted and if the interest preserved was clearly more important than the interest infringed (Article 424 KC).

Contrary to the previous rule (no. 241), this rule also covers sources of danger other than human behaviour (i.e., a threat must come from a thing or an animal).

255. In cases where an act is directed against a thing which was not the source of the danger, a duty to repair damage may arise. An owner cannot object to the use and even damage or destruction of a thing by another person if it is necessary to

434. *See* M. Nesterowicz, E. Bagińska & A. den Exter, *Medical Law in Poland,* 71–81 (Wolters Kluwer, 2011).

435. *See* W. Wagner, in *Polish Civil Law*, vol. II *Obligations in Polish Law*, 190 (D. Lasok ed., Leiden 1974,, 192.

avert danger directly threatening the personal interests of that person or a third party. However, the actor will have to remedy any resulting damage to the owner pursuant to Article 142 §1 KC. This rule of reparation also applies in the case of danger threatening property rights unless the threatened damage is clearly and disproportionately smaller than the loss which the owner could suffer as a result of the thing being used, damaged or destroyed.[436]

§4. OTHERS

256. Pursuant to Article 343 §1 KC a possessor and an actual holder can resort to self-defence to repel a wilful infringement of his possession. A possessor of real estate may immediately, after a wilful breach of his possession, restore the previous status by his own actions; however, when doing so, he cannot use violence against other persons. The possessor of a movable thing, if threatened by the danger of irreparable damage, may immediately, after having been wilfully deprived of possession, use the necessary self-help in order to restore the previous status (Article 343 §2 KC).

436. *Ibid.*, W. Wagner, 193.

Chapter 3. Contributory Fault (Contributory Conduct)

257. Polish law accepts the rule that contributory conduct, regardless of its seriousness, has an effect of reducing the damages but cannot serve as a complete defence to liability. 'Contributory negligence' – as understood in English or American law – is not a term which adequately reflects the approach in Poland. Polish courts assume a conduct to be 'contributory to damage' even when the contributory behaviour of the injured person does not bear the characteristics of fault. The term 'comparative negligence' may therefore be more appropriate, but it raises similar objections.[437]

Article 362 KC stipulates:

> If the injured person contributed to the occurrence or increase of damage, the obligation to redress it shall be correspondingly reduced according to the circumstances, and in particular the degree of fault of both parties.

258. This provision governs both tort and contractual relations. Contribution to the increase of damage is subject to the same principles as contribution to the infliction of damage.[438] The former occurs when the extent of the damage would have been smaller but for the victim's conduct. In general, the victim should undertake reasonable steps in order to minimize the damage.

A distinct duty of the injured person to act so as to reduce damage under pain of refusal of compensation is provided for exclusively in Article 826 §1 KC which refers to property insurance.

In cases of personal injury the aggravation of damage arises from omissions or failures of victims, such as failure to report to a doctor or to undertake treatment.

259. Article 362 KC gave rise to four ways of interpretation:

(1) a mere causal connection between the conduct of a victim and his loss should result in a reduction of damages (*causa concurrens*);
(2) the victim's contribution is legally relevant when his conduct was objectively improper (unlawful);
(3) the victim's contribution is legally relevant only when fault can be imputed to him (*culpa concurrens*);
(4) the victim's conduct is assessed in a manner conditional upon the grounds for liability. If the person liable for damage accounts for his conduct based on fault, then only the fault of the injured person may constitute contributory negligence. If liability is based on risk or fairness, it is sufficient to submit the plea of objectively improper behaviour of the injured person to assume the latter's contribution.[439]

---

437. *See* M. Nesterowicz & E. Bagińska, *Contributory Negligence under Polish Law*, in *Unification of Tort Law: Contributory Negligence*, 149 (U. Magnus, M. Martin-Casals eds, The Hague, Kluwer Law International, 2004).
438. *Ibid.*, M. Nesterowicz & E. Bagińska, 151.
439. *Ibid.*, M. Nesterowicz & E. Bagińska, 150, 155.

In earlier judicial decisions the causal theory (*causa concurrens*) of the victim's contributory conduct prevailed.[440] This position was later modified due to a considerable criticism expressed by most legal scholars. In particular, the 'pure causal approach' was said to necessarily lead to the same result regardless of whether the victim was sound and sane or was a child or mentally ill. The prevailing doctrinal view that contributory negligence is a type of conduct that would be qualified as 'fault' if committed in relation to other persons, was rooted in the idea of justice and equity. Nevertheless, there is no unanimity as to the standard of care for one's own interests. A full spectrum of views (from *culpa in concreto* to *culpa in abstracto*) is represented in doctrinal writings and judicial decisions.[441]

Currently, the second and fourth approaches to contributory negligence have more supporters, although judicial decisions are inconsistent.[442] It is widely accepted that one can contribute to the damage only by a conscious act and not by a reflex caused by fright, or guided by panic in which the victim found himself due to the negligence of the tortfeasor.[443] This notwithstanding, both in judicial decisions and in legal writing there are still many unresolved issues.

260. In cases of strict liability a prevailing test to establish contributory conduct applied by courts is the 'objectively improper conduct' of the victim.[444] This rule was confirmed in the Supreme Court decision of 6 March 1997. The court held that 'additional compensation based on the Civil Code for the family members of the employee who died of larynx cancer (recognized as an occupational disease) may be reduced correspondingly to the degree of the deceased's contribution to the attracting and developing of this disease by long-term cigarette smoking (Article 362 KC)'.[445]

261. According to long established line of judicial reasoning the behaviour of a minor to whom fault cannot be imputed because of his age (*see* Article 426 KC –*supra* no. 49) may justify a reduction in damages from a person liable.[446] Consequently, a court can decrease the amount of damages even for non-faulty contributory conduct in case of traffic accidents involving children aged between 3 and 5. This position has been criticized in legal scholarship.[447]

440. SN of 11 Jan. 1960, OSN 1960, item 92.
441. Cf. SN of 29 Oct. 2008, IV CSK 228/08, OSNC ZD C/2009, item 66.
442. *See* M. Nesterowicz & E. Bagińska, *Contributory Negligence*, 149, T. Pajor, *Uwagi o przyczynieniu się poszkodowanego do powstania szkody*, in M. Pyziak-Szafnicka (ed.) *Odpowiedzialnosc cywilna. Księga pamiątkowa ku czci Profesora Adama Szpunara* (Kraków, Zakamycze, 2004), 161 et seq.
443. SN of 16 Aug. 1956, 4 CR 481/56, *Nowe Prawo* 1956, 181; SN of 29 Jan. 1964, OSPiKA 1965, item 8.
444. *See* E. Bagińska, *A Polish Perspective,* 673.
445. SN of 6 Mar. 1997, II UKN 20/97, OSNP 1997, item 478.
446. SN of 20 Sep. 1975, OSNC 1976, item 151.
447. *See* M. Nesterowicz, *Contribution de la victime dans des accidents de la circulation*, *Acta Universitatis Lodziensis, 44 Folia Iuridica* (1990), 96.

In the judgment of 29 October 2008,[448] the Supreme Court considered a 3.5-year old boy who, while supervised by his 11-year-old sister, was hit by a car when he suddenly entered the street. The court held that Article 362 KC bestows a court with the power to reduce or to refuse to reduce compensation despite a causal contribution of the injured. Each contributory conduct of the victim is a basis for reduction of his damages where there is an adequate causal connection between the victim's behaviour and the final result. Once causation is established, the subjective factors, such as fault, objectively improper conduct, age, sanity, should be balanced in order to reach a decision whether and to what extent the damages should be reduced. Hence, in the first stage a court must establish whether an injured contributed to his/her loss and in the second phase the court decides whether to mitigate the damages. The ground of the plaintiff's liability is one of the elements taken into consideration in the second phase of the assessment, along with all subjective factors. The standard of 'objectively improper behaviour' of the victim should exist separately for a given category of persons. It is doubtful, however, that such a standard can be created for 3-year-old children.

This approach was reiterated as regards minors over the age of 13 in the decision of the Supreme Court of 24 September 2009.[449] According to the court, subjective fault is based on a defined mental relationship of a person with her own conduct. Factors such as free will and foreseeability should be examined. The correct application of Article 362 KC implies that liability has already been established. At the stage of assessing damages courts have the power to reduce or to refuse to reduce compensation despite a causal contribution by the injured person.[450]

The Supreme Court has held, in the judgment of 19 March 2014,[451] that in the circumstances of a particular case the fulfilment of the court's duty to reduce damages on the basis of Article 362 KC may exceptionally contradict the principles of equity (scil. Community life). The cited case concerned an 11-year-old plaintiff who was seriously injured in an accident, when he crossed the road at an unauthorised place, in close proximity to an oncoming motorcycle, moving too fast on the wrong lane. In such cases, even though Article 362 KC does not expressly refer to equity, the decision of the court to deny a reduction of the compensation amount must be considered as permissible. Such a reduction can be considered in the light of Article 428 KC. Pursuant to this provision, where a perpetrator is not liable for damage due to his/her age or mental/physical condition, and there are no persons responsible for his/her supervision, or when redress for the damage cannot be obtained from them, the injured person may demand complete or partial redress for the damage from the perpetrator himself if it follows from the circumstances, in particular from a comparison of the financial circumstances of the injured person and those of the other person, that the principles of community life so require. Thus, this rule can be

448. IV CSK 228/08, OSNC ZD C/2009, item 66, commented by E. Bagińska, in: *European Tort Law 2009*, Nos 26–33 (2010).

449. IV CSK 207/09, OSNC 4/2010, item 58, reported in: E. Bagińska, European Tort Law 2010, Nos 39–44 (2011).

450. *See also* SN of 3 Aug. 2006, IV CSK 118/06 (refusal to reduce damages).

451. I CSK 295/13, OSNC 2015, No. 3, item 34, commented by E. Bagińska & I. Adrych-Brzezińska, *European Tort Law 2015*, Nos 2–8 (2016) similarly in judgment of 6 Aug. 2006, IV CSK 118/06, not published.

applied *per analogiam.* The legal construction offered by the Supreme Court is supported by the similarity of the scope of regulation covered by both discussed provisions and expressed in the fact that in both cases a partial reduction of compensation is based on the principle of equity.

262. In earlier decisions, the Supreme Court held that contribution by parents to damage suffered by their minor child is equated with the minor's negligence under Article 362 KC. This approach was based on the theory of 'family and household relationship',[452] and it was criticized by legal writers. Present court practice agrees with the view that minors cannot suffer the consequences of their parents' contributory negligence to the occurrence of damage, parents may however be held liable towards minors for negligence in supervision.[453]

263. Mentally ill or disturbed persons may not be deemed as victims contributing to damage.[454] The victim cannot contribute to the damage if she/he had no ability of reaching a reasoned decision as to choice of conduct.[455] Contribution and fault have different meanings, as one may contribute to damage without being at fault. This line of argument was continued in a case involving a patient who had left psychiatric hospital facilities by using the regular exit, and subsequently committed suicide.[456]

264. The reduction of the duty to compensate depends on all circumstances of the case. A court must consider in particular the fault of both parties, risks created by the tortfeasor's activity, the conduct of the parties (when liability is based on risk or fairness) and the financial position of the parties. A comparison of the degree of fault of both parties means that the larger the fault of the injured, the smaller the damages. An especially grave negligence of the tortfeasor may justify the allocation of full liability on his part or, alternatively, only a slight reduction of the damages. Correspondingly, a high degree of negligence of the victim will justify a significant reduction of the obligation to redress the damage.[457]

265. Courts usually decrease awards by a defined fraction or by a percentage; a reduction need not be a result of mathematical calculation, but it must always be justified. Accordingly, it is not acceptable to simply reduce the award by 50% if the determination of the degree of the contribution of each party to the occurrence of the damage faces excessive difficulties.[458]

Contributory negligence of the deceased influences the extent of the compensatory claims of ricochet victims.[459] If his exclusive fault or assumption of risk would

452. SN of 2 Dec. 1982, OSPiKA 1984, item 4; SN of 16 Mar. 1983, OSPiKA 1985, item 77.
453. SN of 16 Mar. 1983, I CR 33/83, OSNC 12/1983, item 196; SN of 5 Nov. 2008, I CSK 139/08 not published.
454. SN of 24 Feb. 1962, II CR 363/61, OSN 1963, item 124.
455. SN of 30 Apr. 1952 C 290/52, OSN 1953, item 99.
456. SN of 16 Dec. 1967, OSN 1968, item 167; SN of 19 Nov. 1969, OSPiKA 1970, item 249.
457. SN of 20 Jul. 1964, OSPiKA, 1966, item 33.
458. SN of 3 Feb. 1962, OSN 1963, item 25; SN of 6 Oct. 1964, *Nowe Prawo* No. 4 (1965), 482.
459. *See* A. Szpunar, *Wynagrodzenie szkody*, 71–75.

result in the denial of compensation, the action by the ricochet victim would have to be dismissed as well. The compensation is also reduced when the indirectly injured persons contributed to the damage themselves, e.g., by failure to organize medical help which contributed to the death of the victim.[460]

266. Failure to wear seat belts has an impact on the consequences of accidents. The reduction of compensation due to contributory negligence will be justified in most cases. The criteria for the reduction are provided in Article 362, one being the degree of fault of both parties. Hence, it may be necessary to compare the fault of the tortfeasor (the driver) and the injured party. If the tortfeasor intentionally breached safety rules, for which he was sentenced by a criminal court, such a circumstance should be considered a highly disproportionate to the victim's failure to fasten his seat belt when sitting in the middle of the back seat of the vehicle. However, the injured can be held grossly negligent if he could and should have foreseen the consequences of a possible accident and the consequences of his actions. An adult sitting in the middle of the back seat of a car without fastening his seat belt is particularly exposed to severe injuries in the event of a collision. According to the Supreme Court such circumstances justify the 30% contribution.[461] Likewise, according to case law, riding in a car with a drunk driver justifies the reduction of compensation by 25%,[462] while drinking alcohol with a driver before the ride, and then riding in a car with a drunk driver justifies a 50% contribution to the damage.[463]

460. *See* E. Bagińska, *A Polish Perspective,* 678–679.
461. SN, 16 Mar. 2018, IV CSK 114/17, OSNC – ZD 2019/1 item 13.
462. SN of 6 Jun. 1997, II CKN 213/97, OSNC 1998/1, item 5.
463. SN of 3 Mar. 2017, I CSK 213/16.

Chapter 4. Exemption Clauses

267. Liability in tort cannot be excluded or limited except in cases specified by law. However there is a possibility, sanctioned by the principle of freedom of contract (Article 353^1 KC), of excluding or limiting liability which would arise between two contractual parties. As it was explained above, Poland does not use the *non cumul* principle. Thus, there is a potential for tortious liability in cases of breaches of contract. Contractual parties can agree that both or either types of liability are excluded. Contractual clauses excluding liability, or limiting the scope or amount of available compensation are quite common, especially in certain types of commercial relationships (insurance, services). These clauses are always subject to scrutiny by the following provisions of the Civil Code:

- Article 58 concerning validity of legal acts (which include contracts), which must comply with law and with the principles of community life.
- Article 353^1 concerning limits on freedom of contract (contracts must comply with their nature, with law and with the principles of community life).
- Specific provisions relating to consumer contracts (provisions of the Civil Code implementing the Unfair Contract Terms Directive[464]– Article 385^1–385^3).
- Other provisions prohibiting exclusions or limitations of liability in specific areas of law: for instance the product liability provisions of the Civil Code (implementation of the Product Liability Directive, examined in detail above – *see supra* Part III, Chapter 2) contain a prohibition of excluding or limiting product liability (Article 449^7 KC).
- Liability for intentionally caused losses cannot be excluded (Article 473 §2 KC).
- There are two types of tortious liability which according to the Civil Code (Article 437) cannot be excluded or limited in advance: these are liability for losses caused by enterprises set into motion by forces of nature (such as vapour, gas, electricity.) and enterprises producing or using explosives (Article 435) and liability of a person in possession of a mechanical vehicle for losses caused by the vehicle (Article 436).

464. Council Directive 93/13/EEC on unfair terms in consumer contracts, OJ L 95, 21.4.93, P. 29–34.

Part V. Causation

268. Causation plays a very important role in establishing tortious liability and delimiting its scope. Nevertheless, it has been described as 'an elastic feature which can be stretched and shrunk according to the magnitude of … other requirements of liability'.[465] Often causal considerations are merged with other elements of liability, such as in common law systems with negligence or scope of duty of care, and in fault liability systems with considerations of fault. The latter has certainly been the case in Poland, where general tortious liability is based on fault. One would struggle to find a detailed elaboration of causation in Polish general tort jurisprudence until recently. Conduct of defendants and their potential fault were analysed in great detail, with causation often referred to as a matter of course. This is not to say that courts were ignoring causation. Indeed, they were quite aware of its scope and framework. The Supreme Court declared quite early on that foreseeability of outcome is not to be taken into account when establishing causation, but should rather be examined as part of considerations of fault.[466] Causality, while crucial, was not the primary focus. This approach is currently changing, with greater uses of strict liability. Courts are forced to see causation as increasingly detached from the defendant's conduct and rather linked with some other objectively ascertainable event, such as defect in a product, thus increasing the scope of issues to be considered as part of causation. Courts also need to deal with new forms of liability and more complex cases. They have an extensive range of analytical resources at their disposal. These resources derive from legislation, but even more significantly from legal scholarship.

269. While most European civil codes refrain from defining causation, the Polish Civil Code indeed provides a definition. Article 361, which can be found in Book Three (Obligations) Chapter One (General Provisions) specifies both the meaning of causation and the scope of recoverable damage (the latter is analysed in detail *supra* nos 268 et seq.). Paragraph 1 reads:

> A person liable to pay compensation is responsible only for normal results of the act or omission from which the damage resulted.

465. Cees Van Dam *European Tort Law*, 268 (Oxford University Press, 2006).
466. SN of 10 Dec. 1952, C 584/52, PiP Nos 8–9/1953, 366.

Legal scholars built a very comprehensive theoretical framework around the definition provided by the Code. The theories are similar to those seen in other European legal systems. Causation plays two roles: it is one of the elements establishing liability, and it limits the scope of liability. Scholars set out two approaches or principles which are part of causal analysis: causation in fact (factual analysis) and what is often referred to as causation in law or scope of liability (limiting the scope of events which remain in factual causal connection to those relevant in the eyes of the law). Factual causation is not mentioned in the Civil Code expressly, but it is treated as a crucial element of analysis nonetheless. The rule of *conditio sine qua non* (also referred to as the principle of equivalence of causes) is applied here. It is widely accepted that this approach by itself is not capable of establishing the existence and scope of liability. The principle of adequate causal connection (used for delimiting the scope of causation in law) can meet both aims. The principle is referred to in Article 361 KC, although the latter uses the notion 'normal results'. Adequate causal connection is established by courts with the use of objective criteria provided by life experience and science.[467] It qualifies the results of the *conditio sine qua non* approach to accept only legally relevant causal links. The assessment of what normal results are is done using an objective approach – they are seen from the point of view of the court (not for instance the defendant or an observer's point of view) at the time of adjudication. The approach allows both usual and unusual consequences of a particular event to be within the scope of adequate causal connection. It allows the inclusion of cases where victims suffer particularly severe injuries because of certain peculiar sensitivities (counterpart of the eggshell skull rule).

270. The theoretical analysis which leads to final determination includes the following train of thought: as long as the likelihood of the consequences increases each time the event occurs when compared to the state when the event did not occur, the consequences are within an adequate causal link with the event.[468] The scope of normal consequences extends upon direct as well as indirect results of the event, as long as in the chain of causation no external event which is beyond the defendant's control (*nova causa interveniens*) intervened.

271. The issue of possible multiple contributing factors received attention from both the Polish courts and scholars.[469] The first type of cases are those involving alternative causation: either pure alternative causation or hypothetical alternative causation. Pure alternative causation takes place when only one event actually caused the damage, and yet pointing to the event is difficult or impossible because other events potentially could have caused the damage as well. While some scholars suggest that all those potentially involved ought to bear joint and several liability, it is rather more commonly accepted that proof of causation will fail in such

467. SN of 2 Jun. 1956, 3 CR 515/56, OSN 1957, item 24.
468. M. Kaliński *Odpowiedzialnosc odszkodowawcza* in A. Olejniczak (ed.) *System Prawa Prywatnego: Prawo Zobowiązań. Część Ogólna*, Vol. 6 (Wydawnictwo C.H. Beck, Instytut Nauk Prawnych PAN, Warszawa, 2009), 130.
469. E. Bagińska, *Odpowiedzialnosc deliktowa w razie niepewnosci związku przyczynowego. Studium prawnoporównawcze*, wyd. Dom Organizatora TNOiK, Toruń 2013.

circumstances.[470] The case law accepts the approach of joint and several liability, as for example in the case of a young girl, who lost her eye as a result of an attack by a group of teenagers who had gathered at a bonfire.[471] The attackers shot at the group to which the plaintiff belonged with a sling, using stones and pinecones. One of the stones hit the plaintiff and injured her in the eye. It was not established whose slingshot it was. Five defendants in this case were tried by a juvenile court for assault and battery. Finding all the defendants jointly and severally liable, the court emphasized that the fact that it is sufficient to prove that each individual defendant participated in an assault and battery that resulted in the plaintiff's personal injury. The group of participants in a dangerous game *as a whole* created a dangerous situation leading to the damage and where the actual perpetrator cannot be established, all the members of the group may be considered joint tortfeasors. In addition, it does not matter whether the actions of one party were direct or indirect or whether one party is more responsible or blameworthy than the other. As a principle, the degree of liability of individual persons is not to be identified or differentiated in the main lawsuit, but in separate proceedings.[472]

272. Hypothetical alternative causation encompasses situations where the damage would have occurred even without the tortious event because some other, later event happened (*causa superveniens*). The only reason the latter did not cause the damage was that it was already done. Normally, courts and scholars do not accept such hypothetical causation as defence of the tortfeasor, but it may be relevant in establishing the scope of damages due to the victim.[473] This means that generally a court should disregard the successive event that would have inflicted the same harm anyway. A person obliged to redress damage should be absolved from the obligation to compensate only if the cause imputed to her had ceased to exist before the successive cause occurred.[474] This view is also supported by early judicial decisions.[475]

273. A different position, applied in recent cases,[476] suggests that the general rule should be reversed. This opinion emphasizes the theory of differentiation and the necessity to take account of certain hypothetical causes when assessing the damage. Hence, if a hypothetical state of the victim's patrimony is one of the factors

---

470. M. Kalinski, *Odpowiedzialnosc odszkodowawcza,* at 138.
471. SN of 18 Jan. 2012, I CSK 157/11, OSNC ZD B/2013, item 30, commented E. Bagińska & I. Adrych-Brzezińska, *European Tort Law 2013*, Nos 37–47 (2014).
472. *SeeM Nesterowicz/E Bagińska*, Multiple Tortfeasors under Polish Law, in: WVH Rogers (ed), Unification of Tort Law: Multiple Tortfeasors (2004) 153, 156.
473. SN of 16 Feb. 1965, I PR 330/64, OSNCP 11/1965, item 194. *See* A. Szpunar, *Ustalenie odszkodowania w prawie cywilnym* (1975) 43; W. Czachórski, *Zobowiązania* (2003) 213 f.; B. Lewaszkiewicz-Petrykowska, *Wyrzadzenie szkody przez kilka osob* (1978) 79; M. Nesterowicz/E. Bagińska, *Digest of European Tort Law, vol I: Essential Cases on Natural Causation, National Court Practice and Tort Law* (2007) 524.
474. SN of 28 Feb. 1974, II PR 61/74, OSPiKA 9/1974, item 195.
475. SN of 16 Feb. 1965, I PR 330/64, OSN 11/1965, item 194.
476. SN of 29 Apr. 2010, IV CSK 467/09, OSNC-ZD D/2010, item 116, SN 15 Apr. 2010, II CSK 544/09, OSNC-ZD D/2010, item 113.

taken into account in the assessment of the loss, then all the circumstances subsequent to the tortious event that might or have influenced this state should be considered. A supervening cause belongs to those 'circumstances'.[477] The Supreme Court also held that a hypothetical cause should be disregarded if it would have consisted of legal conduct by the person liable whereas the actual conduct (original cause) violated the legal norms aiming to prevent the plaintiff's damage.

274. There are certain areas of court practice where this issue is particularly visible, i.e., in the claims execution cases and in cases of state liability for illegal expropriation. Recently, the Supreme Court has put limits to the defence of inevitable (inescapable) expropriation, thereby giving preference to the protection of the interests of the victims. In the judgment of the panel of seven judges of 22 January 2013 the Supreme Court confirmed the approach, which accepts the defence of a supervening (hypothetical) cause.[478] This notwithstanding, the court distinguished cases where the hypothetical cause, raised as a defence by the State Treasury, is a hypothetical expropriation of a proprietary right to land. The court underlined that the wrongs committed by the socialist government after World War II in execution of nationalization decrees that had accommodated the interests of former owners by guaranteeing them a right to be compensated were intentional. Such conduct not only breached the protective scope of the said provisions, but was also a method to avoid formal procedures in which the interests of former owners and their procedural rights would have had to be respected. The final result of such procedures was unpredictable to the authorities. Therefore, the fact that a piece of land would have been legally expropriated has no impact on the amount of damages sought in connection with an administrative decision denying a right of a temporary ownership of that land that was issued in patent violation of the law. The decision, which we approve of, thus sends a clear signal that such a defence is neither a proper way to avoid liability by the state, nor a simple method to reduce damages by a hypothetical sum of compensation for expropriation that had never been calculated, nor paid by an administrative organ.[479]

275. The second group of cases involving multiple causative factors are those where a number of causes actually did contribute to the damage. Here it may be clear to what extent each event or person contributed to the damage, but it is also possible that the exact contribution of each is unknown. In both cases, the Civil Code prescribes joint and several liability. This liability is regulated by Article 441 KC. Joint and several liability entails the following effects:

– All persons liable jointly and severally are liable for the entire damage to the victim.

477. *See* SN of 14 Jan. 2005, III CK 193/04OSP 7–8/2006, item 89, reported in E Bagińska, *Poland*, in *European Tort Law 2006,* 373, Nos 5–12 (H Koziol/BC Steininger eds, 2008).

478. 2. SN (Panel of sevenjudges) 22 Jan. 2013, I CSK 404/11, OSNC 9/2013, item 110, commented E. Bagińska & I. Adrych-Brzezińska, *European Tort Law 2013*, Nos 11–24 (2014).

479. E. Bagińska & K. Krupa-Lipińska, 'Hypothetical causation (causa superveniens) in modern court practice', 2 (vol. 38) *Gdańskie Studia Prawnicze* 2017 (in English).

- The victim may take action for the entire damage against only one tortfeasor, a number of them, or all of them. If one of the tortfeasors satisfies the entire claim, the others are released from their liability towards the victim (albeit not towards the person who satisfied the claim). The victim also may take separate actions for parts of damage against each tortfeasor separately.
- The person who redressed the damage has a right of recourse against the others, and the level of recourse depends on the circumstances, and particularly on the fault of the person against whom the recourse is sought and the degree of his contribution to the occurrence of damage.

276. Theoretically, the duty to prove causal link always lies with the claimant. However, courts increasingly use the principle of res ipsa loquitur and various presumptions for the existence of causal link, especially in cases involving personal injuries where proving causation can present significant challenges. Further, it is not required that causal link is proven with complete certainty, but rather with high likelihood of certainty. However, the common law approach of 'more likely than not' would not be possible in Polish tort liability cases. As a matter of principle, courts may utilize any evidence, both direct and offering certainty as well as indirect having a significant degree of probability, in order to establish causation. According to Article 231 of the Code of Civil Procedure courts may deem the facts which have crucial significance for the adjudication of the case confirmed if such a conclusion may be drawn from other established facts. This competence has particular significance in medical malpractice cases. For instance, a court may assume that damage inflicted by infecting a patient with a contagious disease is a result of lack of safety of treatment.[480] Further, courts increasingly use prima facie evidence in cases of uncertain causation involving contracting contagious diseases (HBV virus, HIV or staphylococcus). The Wroclaw Court of Appeal held that the plaintiff demonstrated causation by showing that when entering the hospital he was not infected with any virus and that he could not have contracted it anywhere else.[481] Where a patient was infected with a contagious disease, the defendant hospital may escape liability for damages only by proving a high probability of a different cause of the infection.

480. E Bagińska *Aggregation and Divisibility of Damage in Poland: Tort Law and Insurance,* 21.
481. Judgment of 28 Apr. 1998, I Aca 308/98, in Prawo i Medycyna 12/2002, 147.

Part VI. Remedies

Chapter 1. General Principles

277. The general principles governing remedies in the Polish law of obligations are contained in Articles 361–363 KC. They encapsulate the principle of full compensation, subject to the requirements of causation explained above. Unless law or a contract stipulate otherwise, compensation ought to cover damage sustained by the victim *(damnum emergens)* and the profits he or she would have gained had the damage never occurred *(lucrum cessans)* (Article 361 §2). They establish rules concerning limitation of compensation in cases of contributory negligence (Article 362) (*see* nos 257–266). They also regulate the types of remedies available: the victim can choose either restitution or monetary compensation, unless restitution is impossible, overly difficult or costly, in which case only monetary compensation is available. Article 363 §1 reads:

> The damage shall be redressed, at the election of the injured person, either by restoration of the previous state of affairs or by the payment of an appropriate sum of money. If, however, restoration of the previous state of affairs is impossible or if it would entail undue hardship or excessive costs to the person liable, the injured person's claim shall be limited to a pecuniary payment.

278. Examples of circumstances where restoration of the previous state of affairs (understood as the state of affairs in economic terms which would have existed if the damage never occurred) is impossible are for instance: non-pecuniary damage caused by infringements of personal interests (such as life or health), irreversible damage to or loss of an object, or lost monetary profits.[482] In general, the interests and preferences of the victim in selecting the method of redress are secured at the cost of the preferences of the person liable to redress.[483] Even if the restoration of the previous state of affairs would be more costly than monetary compensation, the former will be the redress method if the victim chooses so. The impossibility, hardship or costs which Article 363 §1 established as exceptions are interpreted rather narrowly.

279. While the victim has a choice of a form of remedy, damage can be redressed only once. The remedy can, however, combine restitution and monetary

482. M. Kaliński *Odpowiedzialnosc odszkodowawcza*, 176.
483. SN of 29 Nov. 1982, I CR 377/82, OSPiKA 1983, No. 11, item 251.

compensation. Further, when bringing a claim the injured person may ask for restitution or monetary compensation, with the understanding that it is not always possible to ascertain the feasibility of restitution at the start of the proceedings.[484]

280. As far as restitution is concerned, here are its most common forms:

- Repair of the damaged object.[485]
- Return of the object to a person who has lost possession or use of it.
- Handing over of non-pecuniary profits obtained from an object, land or building.
- Performance of a service.
- Press announcement or apology (in cases of infringements of personal rights).[486]

281. Monetary compensation is assessed in accordance with prices prevailing at the time of adjudication 'unless special circumstances require that prices existing at another time be taken as the basis for the calculation' (Article 363 §2 KC). It is determined by comparison of the actual state of the victim's economic circumstances and the hypothetical state the victim would have been in if the damage never occurred (the differential method).[487]

282. The principle of full compensation, according to which both the actual damage and lost profits ought to be redressed, can in practice be altered by a number of factors which are strictly regulated by the Civil Code. These phenomena include contributory negligence, statutory or contractual modification and modification by a court. Contributory negligence is regulated by Article 362, which is described in detail above (nos 257–266). The statutory modification of the scope of compensation should more precisely be referred to as modification of the scope of compensable damage.[488] It can take a number of forms:

- Delimitation of the types of compensable damage or objectivization of the method of assessing damage (for instance: Article 481 KC).
- Description of the type of causal link which is relevant in the determination of the scope of damage which should be compensated, thus limiting the scope of damage in comparison with the ordinary approach to causal link (only events within factual causal link – Articles 478 and 714 KC).
- Limitation of the scope of recoverable damage to the actual losses only (Article 438 KC concerning situations where a person suffered loss as a result of attempting to avert danger threatening another person).
- Caps on compensation: there are a number of cases where compensation is capped in Polish law. They include employment law, shipping law, rules concerning hotels, nuclear liability and others arising from ratified international conventions.

---

484. A. Szpunar *Ustalenie odszkodowania według przepisów kodeksu cywilnego,* NP 1965, No. 4, 146.
485. This type of remedy is interpreted widely: for instance the Supreme Court indicated that a destroyed well can be 'repaired' by way of construction of another one, even if the latter is in a different place and has different dimensions (SN of 29 Nov. 1982, I CR 377/82, OSPiKA 1983, No. 11, item 251).
486. M. Kaliński *Odpowiedzialnosc odszkodowawcza,* 177.
487. *Ibid.*, 178.
488. *Ibid.*, 193.

- Other limitations: for instance in the area of product liability law (Articles 449^1–449^{11} KC) damage to the product itself and lost profits cannot be compensated (Article 449^7KC).

Contractual clauses limiting the scope or amount of available compensation were explored above, in the part of the study dealing with exemption clauses (no. 267). These clauses are quite common, especially in certain types of commercial relationships (insurance,[489] or services: for instance holiday services).[490] Clauses extending liability are considerably rarer. Both types of clauses are always subject to scrutiny by the provisions of the Civil Code.

283. Compensation which would otherwise be due according to the rules of tortious liability may be limited (although not entirely eliminated) by a court adjudicating the case (Article 440 KC). The decision to limit compensation is within judicial discretion, but the Code specifies criteria which should be considered: the financial position of the victim and of the person liable. This provision is not used frequently, and it is interpreted narrowly (*see infra* no. 321).[491]

284. The key principle governing compensation is that, unless law specifies otherwise, the injured person should not be overcompensated (the principle of restitution).[492] Compensation ought to be equivalent to and not higher than the damage established using the rules and mechanisms described above: Article 363 §2, the theory of differentiation, the rules of causation and taking into account any contributory negligence. Compensation is not meant to have a punitive character.

285. The forms and scope of monetary compensation for personal injuries are regulated by Articles 444–448 KC. These provisions cover pecuniary and non-pecuniary damage (analysed in detail below). Compensation can take the form of a lump sum or an annuity (the latter in cases where law permits it).

286. Assessment and assigning an exact value to loss is not always easy or even possible, especially with regard to future losses or non-pecuniary losses. Polish law enables courts to use a certain level of flexibility and discretion in such circumstances. Article 322 of the Code of Civil Procedure provides that if exact valuation of loss is overly troublesome or impossible, courts may use their own judgment and determine the amount of damages taking into account all the circumstances of the case. Courts, especially lower level judiciary, are not eager to fully utilize this tool

489. *Ibid.*, 197.
490. *See* Kaliński *Odpowiedzialnosc odszkodowawcza*, 197–200, and M. Nesterowicz *Odpowiedzialnosc cywilna biur podróży* (Warszawa, 1974), 99.
491. *Ibid.*, Kaliński, *Odpowiedzialnosc odszkodowawcza*, 200–201, and J. Rezler, *Naprawienie szkody wynikłej ze spowodowania uszczerbku na ciele lub zdrowiu (według prawa cywilnego)* (Warszawa, 1968), 44.
492. Statutory compensation levels which can exceed actual damage, have been provided in a number of types of cases in the area of contract law, for instance contractual penalties.

and rather opt for seeking additional evidence and further expert opinions.[493] The reasons for this hesitation are related to the fear of the decision being overturned on appeal, and are grounded in the wider, systemic problem of the Polish judiciary described in the first part of this study: hesitation in using own judgment, flexibility and discretion and reliance on expert opinions. This judicial restraint is one of the key causes of delays in the Polish civil proceedings. When occurring in the context of assessment and determination of compensation it has the potential to lead to very significant delays.[494]

493. The same phenomenon can be observed in the application of Art. 440 – judicial modification of compensation (*supra* para. 284 and *infra* para. 322).

494. A. Smieja, *Szczególne zasady naprawienia deliktowej szkody na osobie,* in A. Olejniczak (ed.) *System Prawa Prywatnego: Prawo Zobowiązań. Część Ogólna* Vol. 6 (Wydawnictwo C.H. Beck, Instytut Nauk Prawnych PAN, Warszawa, 2009), 677. On delays in the Polish justice system *see* M. Tulibacka, *The Ethos of the Woolf Reforms in the Transformations of Post-socialist Civil Procedures: Case Study of Poland,* in *The Civil Procedure Rules. Ten Years On,* 395 (D. Dwyer ed., OUP, 2009).

Chapter 2. Kinds of Damages

Explanatory note:

287. Polish legal language and legal doctrine distinguish pecuniary and non-pecuniary damage, as well as compensation of these distinct types of damage, by way of maintaining separate notions for them. *Szkoda* (loss) indicates pecuniary damage and *krzywda* (detriment, *dommage moral*) indicates non-pecuniary damage; *odszkodowanie* is compensation of non-pecuniary damage and *zadoscuczynienie* – compensation for non-pecuniary damage.

§1. Individual and Collective Damage

288. Polish law does not know the concept of collective damage. Thus, while a number of persons who suffer damage as a result of the same or a similar event can seek redress together through a class action or a representative action, damages are still awarded individually to each person. Polish civil law and civil procedure are grounded in the concept of complete redress of individual damage which is sought directly by the victim.

289. The potential for mass claims is significant, especially in the areas of consumer law, competition law and environmental law.[495] While there are arguments in favour of introduction of the concept of collective damage into the Polish legal system, this process would no doubt involve significant systemic changes: within both substantive and procedural laws. There are areas of law (intellectual property law, or company law) where compensation of damage caused to a person can be sought by another person (representative organization). Further, prosecutors and social organizations have been given legitimacy to commence proceedings in the name of citizens, or groups of citizens (e.g., consumers).[496] However, the power to seek redress has purely procedural implications, and does not lead to transfer of a substantive right to compensate the other person. The Polish system of civil law struggles with the idea of mass damage even in the context of the relatively new class action mechanism (since 2010), which was reformed in 2017.[497]

290. The Class Actions Act of 17 December 2009,[498] as amended in 2017, allows for class actions to be brought by a class representative in the name of at least ten people with claims of the same kind based on the same or similar facts. Since 2017 the Act applies product liability and tort liability claims, personal injury,

495. M. Kaliński *Odpowiedzialnosc odszkodowawcza,* 36.
496. M. Tulibacka, *Poland,* in D.R. Hensler, C. Hodges, M. Tulibacka, *The Globalization of Class Actions, The Annals of the American Academy of Political and Social Science*, Vol. 622, 190, 194–195 (Sage, 2009).
497. Article 10 of the Act of 7 Apr. 2017 on the amendment of certain laws in order to facilitate the enforcement of claims, Dz.U. of 2017 item 933.
498. Dz.U. of 2010, No. 7; item. 44 p. 1. In force since July 2010. *See* M. Tulibacka *Poland* for an introduction of the work and the legal position preceding the Act.

including wrongful death cases, claims arising from contractual liability, unjust enrichment and to all other claims if they are consumer claims. Explicitly excluded remain claims for the protection of personal interests (other than personal injury). Clearly, the aim of the new mechanism is to simplify and facilitate actions by large numbers of people seeking compensation. The Act includes a very interesting requirement, which is indeed unique among other class action models. If a suit concerns monetary claims, class litigation is possible only if the amount claimed by each class member has been made equal with the others (this may be done in subgroups of at least two people).[499] The requirement entails a detraction from the idea of full compensation. Some class members will need to modify their claims and adjust them to the amounts claimed by other class members. In practice this means decreasing the claim amount to the level of the lowest in the class or subgroup, because courts will not award compensation above the actual damage. In spite of this attempt at approaching damages more 'globally', the Act does not detract from the main premise of compensatory rules: each class member is to be awarded damages individually.

During the relatively short period of experience, important limits of this mass litigation instrument could be observed with respect to tort claims. In a judgment of 28 January 2015[500] the Supreme Court clarified the meaning of the notion 'Defendant's liability' under the Class Action Act. The case was a seminal class action lawsuit arising from a 2006 building catastrophe which took place when an exhibition hall collapsed, killing or injuring tens of people. The families who lost their relatives filed a class action against the State Treasury, the Chief Inspector of Building Inspection and Mayor of the City of C. They claimed compensation for deterioration of their living situation based on art 446 §3 KC. The Court of Appeal found the class action inadmissible for lack of the requirement of a 'same claim'. However, the Supreme Court held that the requirement of 'the claims of one kind' means that all the plaintiffs demand damages or demand the determination of a legal relationship or a right. Even if the plaintiff only seeks to determine the liability of the defendant, he needs to formulate the pecuniary claim (with no precise quantum), which will be examined later in the individual proceedings. A court should be able to determine whether such a claim falls under the scope of the Class Action Act. If the court examining a class action is able to establish the liability of the defendant, the judgment serves as a prejudgment for the future individual cases. This prejudgment establishes the liability of the defendant for a particular action, but it does not establish the fact that each of the plaintiffs suffered particular damage in a particular amount. All these facts, including damage, its extent, the causal link between the defendant's conduct and the damage suffered or fault are to be established in the individual proceedings of each member of the group.

In line with the above case the 2017 amendment specified, among other things, that the class action may only aim to determine (declare) of the defendant's liability for certain event(s). In such a case the court establishes all elements of the factual

499. Article 2 §1 and 2 §2.

500. I CSK 533/14, OSNC 2015, Nos 7–8, item 97, reported in E. Bagińska & I. Adrych-Brzezińska, *European Tort Law 2015*, Nos 65–69 (2016).

and legal situations, which are common to all the participants. Individual claims for compensation need to be indicated as to its kind in the motion for the action and can be sought individually.

§2. Direct and Indirect Damage

291. Both direct and indirect damage can be recovered in Polish tort law, as long as they meet the criteria of having been normal consequences of the action or omission from which the damage resulted.[501] In fact, the distinction between direct and indirect damage, albeit mentioned by scholars, does not play an important role in Polish civil law which rather operates based on the principle of full compensation limited by the rules of adequate causation.[502] It is absorbed into discussions of other aspects of compensation of damage in tort law.

The dichotomy can be seen as reflecting the causal relation between the damaging conduct and the damage, or alternatively as focusing on the persons directly injured and those who suffered losses indirectly (for instance by death of a family member). The Civil Code expressly provides for compensation for certain persons who indirectly suffer losses following from a tort (victims *par ricochet*). These are family members and other people in close relationship with a person directly harmed . The legal position of indirectly injured parties if the victim of a tort dies is regulated by Article 446 §1–§4 KC. These rules apply only in personal injury cases. Such persons, provided that they are next of kin, have their own claims for compensation and bereavement claims. Other persons, unrelated to the deceased as well as those who have contractual claims against the deceased, are not entitled to compensation. In property damage cases an indirectly injured person can sue the tortfeasor for compensation provided that the premises of liability are met, in particular the consequences of the tortious conduct infringing upon his/her rights or legally protected interests must meet the test of adequate causation (Article 361 §2 KC).

Further, the direct/indirect damage dichotomy may refer to goods and interests directly damaged, as well as other interests of the victim (for instance lost profits).

It must be pointed out that the Code-established rule of full compensation may sometimes be derogated from. This point was examined above: a legal provision, a contract, or a court may modify the scope of compensation (*supra* no. 282). Here is where the distinction between direct and indirect damage plays an important role. Thus, in certain types of relations (such as insurance, and specifically – property insurance) parties may decide that only direct damage can be compensated.[503]

501. M. Kaliński *Odpowiedzialnosc odszkodowawcza,* 100.

502. *Ibid.*, 104. Also: L. Stecki *Problematyka odpowiedzialności za szkodę pośrednią*. In S. Sołtysiński (ed.) *Problemy kodyfikacji prawa cywilnego (studia i rozprawy)* (Poznań, 1990), 293, and A. Szpunar *Odszkodowanie za szkodę majątkową. Szkoda na mieniu i osobie* (Bydgoszcz, 1998), 47.

503. M. Kaliński, *Odpowiedzialnosc odszkodowawcza, 197.*

§3. Pecuniary and Non-pecuniary Losses

292. Polish tort law allows recovery of both pecuniary and non-pecuniary losses, albeit redress of non-pecuniary losses is only possible in cases specified by law.

Pecuniary losses concern property or other interests of the victim as long as the interests have some monetary value. Non-pecuniary losses are those which result from infringements of a person's personal interests but do not have monetary value. Pecuniary losses can follow either property damage or infringements of personal interests. Thus, infringements of personal interests can result in both pecuniary and non-pecuniary losses. Property damage has an exclusively pecuniary character, and non-pecuniary losses resulting from property damage cannot be recovered.

293. The scope of pecuniary losses which can be compensated in Polish tort law is regulated as follows by Article 361 §2 KC:

> In the absence of any legal or contractual provision to the contrary, damages shall include the losses suffered by the injured person and the profits which he would have gained had he not sustained the damage.

294. The notion of pecuniary damage was further shaped by courts and doctrine. While actual losses are deemed to be the type of direct damage, lost profits are as a matter of principle treated as indirect damage .[504] Actual losses may take form of depletion in a person's patrimony or increase of a person's debts or obligations. They also include costs incurred by the victim in order to restore his property to the previous state.[505] Lost profits can be redressed as long as there is a high probability that they would occur. While no absolute certainty is necessary (absolute certainty is obviously impossible to achieve in cases when one attempts to predict potential future profits), anything less than high probability would mean that this category of loss becomes 'loss of chance', which is not normally redressed in Polish tort law (*see infra* no. 313).

295. The only cases where loss of chance may result in compensation are linked to personal injuries and death, and involve non-pecuniary benefits. Article 444 §2 KC prescribes the possibility of the victim of personal injury to demand compensation for diminished future prospects. Further, according to Article 446 §2 KC the family of a victim who died may demand compensation for their diminished standard of living. While there are arguments in favour of allowing redress in cases of loss of chance, this would involve changes in the Civil Code which at present remains quite inflexible on the matter.

296. Compensation of non-pecuniary losses existed in the Polish legal tradition since the old Code of Obligations of 1933. The Code contained a provision specifying circumstances when they were recoverable. The 1964 Civil Code also had

504. M. Kaliński, *Odpowiedzialnosc odszkodowawcza,* 104.
505. *Ibid.*, Kaliński, 91.

such a provision, albeit it was relatively limited in the light of the popular understanding (disapproved of by prominent scholars) that compensation of non-pecuniary losses is not entirely compliant with socialist ethics.[506] Non-pecuniary losses could be compensated only in cases of personal injuries, deprivation of liberty and sexual misconduct towards women. With the evolution of Polish tort law, especially recently, came a much greater emphasis on compensating non-pecuniary damage. The number of legislative provisions allowing such compensation has been steadily increasing. At present, cases where non-pecuniary damage can be compensated include:

- Personal injury (which in the Polish Civil Code means infringement of a personal interest) – Article 445 §1KC.
- Infringements of other personal interests (such as privacy or dignity) – Articles 23, 24 and 448 KC.
- Deprivation of personal liberty – Article 445 §2 KC.
- Sexual assault or sexual misconduct (against females or males) – Article 445 §2 KC.
- Persons in close relationships with the victim in case of death – Article 446 §4 KC.
- Persons in close relationships with the victim in case of a serious and permanent bodily injury or damage to health resulting in the inability to establish or continue a family relationship – Article 446^2 KC.

297. There are several provisions in the area of healthcare law which allow for compensation of non-pecuniary losses, including an infringement of patients' rights (Article 4 of the Act of 6 November 2008 on Patients' Rights and the Patient Ombudsman[507]), breach of confidentiality, disclosure of personal data and information about an insured person and compensation for a blood donor. The workers' compensation scheme) also allows for recovery of non-pecuniary losses. Other areas of law where non-pecuniary damage can be compensated (these are beyond the scope of this study) are election rules, copyright law, patent law and criminal law.[508]

298. Whilst most of the provisions mentioned above are relatively new (introduced after 1989), they reflect the contemporary tendency to increase the scope and instances of recovery of non-pecuniary damages. The most significant transformation has been linked to the concept of personal interests (*dobra osobiste)* and their protection. The concept was explained earlier in this study, in the part concerning injury to reputation and privacy. It includes health (thus – every case of personal injury is also a case of an infringement of personal interests), liberty, dignity, freedom of conscience, name, image, privacy of correspondence, inviolability of the home, scientific, artistic, creative and inventive achievements (Article 23 KC). The

506. Z. Radwański, *Zadośćuczynienie pieniężne za szkodę niemajątkową. Rozwój i funkcja społeczna* (Poznań, 1956), 166.
507. Dz. U 2009, No. 52, at 417 and No. 76, at 641.
508. E. Bagińska & M. Nesterowicz, *Non-pecuniary Loss under Polish Law.*

list is non-exhaustive. Following the 1996 amendment of the Code,[509] Article 24 provides that a person whose personal interest is threatened by another can demand that the action ceases. If an infringement already occurred the victim may demand that its effects are rectified, which can entail in particular: a statement, compensation, or a sum of money paid to a social cause. Articles 445 and 448, which further specify conditions for assessing and awarding damages for non-pecuniary losses, also apply. Article 448 provides that in cases of infringements courts may award compensation of non-pecuniary loss or hold that a sum of money should be paid to a social cause specified by the victim, in addition to other remedies prescribed by law. Article 445 allows compensation of non-pecuniary losses for victims of personal injuries, deprivation of property and sexual misconduct.

299. Article 448 refers to all personal interests, and Article 445 (*lex specialis* in relation to the former provision) applies specifically to personal injuries, deprivation of property and sexual misconduct. Pursuant to Article 448 KC, in the case of an infringement of a personal interest, a court may award an injured person an adequate sum as compensation for non-pecuniary loss or, if the victim so demands, an appropriate sum for a designated social cause, irrespective of other means necessary to eliminate the effects of the damage caused. The actual content of Article 448 KC was shaped in 1996.[510] Until then, intentional fault was a premise of the claim and the Polish Red Cross could be the only beneficiary of an award. Historically, this type of claim was not considered an indemnity for non-pecuniary loss, but rather a sort of private penalty to be paid to the mentioned institution. Courts held that this claim played an explicit preventive role, punishing the wrongdoer for his malice in the interference with personal interests of another.[511] Since 1996 the courts and doctrinal views have been clearly divided on the issue whether the claimant whose personal interests are violated may present two claims for non-pecuniary loss, i.e., one for his account and one for a designated social cause. According to the dominant view, victims have a choice between the two claims. Article 448 KC in its present wording regulates one and indivisible claim for redress of non-pecuniary loss. Therefore, in several decisions courts held that the norm contains an alternative that excludes the accumulation of claims.[512] However, in a number of other decisions the Supreme Court followed the opposite view.[513]

300. The recent Supreme Court resolution of 9 September 2008[514] emphasizes the difference in functions and structure between the two claims embraced by Article 448 KC. Although both claims provide for pecuniary redress, the means of reparation of moral harm varies, and hence they are not identical claims. The money paid to the injured is a different means of redress than his satisfaction caused by

509. Act of 23 Aug. 1996, Dz.U. 1996, No. 114, item 542.
510. *Ibid.*
511. SN (Full Civil Chamber), 8 Dec. 1973, OSN 1974, 145.
512. *See* SN of 1 Apr. 2004, II CK 115/03, unpublished, SN of 17 Mar. 2006, I CSK 81/05 unpublished.
513. *See* SN of 16 Apr. 2002, V CKN 1010/00, OSNC 4/2003, item 56; SN of 17 Mar. 2006, I CSK 81/05, OSP 3/2007, item 30; SN of 19 Jun. 2007, III CZP 54/07, OSN-ZD B/2008, item 36, reported in E. Bagińska, *European Tort Law 2008*, No. 5. (2009).
514. III CZP 31/08, OSNC 3/2009, item 36.

making the wrongdoer pay a sum of money to a social cause. The Supreme Court confirmed the minority interpretation of Article 448 KC, according to which an aggrieved party may demand payment of damages for both himself and a social institution in order to reach full satisfaction. This interpretation of the provision seemingly shows a more modern approach to the protection of personal interests. If an aggrieved party would achieve full satisfaction by demanding payment of damages for both her and a social institution, the law should enable her to make such claims. It is for the courts to put reasonable limits to the application of the *cumul* of claims.[515]

301. Article 445 KC allows compensation of non-pecuniary losses for victims of personal injuries, deprivation of liberty and sexual misconduct. Liability for personal injuries is explored in more detail in a further part of this study (*infra* Part VI, Chapter 4). Below we introduce the remaining two types of infringements and briefly explain the scope of recovery of non-pecuniary damage in the area of health law.

302. In cases where a person is prevailed upon by deceit, violence or abuse of a relation of dependency to submit to an immoral act a court may award compensation for non-pecuniary harm. In practice, most cases concern rape committed on a woman, a minor or a mentally disabled man. In the judgment of 21 March 1979[516] the Supreme Court held that 'compensation for moral harm inflicted upon a woman through an immoral act is justified regardless of the results of the act'. However, the results may have some importance for assessment of damages.[517] Scholars argue that compensation should not cover further consequential losses, for instance a breach of promise of marriage, the breakup of marriage, or loss of future life prospects. In establishing the appropriate amount of compensation, courts take into account the type and the manner of infliction, gravity of pain and suffering, particularly severe mental trauma (for a very young persons), feelings of shame and humiliation, disturbances in intimate relations, acquiring of a venereal disease, etc.[518]

303. Cases concerning recovery for deprivation of liberty are not common. They do not necessarily concern arrests or being held in a prison. The Supreme Court held that damages can be recovered for having been put in a psychiatric hospital against one's will.[519]

The assessment of compensation due in such cases includes the duration and manner of deprivation of freedom and the motives of infringement. The Appellate Court in Katowice in the judgment of 28 November 1996[520] held that a construction company was liable for moral damage to its workers whom it sent to work in Germany without getting an official authorization for work or a residence permit.

515. E. Bagińska & M. Nesterowicz, *Non-pecuniary Loss under Polish Law.*
516. IV CR 68/79.
517. *See also* E. Bagińska & M. Nesterowicz, *Non-pecuniary Loss under Polish Law*, Nos 48–49.
518. *Ibid.* Bagińska, Nesterowicz.
519. SN of 15 Nov. 1979, [1981] OSPiKA, 26.
520. OSA, 1998, item 28.

As a result the workers were arrested by the police, kept in detention for over 30 hours, and deported to Poland with a lifelong ban on entering Germany.

304. Compensation for deprivation of liberty arising out of unjust conviction, arrest or detention is regulated by Article 552 of the Code of Criminal Procedure (*see supra* no. 101). Its purpose is to cover pecuniary damage and moral harm, thus the existence of a decline in the financial situation of the claimant has no influence on the indemnity for non-pecuniary harm.[521]

305. Another important provision concerning non-pecuniary losses is Article 8 of the Act of 23 February 1991 on declaring void the decisions rendered against persons prosecuted for activities performed for the benefit of the independent Polish State[522](*see* no. 103).

306. Polish health law enables patients to recover non-pecuniary damage in a number of cases. First of all, the catalogue of patients' rights is contained in Chapters 2–11 of the Act of 6 November 2008 on Patients' Rights and the Patient Ombudsman.[523] It includes the right to medical services, the right to information, the right to informed consent (with a specific regulation concerning minors and mentally incompetent patients), the right to intimacy and protection of dignity, the right to confidentiality, and the right of access to medical documentation, a right to object to an opinion or decision of a doctor. The Patients' Rights Act proclaims a claim for compensation in Article 4. A person harmed by a negligent breach of patients' rights may claim pecuniary compensation for moral damage in an action based on Article 448 KC (Article 4 section 1 of the Act). In a case of breach of the right to die in dignity, a spouse, the next of kin or a guardian may claim a sum of money to be paid for the benefit of a charitable institution (Article 4 section 2). The pecuniary protection is limited to the right to safety of valuables deposited in a hospital, the right to information about the scope and type of healthcare services offered by healthcare providers and the right of patients to access their medical records (Article 4 section 3 of the Patients' Rights Act). In all three cases an aggrieved patient has no claim for a pecuniary redress of non-pecuniary loss. Thus, the patient will need to make use of other available remedies, be it of an administrative nature (both an individual action and an action for the infringement of patients' collective rights) or a general contractual claim. This ground of awarding damages for non-pecuniary loss has gained significant importance in Poland. In the judgment of 27 November 2019,[524] the Supreme Court extended the protection of Article 4 of the Patients' Rights Act to a Father's Right to Information about Child's Congenital Disorder. While the Court of Appeals dismissed the father's claim arguing that the father of the child was not a patient within the meaning of the Patients' Rights Act, and therefore had no legal standing, the Supreme Court held that each parent had the same rights to information about the condition of their children and a broad

521. SN of 24 Apr. 1972, OSNKW 9/1972.
522. Dz.U. of 1991 No. 34, item 149.
523. Dz. U 2009, No. 52, at 417 and No. 76, at 641.
524. II CSK 491/18, OSNC-ZD 2020/3, item 54.

understanding of 'patient' should be adopted. The plaintiff was present both during the prenatal tests and at the childbirth, when he learned of the physical defect of the child. He therefore suffered psychological harm similar to that of his wife and mother of their child. The right to information is a personal right. The lack of a proper diagnosis of a serious foetal defect prevented the plaintiffs from receiving psychological assistance already in the prenatal stage. Hence, the father of the child should be regarded as an injured party in the meaning of Article 4 of the Patients' Rights Act. Moreover, the Supreme Court also approved the concept of awarding compensation on the basis of the Civil Code rules concerning the violation of personal rights, more specifically of mental health and dignity of the father (Articles 24 and 448 KC). It should be noted that the recognition that the child's father is a patient in light of the Patients' Rights Act raises serious doubts, as the health services were provided exclusively to the mother and the child. The statutory definition of a patient is precise and sufficiently broad but not broad enough to be extended to the father of the unborn child.[525] Thus, the correct basis for the father's claims is the infringement of his personal rights.

307. The Act of 7 January 1993 on Family Planning, Fetus Protection and Conditions of Permission of Abortion[526] (Article 4c) imposes on persons carrying out activities regulated by the statute (i.e., physicians performing abortions or giving medical advice to a pregnant woman) a duty to keep secret all information provided in connection with the activities. Negligent breach of confidence entitles an injured person to compensation for non-pecuniary loss.

308. Article 12 of the Blood Shield Statute of 22 August 1997 allows blood donors who sustain bodily injury or disturbance of health ensuing from the procedures of acquiring blood or immunizing to claim redress according to the provisions of the Civil Code. It refers to Articles 444 and 445 KC. Thus an injured blood donor can claim compensation of pecuniary and non-pecuniary losses.

309. While compensation of non-pecuniary damage can only be awarded in cases specified by law, whether or not to award such compensation and how much to award is left to judicial discretion, with a number of reservations. First of all, in cases where compensation can be awarded, it can be denied only on the basis of ascertainable objective criteria. For instance when the damage was insignificant and the tortfeasor was not at fault, or when the victim contributed to the damage to a large extent,[527] or when personal injury was a result of criminal conduct of the victim.

525. See comment to the reported judgment by *N Karczewska-Kamińska*, OSP 12/2020, 10.
526. Dz.U. No. 17, item 78.
527. SN of 31 Oct. 1960, published in OSN 1962, item 128.

§4. Pure Economic Loss

310. The concept of pure economic loss is not often used by Polish legal scholars. It is not seen as relevant in the light of the wide scope of the provisions of the Civil Code concerning liability in tort. The provisions, explored above, elucidate the principle of full compensation within the limits of adequate causation. They do not exclude pure economic loss. As a matter of principle, pure economic loss is seen as a type of pecuniary loss which occurs irrespective of any infringement of someone's rights. Examples given in scholarly writings concern cases of unfair competition or sharing know-how.[528] While Polish tort law does not exclude the possibility of compensation of such losses, they may well be very difficult to quantify.

§5. Actual and Future Damage (Lost Profits and Loss of Chance)

311. The approach of Polish tort law to actual losses and lost profits was explained above (*supra* no. 291). Both constitute important parts of recoverable damage, and the Civil Code provision concerning full compensation (Article 361 §2 KC) refers to them expressly. When awarding compensation to victims of torts, courts may include compensation of future damage (including lost profits) as long as at the time of adjudication there is a high probability of it occurring.[529] In cases when such future damage cannot be assessed accurately, courts tend to issue declaratory judgments which confirm the tortfeasor's liability for such damage. There is no possibility, however, of a tort claim for redress of future damage only. Future damage must be linked to some other loss which already occurred.

312. The concept of future damage is particularly significant with regard to personal injuries, where some consequences of the injury may be unknown or have not yet materialized at the time of adjudication. The Civil Code contains mechanisms which enable a victim of personal injury to receive a temporary annuity until the extent of damage to health is fully known in cases where the damage already occurred but its extent is not yet known. This is not future damage, but rather existing damage which cannot yet be quantified. It is explored further below, in the part of this study devoted to redress of personal injuries (nos 342 et seq.). As far as future damage is concerned, the Code contains no precise answer, but judicial practice confirms that in personal injury cases liability for future damage may be added to the claim of compensation for damage which already occurred. The Supreme Court issued a legal principle to this effect on 17 April 1970.[530] The victim's ability to make such a claim was recently questioned before the Supreme Court in the light of the amendment of the Civil Code in 2007.[531] The amendment, mentioned above (*see* no. 235) meant that the limitation period for personal injury claims in tort does

528. M. Kaliński, Odpowiedzialnosc odszkodowawcza, 100–101.
529. SN of 17 Jun. 1963, III CO 38/62, OSPiKA 1965, No. 9, item 196. *See*, however, M. Kaliński, *Odpowiedzialnosc odszkodowawcza,* 155 for arguments against the possibility of establishing liability for future damage.
530. III PZP 34/69, published in OSN*: Izba Cywilna/Pracy* 1970, No. 12, item 217.
531. SN of 24 Feb. 2009, III CZP 2/09.

not start running until the victim learnt of the injury and the person liable (Article 442^1§3). The risk of claims being time-limited has always been a very significant argument in favour of inclusion of future losses in judicial decisions concerning personal injuries. With the now existing possibility to bring additional claims at any time in the future as long as it is within three years since the victim has knowledge of the damage, the need to cater to future damage at the time of making the first decision in the case lost some of its urgency. Nevertheless, the Supreme Court saw such future claims as very problematic because passage of time entails that some evidence is lost or more difficult to obtain. Potential future suits may be ineffective because the victim's task of proving all the necessary requisites of a tort is likely to become much more onerous. Thus, the Supreme Court reaffirmed the importance of the possibility of claiming liability for future losses.

313. Another crucial issue linked to the distinction between actual and future damage is the phenomenon referred to as 'loss of chance'. While in other legal systems loss of chance may be examined within the scope of causation, Polish courts see it in the context of damage.

In Polish legal scholarship loss of chance, loss of expectations or *prejudice eventuel* are treated as one category and seem to be excluded from the scope of compensation (*see also supra* no. 282). The only cases where loss of chance may result in compensation are specifically provided by the Civil Code. They are linked to personal injuries and death, and involve non-pecuniary benefits. Article 444 §2 KC prescribes the possibility for the victim of personal injury to demand compensation for diminished future prospects. Further, according to Article 446 §2 the family of a victim who died may demand compensation for their diminished standard of living. Within this category the courts award compensation for lost chances to obtain certain financial means from the deceased, in addition to the pecuniary losses covered by an annuity (Article 446 §2 KC – *see infra* nos 358, 362).[532]

As mentioned above, courts approach loss of chance cases from the perspective of damage rather than causation. In personal injury cases, the standard of proof is lowered to a sufficient degree of probability. Courts tend to declare that a late diagnosis resulting from negligence of a medical service provider is causally linked to a loss (or diminution) of chance of healing. A reduction in chances of healing constitutes a standalone harm of 'lost chances' for which the victim should be fully compensated. In the case of a refusal to perform medical treatment, the patient's harm is not just a deterioration of his health, but also maintaining the existing disturbance, if it could have been eliminated had the treatment been carried out (loss of healing).[533]

Polish courts have awarded damages for a lost chance of healing or a lost chance of improvement of the patient's condition either under the head of pecuniary damage (in the form of an annuity) or as compensation for non-pecuniary loss. For example, in the case where a patient lost capacity to have more children as a result

532. *See* E. Bagińska, *Causal Uncertainty and Proportional Liability in Poland*, in *Proportional Liability: Analytical and Comparative Perspectives,* 253, Nos 41–46 (I. Gilead, M.D. Green, B.A. Koch eds.,De Gruyter Berlin, 2013).

533. SN of 11 Dec. 2002 I CKN 1386/00 unpublished, *ibid.*, E. Bagińska *Causal Uncertainty.*

of medical malpractice during the delivery of the first child, the court awarded compensation for a 'loss of a chance to give birth to a child'.[534] The extent of compensation is not related to any percentage of probability, but it is left to the discretion of the court.

In the judgment of 17 June 2009,[535] the Supreme Court ruled that negligent omissions of healthcare providers could lead to damage in the form of lost or reduced chances of improving one's health condition (in this case a minor lost his chance to reduce the disability for which no one was at fault). The plaintiff was awarded both compensation for non-pecuniary loss and an annuity.

As regards the loss of the chance to obtain gains, a vast majority of legal scholars traditionally reject such claims, albeit with various justifications. The key argument is that chances to obtain gains fall outside of the scope of normal causal consequences (i.e., fail to meet the adequate causation standard). A much stronger point is the failure to meet the standard of proof (here: a high probability standard) when one has to reconstruct a purely hypothetical situation. The prevailing line of court practice follows the legal scholarship.[536] If a victim proves with a sufficiently high probability that he could have obtained the profits but for the damaging event, his loss will be compensated. However, if he fails on evidence, the court will classify the loss as potential damage or a loss of chance, or loss of (subjective) expectations and dismiss the case.[537]

§6. Other Costs

I. Cost of Legal Opinions

314. Polish courts consider the costs of legal opinions as an element of damages. The Supreme Court held that the cost of legal opinions procured in connection with administrative proceedings which led to the annulment of an unlawful decision were part of *damnum emergens* if they were adequately causally linked with this decision.[538]

II. Costs of a Legal Representative in Pretrial (or Insurer's Liquidation) Proceedings

315. In early case law the claims for refund of the cost of a legal representative retained in pretrial proceedings were accepted on the basis of an adequate causation requirement, understood as covering necessary and rational costs. In a number of recent cases, and in particular in the decision of 20 February 2002, the Supreme

534. SN of 1 Sep. 1978, CR 510/77, OSN 11/1978, item 210, *ibid.*, No. 43.
535. SN of IV CSK 37/09, OSP 9/2010, item 93, Cmt by *M. Nesterowicz*, OSP 9/2010, 657.
536. For instance: SN of 18 Apr. 2002, II CKN 1216/00, OSNC 4/2003, item 58.
537. *See* E. Bagińska, *Causal Uncertainty*, No. 46.
538. SN of 19 Jun. 2008, V CSK 18/08 Lex No. 424431.

Court held that lack of an adequate causal link between the costs and the damage in the circumstances of the case merited the dismissal of such a claim.[539]

The position was ultimately settled in 2012. In response to a preliminary question of the Ombudsman for the insured, the Supreme Court ruled that justifiable and necessary costs of a representative incurred by the injured party in pretrial proceedings might constitute, in the circumstances of the particular case, a reparable pecuniary loss covered by compulsory third party liability motor insurance.[540] According to the Supreme Court, Article 34 section 1 and Article 36 section 1 of the Law on Compulsory Insurance indicate the sources of insurers' liability.[541] They do not restrict liability to the explicitly mentioned direct losses to the exclusion of adequately connected indirect pecuniary losses. The only limit to an insurer's liability is the guarantee sum (Article 36 section 1 of the Law).

316. The costs of a representative in pretrial proceedings need to be necessary and justified by the amount of work. In addition, services should be performed by a person with adequate qualifications. These requirements result from the creditor's duties to prevent and reduce damage (Articles 354 §2, 362 and 826 §1 KC). Most importantly, whether the costs of a proxy in pretrial proceedings constitute damage in adequate causal connection with an accident should therefore be evaluated on a case-by-case basis. The injured party's mere inconvenience in making a claim is not causally relevant, because this is a non-compensable non-pecuniary loss. Causally relevant legal representation might be recoverable when the victim's state of heath, personal skills or life situation justifies the necessity of such representation for efficient and economically profitable pursuit of proceedings. Although the injured party incurs these costs voluntarily, her decision is not free but rather forced by the circumstances.

317. In the cited judgment of 13 March 2012 the Supreme Court emphasized, obiter dicta, that its ruling can also apply to other forms of useful and paid-for assistance which the injured party may need in pretrial proceedings (for instance legal advice to properly formulate claims and present adequate evidence, an expert opinion on the scope and amount of the loss, other help in collecting and presenting evidence, as well as other activities necessary in pretrial proceedings).

539. SN of 11 Jun. 2001, V CKN 266/00, OSP 3/2002, item 40; SN of 20 Feb. 2002, V CKN 908/00, not published; SN of 7 Aug. 2003, IV CKN 387/01, not published.
540. SN of 13 Mar. 2012, III CZP 75/11, OSNIC 7–8/2012, item 81, commented by E. Bagińska, K. Krupa-Lipińska, *Poland,* in *European Tort Law 2012*, Nos 16–22 (2013).
541. According to Art. 34 sec. 1 and Art. 36 sec. 1 of the Law on Compulsory Insurance, compensation from the third-party liability motor insurer is due if the possessor or driver are obliged to compensate for this loss because the operation of a vehicle resulted in death, bodily injury, health disorder or loss, destruction or damage to property.

§7. MITIGATION OF DAMAGES

318. It follows from Article 362 KC that contribution to an increase of damage is subject to the same principles as contribution to causing damage in the first place. The former entails that the extent of the damage would have been less significant but for the injured person's conduct.

In personal injury cases, omissions by injured persons following the occurrence of damage are relatively frequent. If necessary efforts to prevent further consequences of the accident are not undertaken (for instance failure to report to a doctor, failure to start medical treatment, or failure to start another job corresponding to lower skills and strength resulting from partial health deterioration), a court will usually consider this failure to act as contributory to the increase of damage.[542]

319. Specific problems may arise regarding refusals to undergo a medical operation. Initially, the Supreme Court assumed that an injured person could not be forced to undergo an operation aimed at full or partial restoration of the working capacity. Hence, the refusal could not cause a reduction of damages as the injured person may be mentally unprepared for an operation.[543] In another judgment the Supreme Court held that the tortfeasor could not force the injured person to undergo an operation under the threat of facing a reduction of compensation. If the position was different, it would entail reversal of the roles of the parties – the tortfeasor would appear as a victim, and the injured person as the tortfeasor of a new harm caused by his refusal to undergo an operation.[544] In subsequent cases, however, the Supreme Court mitigated its position.[545] It decided that in the light of the current state of medical knowledge, some diseases and injuries could be subject to verified and commonly available methods of pharmacological and surgical treatment which generally bring about positive results. It is also known that the same diseases and injuries may cause much more serious and sometimes irreversible consequences when left untreated. A special sensitivity of the victim certainly deserves to be protected by law, although the protection should remain within reasonable limits and be justified in a wider context of social justice and fairness.[546] To summarize, the victim's refusal to undergo medical treatment which generally tends to bring successful results and improvements in health should be assessed considering all the circumstances. Refusals shall be based on reasons understandable at least to experts and supported by actual reactions of the human body.[547]

320. As concerns property damage, contributory negligence may occur when the injured person fails to undertake the activities necessary to decrease the size of the damage.[548] A distinct, positive duty of the injured person to act so as to reduce damage under pain of refusal to be paid compensation is provided for exclusively in

542. *See* M. Nesterowicz & E. Bagińska, *Contributory Negligence*, 151–152.
543. SN of 15 Mar. 1961, OSPiKA 1962, item 10.
544. *See* M. Nesterowicz & E. Bagińska, *Contributory Negligence*, 151–152.
545. SN of 11 Jan. 1978, OSPiKA 1979, item 17.
546. *See* M. Nesterowicz & E. Bagińska, *Contributory Negligence*, 152.
547. *Ibid.*
548. SN of 11 Mar. 1974, OSN 1974, item 202; SN of 28 Feb. 1975, OSPiKA 1977, item 129.

Article 826 §1 KC, which refers to property insurance and stipulates: 'In the event of an accident, the insured party shall be obliged to undertake all available measures to reduce the damage to the insured property and to protect directly threatened property against damage.'

The possessor of a damaged car may elect where to have it repaired, based on criteria such as high professional standard, authorized spare parts. Although he has no duty to search for the cheapest service, the compensation should only cover indispensable and economically justified costs of repair. Prices charged by a garage are economically justified regardless of whether they deviate (in plus) from the average market prices of a certain type of services.[549]

321. As to ad hoc mitigation of damages (ad hoc reduction – Article 440 KC – *see also* nos 271, 337), in relations between natural persons, the scope of the duty to redress damage may be limited according to the circumstances of the case. This can be done if, having regard to the financial circumstances of the injured person or those of the person liable for damage, the principles of community life (principles of fairness) require such limitation.

549. SN of 13 Jun. 2003, IV CZP 32/03 OSN 4/2004, item 51.

Chapter 3. Assessment and Compensation of Damages

§1. Objective Versus Subjective

322. It should be recalled that Polish courts apply the theory of differentiation (differential method) in assessing damage. Thus, property damage consists of the difference between the present state of the property of the victim and the state which would have existed had the event causing the damage not occurred.[550]

323. According to Article 361 §2 KC, damage shall be fully compensated. The compensation for a damaged chattel is, first of all, based on objective standards. For example, the value of a thing in need of repairs is represented by its market value. Further, a decrease in the value of assets (e.g., monies) may be considered a material damage. For example, 'real loss' (positive damage) may consist in diminution in the value of the sums paid as public duties that occurred in the period between the payment and the refund (the latter grounded in the unlawfulness of the decisions ordering payment). According to the Supreme Court, interest rates may serve as an objective yardstick of such loss (interest plays a compensatory function) only if they do not exceed the inflation rate, which may appear to be a better, more certain criterion.[551]

324. The Code of Obligations of 1933 provided (Article 160) that in the case of pecuniary loss, damages are established according to market prices and in cases of intentional fault or reckless negligence of the tortfeasor account should also be taken of the special value a chattel had for the victim (*pretium singulare).* This rule (borrowed from the Austrian Civil Code) was not inserted into the Civil Code of 1964. Nevertheless, after 1964 legal scholars still accepted the view that in cases of damage or destruction of a movable, pecuniary compensation should also be based on its utility to the injured. Today, the special value (*pretium singulare*) is recognized through the principle of full compensation (Article 361 §1 KC). If damages are to fulfil the aim of full reparation, the individual situation of a victim must be taken into account. Courts follow this interpretation.

The special emotional value (*pretium affectionis*) which the damaged or destroyed chattel presented for the victim is not taken into account (for instance in the case of destroyed letters from a relative or of loss of a dog).[552] *Pretium affectionis* is regarded as non-pecuniary loss but no legal rule provides for its compensation.[553] Taking into account the evolution of jurisprudence, one may expect that

550. *See*, e.g., SN of 11 Nov. 1957, 2 CR 304/57, OSNC 3/1958, item 76; SN of 19 Mar. 1998, III CZP 72/97, OSNC 7–8/1999, item 133.
551. SN of 16 Apr. 2002, V CKN 960/00 OSNC 5/2003, item 63.
552. *See* A. Szpunar, *Odszkodowanie za szkodę majątkową* (1998) 57; Z. Radwański, A. Olejniczak, *Zobowiązania – część ogólna* (8th Edition, 2008), 104.
553. *See* T. Wiśniewski in: *Komentarz do kodeksu cywilnego, Zobowiązania*, vol I (1996), 56.

in the future courts will consider the sentimental value of domestic animals when they are lost or injured due to a tort, because an animal is not a chattel under the law on the protection of animals.[554]

325. Particular problems arise as regards compensation for damaged vehicles. Currently, courts maintain that if despite the repair the car's value is reduced compared to the market value of an undamaged car, compensation should embrace both the repair costs and the difference in value.[555] In the seminal judgment of 12 October 2001,[556] the Supreme Court pointed to the transformation of the Polish economic system into a free market economy and held that the measure of damages in cases of destruction of a chattel should be based on its market value. One should not consider individual prices that can be negotiated at the point of sale. The average market price is the correct point of reference. It is irrelevant whether the thing was destined for sale or for use by the victim. In a market economy, every chattel of economic value may be sold at any time.[557]

326. Traditionally, courts understood Article 363 §1 KC as providing a duty to repair damage formed as an alternative obligation (i.e., where it is the creditor, not the debtor who makes the choice of remedy). Thus, once the victim chooses the manner of redress (e.g., restitution), the claim for compensation is extinguished.[558] Both claims (performances) could not be combined, as it would be against the clear language of Article 363 KC. The interpretation suggested in 2001 by the Supreme Court provides a possibility of claiming both restitution and compensation. This interpretation has prevailed in present judicial practice.[559]

§2. Concrete Versus Abstract

327. There are no standard rates or other standard rules concerning compensation. Damages are evaluated on a case-by case basis. Hence, for example, compensation should be determined in accordance with prices offered by professional car dealers in the victim's country of residence (if the victim resides abroad), and not in accordance with the prices of similar cars available on the Polish second-hand market. The fact that the damaging event took place in Poland is random and as such remains irrelevant for the establishment of the plaintiff's pecuniary loss which took the form of the destruction of his car.[560]

---

554. The Act of 21 Aug. 1997, consolidated text Dz.U. 2013, item 856.
555. SN of 3 Feb. 1971, III CRN 450/70, OSNCP 11/1971, at 205.
556. SN of 12 Oct. 2001, III CZP 57/01, OSNC 5/2002, item 57, commented in E. Bagińska, M. Nesterowicz, *Comment to the Case in Digest of European Tort Law, Essential Cases on Damage,* vol. 2, Nos 1–5, 102–103.
557. *See* E. Kowalewski & M. Nesterowicz, Comment to the SN of 12 Oct. 2001 (III CZP 57/01), [2003] Prawo Asekuracyjne 3, 69.
558. *Ibid.*
559. *See* in general E. Kowalewski (ed), *Odszkodowanie za ubytek wartości handlowej pojazdu poddanego naprawie* (TNOIK, Toruń, 2012).
560. SN of 19 Mar. 1998, III CZP 72/97, OSNC 7–8/1999, item 133.

328. In the case of diminution of someone's working capacity, damage must not be purely theoretical (abstract). Some concrete pecuniary consequences of the loss must be demonstrated. Accordingly, this element of damage should be understood as the difference between what the victim could have received from her work if the damaging event had not occurred and what she actually receives after this occurrence. The income of a victim of personal injury is not to be compared to her pre-accident earnings, but to what she would have earned at the time of adjudication if there had been no accident. It is sufficient that the victim proves a high probability of receiving the income.[561]

§3. Methods of Assessing Damage

329. The amount of damages is generally determined according to prices on the date when the extent of the damage is established (date of adjudication), unless particular circumstances demand that prices in force on another day be adopted as the basis (Article 363 §2 KC). When issuing a judgment and assessing damages, courts take account of all the circumstances present on the date the trial is closed (Article 316 KPC).

By way of exception and where extraordinary circumstances so justify, a court may evaluate the damages on the basis of prices existing at another moment. In the decision of 12 January 1976[562] the Supreme Court held that a substantial change in prices that occurred between the date of infliction of the damage and the date of judgment could justify a derogation from the rule prescribed in Article 363 §2 KC. In this case, the plaintiff's car burnt in an accident. At the time of adjudication, the car manufacturer no longer produced the model and the prices of used vehicles of this type went down significantly because of availability of new models. The court held that the substantial decrease in the prices of used vehicles between the date of event and the date of judgment, together with the fact of a total loss of the Plaintiff's car, were 'extraordinary circumstances'. They justified the departure from the ordinary principle of Article 363 §2 KC and the award of damages according to the prices on the date of the harm.

Another exceptional case involved a plantation which was partially destroyed by a pollutant emitted by the defendant. Compensation was determined on the basis of prices prevailing at the time when the plaintiff's harvest would normally be sold.[563]

330. Since damages are to fulfil the aim of full reparation, the individual situation of a victim must be taken into account. For example, the stolen car's market price on the day when the court adjudicated the claim shall be decisive, rather than the car purchase price paid by the plaintiff or its market value on the day of the theft.[564] Compensation should enable the plaintiff who lost a thing to purchase a similar one. The measure of the damages when a chattel is destroyed should be

561. *See*, e.g., Court of Appeals in Katowice of 16 Dec. 2004, I ACa 1097/04, OSA 10/2005, item 38.
562. II CR 690/75, OSPiKA 3/1977 item 56.
563. SN of 24 Jan. 1983, OSN 1983 item 123.
564. SN of 15 Jan. 1998, III CKN 322/97, OSN 7–8/1999, item 129.

based on a market value of the chattel, regardless of how it was to be used by the victim. By way of exception only, in a case of destruction of a chattel damages may embrace the price for which it could have been sold had it not been destroyed. This would be allowed only if it were established that the chattel was destined for sale and not for normal use by the victim.

331. As regards traffic accident liability insurance, the scope of liability of a car possessor or a driver determines the scope of compensation (up to the guaranteed limit).[565] Thus, the general rules of the Civil Code regarding remedies find their application here. The duty to remedy the damage to property arises at the moment of its infliction (here: a traffic accident), regardless of whether the injured party actually repaired the damaged thing or wishes to do so later. The loss exists from the moment of the event until the payment of compensation as determined according to law. Hence, whether a car was in fact repaired is irrelevant for determination of the compensation payable by the insurer. In the context of traffic accident liability insurance the injured person cannot demand that his/her car be returned to its previous condition, but is entitled only to a payment of money. This payment must make up the difference between the present patrimonial standing of the injured and the standing that would exist if the event causing the damage did not occur. It is a claim for compensation of the loss suffered and not a claim for the cost of repair. However, typically, redress of property damage is based on the replacement value or the cost of repair.

332. If the repair costs are incurred before the assessment of damage, the compensation may be determined as the equivalent of the hypothetically determined costs of restoring the vehicle to its previous condition. If the insurer demonstrates that such a calculation exceeds the value of the damage, then the compensation may be reduced. If the aggrieved party who did not repair the damage is entitled to compensation, this should also be the case for the aggrieved party who repaired it before the evaluation of compensation. The hypothetical cost of the repair is a yardstick of the amount of compensation payable to the victim since, irrespective of the repair of the vehicle, it should correspond to the cost of restoring the vehicle to its value prior to the accident. If the injured party cannot provide any proof of the cost of the repair (e.g., invoices), the cost of the repair should be determined on the basis of an expert opinion.[566]

Several other issues in this area were settled by judicial decisions. They concern the scope of reparable pecuniary damage and are as follows:

- Indemnity to be paid by an insurer covers the indispensable and economically justified costs of repair reflecting the prices applied on the local market. If the election of a garage by the claimant is not questioned, the prices used by the garage should be the basis of damages. The Supreme Court rejects the average price approach to indemnity by third-party insurers, although it takes into account the aspect of territoriality. The prices (of labour, spare parts, or materials used in

565. *See* Art. 36 of the Act of 22 May 2003 *on compulsory insurance.*
566. SN of 7 Dec. 2018, III CZP 51/18, OSNC 9/2019, item 94.

the service) applied by a garage must reflect prices in the local market of car services, be it the place of residence of the claimant or the place where the car was damaged.[567]

- There is no ground for a deduction from the amount of compensation on account of wear and tear if the victim claims restitution *in integrum* (providing the invoices for the repair service). If an insurer proves that the repairs will lead to an increase in the vehicle's market value, the compensation may be reduced by the increment.[568] This approach can be found in Supreme Court judgments and in some judgments of lower courts.[569] One may speak of unjustified enrichment of the injured party only when the new part increased the vehicle's market value as a whole. The insurer should calculate compensation including the costs of new parts if they were necessary to repair the car.
- According to the Supreme Court Resolution of 17 May 2007,[570] compensation from a traffic liability insurer calculated on the basis of prices of spare parts and service includes VAT to the amount which would be due for payment by the victim (i.e., it will depend on whether the victim is a VAT payer and can reduce the amount of tax due). VAT is a component of the price, thus it should be treated as an element of damages when they are determined according to prices of goods or services on the date of adjudication (Article 363 §3 KC). Pursuant to Article 17a of the Act on Insurance Activity, if the claimant who is not a VAT payer presents the insurer with an invoice for the repair of the 'traffic damage', the insurer is obliged to include VAT in the scope of compensation. This provision was used by insurers to deny the reimbursement of VAT in a situation not covered by it. In the cited ruling of 17 May 2007 the Supreme Court held that any controversy surrounding this norm should be disposed of in view of the Civil Code rules on compensation of damage as well as in view of Article 36 of the Act on Compulsory Insurance.[571] Hence, if the claimant is not a VAT payer the insurer must include VAT in compensation.
- The assignee who acquired a claim for compensation is entitled to demand reimbursement of the reasonable costs of an expert's opinion if the expertise was necessary to claim compensation under the third-party liability insurance scheme[572].

567. SN of 13 Jun. 2003, IV CZP 32/03 OSN 4/2004, item 51, SN of 7 Dec. 2018, III CZP 51/18, OSNC 9/2019, item 94.
568. SN of 12 Apr. 2012, III CZP 80/11, OSNIC 10/2012, item 112, commented by E. Bagińska, K. Krupa-Lipińska, *Poland,* in European Tort Law 2012 (2013), Nos 23–30.
569. *See* SN of 20 Oct. 1972, II CR 425/72, OSNIC 6/1973, item 11; SN of 5 Nov. 1980, III CRN 223/80, OSNIC 10/1981, item 186: 'An increase in the market value of a vehicle after a repair might be considered only when the repaired parts were damaged before the accident or if the repair led to an improvement of the vehicle in relation to its prior state.'
570. III CZP 150/06, OSN 10/2007, item 144, commented by E. Bagińska, in *Poland,* in *European Tort Law 2007*, Nos 54–61 (2008).
571. Article 36 stipulates a duty to pay indemnity and provides for the maximum liability of the insurer under third-party traffic insurance.
572. SN of 18 May 2004, III CZP 24/04, OSNC 2005/7-8, item 117, SN of 29 May 2019, III CZP 68/18, OSNC 2019/10, item 98.

There is an adequate causal link between a procurement of the expertise regarding the scope of repairs and their cost and a traffic accident. As a consequence, the cost of such an expert opinion falls within the scope of the loss, which should be covered by the liable tortfeasor.

In the case of an injured party itself bearing the cost of the expert opinion before the assignment of the claim for compensation, the claim for reimbursement of these costs forms an integral part of the entire loss. If, however, the assignee later incurred the costs of the expertise, it has its own claim for reimbursement. In order to pursue the claim against the insurer, it should be assessed whether the costs were necessary, reasonable, and sufficiently justified.[573]. It is relevant to determine whether the victim (or the assignee) operates a business and therefore has the knowledge, equipment or personnel required for the evaluation of damage to vehicles and so may not need expert experience. Thus, this part of the loss will not be reimbursed if the expertise was provided in order to determine the profitability of the purchase of the claim in question, as well as if the assignee herself, being a professional, could determine the amount of damage. In such a case the costs will not be considered necessary and reasonable, so no reimbursement will be due.

333. Polish courts are obliged to provide a detailed justification of the award of damages and explain all heads of damage. In practice, courts identify particular claims (corresponding to the elements of damage) in separate points of an award (e.g., a one-off compensation for medical expenses and other pecuniary losses, such as an appropriate annuity if the victim lost the ability to work). In particular, compensation for pecuniary and non-pecuniary damage must always be listed as separate elements of an award. A court may not grant these two components of the entire damage in one all-inclusive sum.

334. Article 322 of the Code of Civil Procedure may be viewed as relaxation of the burden of proof concerning damage. According to this rule, 'if in the case of a claim for damages a court deems it impossible or extremely difficult to prove accurately the amount of the claim, it may adjudicate a relevant amount of money in accordance with its evaluation based on the consideration of all circumstances of the case' (*supra* no. 286). This competence is often used in respect of *lucrum cessans* and in personal injury cases. In the first situation, it is sufficient to prove that the plaintiff had an actual possibility to gain certain profits and that he did not gain them due to the consequences of the damaging event.

335. If at the moment of adjudication the damage cannot be assessed precisely, the court may issue a declaratory judgment that would proclaim the defendant's liability for future damage (*see supra* no. 312).[574] This is particularly justified in the case of minors. Once the 'new' damage has occurred, the victim may file a new claim in court (e.g., for an annuity or for a new non-pecuniary loss). With respect

573. SN of 2 Sep. 2019, III CZP 99/18, Monitor Prawniczy 2019/19, 1019, commented by E. Bagińska, P. Wyszyńska-Ślufińska, in *Poland,* in *European Tort Law 2019*, Nos 22–28 (2020).
574. SN of 7 Aug. 1969, OSN 1970, item 217.

to damages for non-pecuniary loss, compensation also covers future harm which is certain to occur or which can be foreseen at the moment of deciding the case. A final adjudication may not be modified or reconsidered since it is subject to the principle of res judicata. Thus, in case of a further decline in the victim's health no additional award is allowed unless there appears a new injury that could not have been foreseen based on the facts of the adjudicated case.[575] On the contrary, if the adjudicated award was symbolic (e.g., PLN1), whether in civil or criminal proceedings, the injured party has a valid claim for non-pecuniary loss unless the judgment states that the symbolic award makes up fully for the sustained damage.[576]

336. When awarding an annuity to the victim (in a personal injury case) on the grounds that his needs have increased or his future prospects have been diminished (Article 444 §2KC – *see infra* for analysis – no. 346 ff), a court usually makes an overall assessment of different elements of pecuniary damage. The annuity must be 'appropriate', therefore the court has a margin of discretion. If at the time of adjudication the damage cannot be accurately assessed, the injured person may be awarded a temporary annuity.

§4. Equitable Limitation of Damages

337. A Polish court does not have the general power to reduce the amount of damages on account of lesser degree of fault of the tortfeasor, his or her wealth, or the other circumstances of the case. The same rule concerns the increase of the amount of damages.

338. However, *ius moderandi* (ad hoc reduction, mentioned *supra* nos 283 and 321) is provided in Article 440 KC. In relations between natural persons, the scope of the duty to redress damage may be limited according to the circumstances of the case if, having regard to the financial circumstances of the injured person or those of the person liable for damage, the principles of community life (principles of fairness) require such limitation. This rule should be interpreted strictly. Polish courts rarely apply Article 440 KC, mainly because of its limited personal scope of application.[577] It concerns only natural persons who are not insured. A court may reduce the award taking into account all factors, including the economic position of the parties and the degree of the tortfeasor's fault. The fundamental precondition for the reduction is the poor economic situation of the person liable. Assessment is to be made on the basis both of the actual income and of the earning capacity of the tortfeasor. The fulfilment of this requirement alone is not sufficient. It must be reinforced by the principles of community life (*see supra* no. 22 for an explanation of the meaning of this general clause).

There are some further limitations to the use of *ius moderandi*. It is not applied in cases of intentional fault, gross negligence or personal injury, since this would be

575. SN of 27 Nov. 1967, III PZP 37/67, OSN 7/1968, item 113.
576. SN of 23 Nov. 1966, [1967] OSN of 94; SN of 24 Nov. 1966, OSN 1967, item 47.
577. There are also problems with its practical application – *see supra* para. 308.

contrary to the principle of fairness. It also does not apply in cases where the person liable has a liability insurance cover.[578] Article 440 KC does not permit a total release of the liable person from the legal obligation to repair damage. Courts have not approved of applying the provision by analogy to cases where one of the parties is a legal entity.

The Supreme Court ruled that the principles of community life do not support mitigation of damages in the case where the breach of duty by the defendant physician was so grave as to constitute a criminal offence and the extent of irreversible personal injury effectively precluded a child from living a 'quality life'. The court emphasized that the cap on the doctor's civil liability insurance was not a reason for reducing compensation, as it had been the defendant's own choice to procure such a low insurance cover.[579]

The wealth of the person responsible cannot be a factor for increasing the award of damages.

339. The level of fault is normally not taken into account in the determination of damages. There is, however, an exception to the general rule. In assessment of damages for non-pecuniary loss courts must take into consideration all circumstances that influence the extent and the gravity of the damage. According to the established line of argument in judicial decisions, moral suffering may well be enhanced by the tortfeasor's insensitive behaviour after the tortious act or omission (for instance failing to undertake any actions aimed at diminishing the damage).[580] It is considered that a high degree of a doctors' fault should result in an increased quantum of damages. This approach is applied in medical malpractice cases, where moral harm was particularly enhanced by obviously unnecessary procedures leading to a permanent disability or the mutilation of a patient, as well as by the loss or reduction of chance to recover or survive.[581]

§5. Methods of Payment

I. Lump Sum

340. In Polish civil law, payment of damages as a lump sum is a rule as concerns damage to property (things) as well as pecuniary damages in personal injury cases (such as the cost of treatment, or outstanding annuities). Non-pecuniary damages are always paid as lump sum.

If the victim asks for compensation in the form of an annuity, the judge cannot award a lump sum ex officio. In personal injury cases pursuant to Article 447 KC, a court may, for important reasons and upon the victim's demand, award a lump sum instead of an annuity or a portion of it. In particular, this applies to a case where the

578. *See* M. Nesterowicz et al., *Kodeks cywilny z komentarzem [The Civil Code with a commentary]*, vol. 1 (1989), 438.
579. SN of 26 Jan. 2011, IV CSK 308/10, OSP 11/2011, item 112.
580. SN of 9 Jan. 1978, OSN 1978, item 210.
581. *See*, e.g., the judgment of the Regional Court in Bydgoszcz 19 Jul. 1999, I C 1150/98, OSP 4/2002, at 59 SN 10 Mar. 2006, IV CSK 80/05, OSP 1/2007, item 11.

injured person became disabled and the award of a lump sum would help him engage in another profession. The victim has the burden of establishing the 'important reasons'. The courts use a restrictive interpretation of this provision. The assessment of a lump sum is based on the annuity to which the plaintiff would be entitled. The payment of a lump sum must be equivalent to the obligation to pay an annuity (hence as long as the victim is entitled to an annuity, a lump sum may be requested).

II. Annuities

341. An annuity is a method of redress of pecuniary losses stemming from personal injury. If a victim loses his ability to work completely or partially, or if his needs have increased (e.g., permanent expenses for treatment or care and assistance by third persons), or his future prospects have diminished (e.g., inability to carry out a profession or obtain specialization), he may demand an appropriate annuity from the person obliged to redress the damage. Any of these conditions, whether alone or concurrent with others, constitutes a sufficient ground for the claim (Article 444 §2 KC – *see supra* no. 335).

The part of the damage in question is described as the emergence of a need to bear expenses (e.g., the cost of a special diet, or of an additional nursing aid). The tortfeasor must pay compensation in the form of an annuity regardless of any other person's existing commitment to supply the victim with care, assistance, or means of maintenance. In cases where a family member renders care personally the courts limit the damages to the cost of nursing and care that would have to be paid if the care could have been rendered by a professional third party.[582] An annuity for the increased needs aims to cover future expenses. The injured person is entitled to an annuity as long as the above expenses stem from his personal injury and are justified in a given situation, regardless of whether they have actually been incurred.

In a case of diminution of working capacity, damage consists of the difference between the income which the victim could have received from his work if the accident had not occurred and the income he is actually able to receive after the accident with his diminished working capacity (in addition to social benefits).

In the case of the victim's death a mandatory annuity may be requested by a person with respect to whom the deceased had the statutory duty of maintenance (provided for in the Family and Care Code) computed in relation to the needs of the injured and to the earning and financial possibilities of the deceased for the time of the likely duration of the said duty (Article 446 §2 sentence 1). This type of annuity may not exceed the sum that the latter would have been obliged to pay as maintenance.

An optional annuity may be claimed by other related persons (e.g., a life partner, or a family member to whom the deceased owed no duty of support) whom the deceased voluntarily and permanently supplied with means of maintenance if it follows from the circumstances that this is required by the principles of equity (Article 446 §2 sentence 2). The nature of claims for an annuity is compensatory; they are not maintenance claims.

---

582. SN of 4 Oct. 1973, II CR 365/73, OSNC 9/1974, item 147.

The victim's contributory negligence justifies – on the basis of Article 362 KC – the reduction of damages to be awarded to the close persons (*supra* no. 257).

342. Based on Article 907 KC the person responsible or the victim may ask the court to adjust the amount or duration of the annuity or to discontinue it completely if circumstances change (e.g., when the victim's earning capacity increases).

Chapter 4. Personal Injury and Death

343. In the context of tort law, the Polish Civil Code regulates redress of personal injury and death in much more detail than redress of property damage. The former type of damage is generally referred to as 'damage to a person' (*szkoda na osobie*). Its two crucial elements are: infringement of a personal interest, and the resulting damage. The concept of personal interests was explored in some detail above (*supra* nos 116 and 290). Here it is useful to recall that Article 23 KC contains a non-exhaustive list of those interests which includes health. Injuries and death resulting from a tortious act are thus infringements of personal interests (albeit of course the concept of personal interests reaches much further than a person's bodily integrity). Both pecuniary and non-pecuniary damage linked to such infringements can be redressed.

344. The notion of personal injury was not given a detailed definition. Nevertheless, the Code does provide a short description in Article 444 which includes 'bodily injury or damage to health'. Thus, it is clear that any physical injuries are covered, and so are any circumstances where a person's internal organ or organs are not functioning properly even though no apparent injury occurred. The latter types of damage to health include mental conditions and even mental trauma. In the judgment of 25 April 1961 the Supreme Court held that a woman could recover compensation for mental trauma sustained in connection with deaths of two of her friends in a motor traffic accident even though she suffered no physical injury.[583] In 1971 the court granted compensation to a person who suffered mental disorder triggered by noise produced by an adjacent mine exceeding legally permitted levels.[584]

§1. Pecuniary Losses

345. The Civil Code has different provisions applying to compensation of pecuniary losses for personal injury and for death. These provisions specify in some detail what forms of remedies are available, what is recoverable, by whom and at which point in time. They are accompanied by a large number of judicial decisions and doctrinal writings.

I. Personal Injury

346. Article 444 §1 KC specifies that all costs arising from bodily injury or damage to health shall be recoverable. It does not provide a list of recoverable costs, but it does mention two important types: costs of treatment, and costs of training for an alternative occupation in cases of disability. The provision stipulates that both these types may be payable in advance (instead of a later reimbursement of costs paid by

583. Published in OSPiKA 1962, item 200.
584. SN of 24 Feb. 1971, OSN 1971, item 182.

the injured person) if requested by the victim. Judicial decisions and scholarly writings explored in much more detail what the notion 'all costs' entails. It is interpreted widely, and includes hospital treatment, doctors, nurses and other medical practitioners' visits, travel and accommodation related to treatment, expenses relating to rehabilitation, purchasing medicines, implants, other medical devices and any other equipment necessary for treatment or everyday life of the victim (such as a pair of glasses, a hearing aid, a wheelchair, or a special needs vehicle required by the victim for attending treatment and carrying out business activities).[585] It also extends upon differences in pay suffered by a person unable to work for a period of time.

347. A panel of seven judges in a judgment on 19 May 2016[586] confirmed the coverage of the cost of private health care by a tortfeasor (and in particular by insurers in traffic liability insurance) pursuant to Article 444 §1 KC. The Supreme Court analysed in great detail the established court practice, including a precedent decision of 13 December 2007,[587] in which it was held that the plaintiff must only prove that he has a valid claim for all necessary costs arising from a tort.

348. As the aim of the principle of full compensation must be achieved as far as possible, all costs which fulfil this aim will be considered as justified and reasonable. The injured person is not obliged to opt for a state-provided doctor or hospital if resorting to private health care, including foreign healthcare providers, will guarantee the effectiveness of treatment and/or rehabilitation in particular circumstances of each case. The private system may offer access to the latest and most effective treatment methods and the long queues in the public system do not allow the victim a quick recovery. The doctrine and earlier case law stresses that the starting point of analysis should be whether the private alternative could realistically, based on sound medical prognosis, improve the patient's chances of recovery from a serious medical condition.[588] It does not matter whether the cost has already been borne or is demanded by the injured for future medical services. The court emphasizes that a victim of a tort has no duty to use the public healthcare system in order to restore his/her health condition to the previous state and moreover, does not need to prove that particular treatment was necessary for his/her condition. If an insurer invokes the victim's duty to reduce damage, then he must prove that fact. The insurers' practice demanding a particular form of evidence from the injured (e.g., medical statements) to prove that the privately sought medical service was necessary and reasonable in a given case is wrongful.

The provision of Article 444 §1 KC covers expenses paid out directly by the victim as well as by other persons (for instance the victim's family), albeit they are all included in the victim's claim. Family members of an injured person normally do not have claims on their own right for expenses they covered. The question whether

585. SN of 14 May 1997, II UKN 113/97, OSP 1998, No. 6, item 121.

586. III CZP 63/15, OSNC 11/2016 item 125, commented by E. Bagińska & K. Krupa-Lipińska, in: *European Tort Law* Nos 77–81 (2017).

587. I CSK 384/07, OSP 2/2009, item 20, *see E Bagińska*, Poland, in: *European Tort Law 2009* 475, No. 66 (2010).

588. SN of 26 Jun. 1969, II PR 217/69, OSN 1969, No. 3, item 50.

the injured party may claim the costs of (full or partial) care of close relatives in a situation where such care is provided free of charge (in a full or partial manner) and is not connected with the loss of any income by the person providing the care, causes divergences in the jurisdiction of common courts and in the doctrine. This issue was positively resolved by the Supreme Court in the resolution of 22 July 2020,[589] ruling that 'an injured person who has suffered a bodily injury or health disorder may claim, on the basis of Article 444 §1 of the Civil Code, compensation for the costs of unpaid care provided by close persons'. The court recognised the fact of need for care as a damage; in other words, increased needs of a person who sustained bodily injury or disorder of health are included in the costs of treatment under Article 444 §1 of the Civil Code. He stressed that care provided by relatives always has an objectively measurable economic value and that the free form of care is often used by indigent persons. In the opinion of the Supreme Court, 'it is difficult to consider as fair the solution (...) differentiating the legal situation of the injured depending on whether they used the care for a fee or – due to lack of adequate resources – the care of their relatives without incurring expenses for it'. The court was guided by the results of linguistic, systemic and purposive interpretation as well as considerations of legal policy. Denying compensation for unpaid care could encourage abuse and the circumvention of the law by making fictitious legal transactions between relatives.

349. Injured persons may receive compensation in a form of a lump sum or an annuity (*see supra* nos 339–341). The latter is available when the person partially or completely loses her ability to work, when her needs increase or when her future prospects are diminished (Article 444 §2 KC). Either of these three conditions is sufficient for demanding an annuity. With regard to the loss of ability to work, the sums are to reflect the shortfall in income taking into account what the injured person would be expecting to earn if the injury did not occur. Compensation may cover employment income or business profits. An annuity can also be awarded to a person who is not employed but runs a household (usually a stay-at-home mother).

350. An increase in a person's needs may occur whether or not the ability to work was lost. Such increases may simply entail additional expenses which the person is faced with, for instance the need to be on a special diet or to require regular medical attention. Diminution in future prospects is a notion which does not receive wide application, and it is clear from judicial decisions and academic writings that the prospects must be very realistic indeed. For instance, young persons who have not yet reached maturity are not normally entitled to compensation for such loss. An exception would be someone who has a particular ability or talent and the prospects for a future career in this area are quite clear.[590] Instead of seeking annuity for loss of future prospects it would be advisable in all other cases to ask for determination of liability of the tortfeasor for future losses (*see supra* nos 311–313).

---

589. III CZP 31/19, OSNC 2021/4, item 22.
590. A. Smieja *Szczególne zasady naprawienia szkody na osobie*, 694.

351. The latter statement refers to a crucial issue concerning many personal injury cases. There are a number of reasons why at the time of adjudication it may be impossible to assess the precise extent of injuries and damage to health. First of all, there is the situation evoked in Article 444 §3: when at the time of adjudication the extent of the damage cannot yet be assessed, a temporary annuity may be awarded. This would be the case for instance when the future prospects of the victim are dependent upon the results of a medical procedure, and yet this procedure cannot be performed until the victim's general condition improves. Second, there are cases where the damage already occurred and its extent is relatively clear, but it is impossible to determine its exact scope or assess its money value. The courts can in these conditions use discretion and award the sum they see adequate taking into account all the circumstances, using Article 322 of the Code of Civil Procedure (*supra* no. 286). Lastly, there is the issue of future loss: when at the time of adjudication not all the harmful effects of the tort materialized. Polish tort law is not meant to compensate those who have not yet suffered losses but are merely expecting them in future. However, in cases where damage already occurred and yet some losses are highly probable to occur, the claimant may ask for determination of liability for future losses (*supra* nos 310–313).[591] In circumstances where at some time in the future circumstances change (for instance the victim's health deteriorates significantly), either of the parties may request modification of the annuity. (Article 907 §2 of the Civil Code – *see supra* no. 340).

352. The actual amounts awarded to personal injury victims with regard to pecuniary losses may seem relatively insignificant, especially when compared with amounts awarded for similar injuries in the US. Nevertheless, they are meant to reflect the true cost of medical care, treatment and rehabilitation in Poland. A large part of such costs is borne by the state-funded healthcare system.[592] The specific feature of Polish health care, however, is the relative importance and popularity of private medical care which exists alongside the state-funded system. The latter tends to suffer from limited resources sometimes leading to delays in provision of care and, for obvious reasons, opts for the most cost-efficient (which does not necessarily entail the best) care. Private health care offers an attractive alternative. The question which Polish judiciary face in personal injury cases is: to what extent should the tortfeasor cover the costs of such private medical care? Could the injured person recover the costs of using a private doctor or a hospital if opting for a state-provided doctor or a hospital would mean a long waiting time? If the private system offers access to the latest and more effective treatment methods and the state system does not, could the victim choose the former and recover the costs from the tortfeasor? The answer depends on the circumstances of each case, but the starting point of analysis should be whether the private alternative can realistically, based on sound medical prognosis, improve the patient's chances of recovery from a serious

---

591. Supreme Court Decision of 24 Mar. 2009, III CZP 02/09.
592. For a detailed analysis of the healthcare system in Poland – *see* Mirosław Nesterowicz, Ewa Bagińska, André den Exter, *International Encyclopaedia of Laws. Medical Law,* Supplement 51 (Herman Nys ed., Poland, 2011).

medical condition. The more serious the condition, the more likely it is that a private alternative will be acceptable to a court, as was the case when a person's eyesight was threatened.[593]

II. Death

353. In cases where personal injuries led to death, the Civil Code prescribes a number of remedies which include reimbursement of costs of treatment and funeral to those who paid them, annuities for family members and compensation of pecuniary and non-pecuniary losses of family members (indirect victims – victims *par ricochet)*.

354. First of all, the person liable ought to refund the costs of treatment and the funeral expenses to whoever has incurred them (Article 446 §1). While there is no limitation on the potential scope of persons who can be reimbursed (for instance the person does not need to be a family member), the payment must be related to money already spent and cannot be required in advance, before the costs were incurred. Thus, the costs of building a tombstone cannot be recovered before the tombstone is constructed and paid for.[594]

355. Further, those in respect of whom the deceased had a statutory duty of maintenance have the right to an annuity from the person liable (*see supra* no. 340). This type of annuity is referred to as a 'mandatory annuity', because if all the conditions for tortious liability specified in the provision applicable in the case are met the court must make an award. Duties of maintenance are regulated by the Family and Care Code of 1964[595] and include descendants, and in some cases siblings, other relatives and divorced or separated spouses.[596] With regard to actual spouses the position was clarified by the Supreme Court's decision of 20 December 1990.[597] The obligation to satisfy the financial needs of the family rests upon every married person (Article 27 of the Family and Care Code). This of course extends upon situations where one of the spouses does not work and runs the household, bringing up children. However, until the Supreme Court Decision mentioned above it was generally accepted that tortfeasors who caused death were not liable to pay an annuity to the surviving spouse where the latter was working or at least was capable of working and there were no dependent children. Maintaining the latter's lifestyle was not seen as an adequate basis for an obligation to compensate. In the 1990 decision, the court held that spouses can be awarded annuity until they are in a financial position to sustain themselves and their family.

593. SN of 26 Jun. 1969, II PR 217/69, OSN 1969, No. 3, item 50.
594. SN of 4 Jun. 1998, II CKN 852/97, OSN 1997, No. 11, item 196.
595. Act of 25 Feb. 1964, published in Dz.U. of 1964, No. 9, item 59. Later amended.
596. Family and Care Code, Arts 128–134, and 60.
597. II PR 61/90, published in PiZS 1991, Nos 5–6, p. 64.

For all those who are entitled to payments, the annuity is assessed taking into account the needs of the claimant and the earnings and financial means of the deceased.

356. An annuity may also be claimed by persons who were in a close relationship with the deceased and whom he voluntarily maintained on a regular, long-term basis (Article 446 §2). This type of annuity is referred to as a 'voluntary/facultative annuity'. The court can award a voluntary annuity as long as the principles of community life so require (considering the financial position of both parties, the relationship between the deceased and the beneficiary and the context in which the voluntary support was taking place, especially its purposes). This provision is particularly relevant in case of cohabitees.

357. The Code also allows immediate family members of the deceased to claim compensation for a considerable deterioration of their living standards (Article 446 §3) and for non-pecuniary damage (Article 446 §4 – *see infra* §2). The compensation extends upon the damage which is not base for an annuity. These are types of pecuniary damage in a broad sense, often difficult to assess exactly, as well as non-pecuniary damage, both leading to substantial deterioration of an immediate family member's financial position. For example, loss of maternal care and support constitutes a worsening in the child's situation, and merits the indemnity on the basis of Article 446 §3.[598] Such losses include not only changes in the actual economic position, but also losses of the realistically foreseeable prospects for the improvement of the living conditions: for instance death of a son whose financial help in the near future could be counted on by his parents,[599] or death of a person thanks to whom the claimant planned to improve his living conditions.[600] Although in general mere grief is not to be compensated, a severe mental trauma (for instance in case of the spouse's or the long-time partner's death), or feeling of solitude (for instance loss of mother by a minor) may increase the degree of the decline in one's quality of life and therefore should merit an award.

§2. Non-pecuniary Losses

358. According to Article 445 §1 KC the victim of personal injury may demand an appropriate sum as compensation of non-pecuniary losses related to the sustained injury. This provision applies in particular to physical suffering and moral damage resulting from injury. Further, it also applies when no injury occurred to the person concerned and the only type of detriment is moral suffering and trauma. For instance, the mother who suffered neurosis following her son's death in a tragic accident.[601] Another example involves a case when a surgeon negligently left a metal surgical tool under the patient's scalp, which became assimilated within the

598. SN of 6 Feb. 1968, OSN 1969, item 14.
599. SN of 13 May 1969, OSPiKA 1969, item 122.
600. SN of 8 Jul. 1974, OSPiKA 1975, item 204.
601. SN of 8 May 1969, OSN [1979] 129.

brain tissue. No actual injury occurred and the patient did not consent to another operation. The Supreme Court held that while the claimant had a reasonable fear of the possibility of injury in future, moral trauma resulting from the fear was sufficient to merit an award of compensation.[602]

359. Everyone may demand redress of non-pecuniary loss. This extends to a foetus' (*nasciturus)* claim for prenatal damages (Article 446^1 KC). The latter claims can be made against a third person or against the mother.

360. The manner in which the amount of compensation is determined is based on objective standards (*see supra* no. 323). Thus, it is relatively unimportant whether the victim is, because of her mental state, unable to realize the full impact of what happened, or whether the victim has particularly acute sensitivity and thus suffered a much more intense mental trauma. On the contrary, courts consider circumstances of a particular case in assessing compensation, and in particular: the degree of physical and mental suffering and how long it lasted, how permanent the injuries are, what the future prospects are concerning life expectancy and quality of life (for instance regarding social life, travel or work) and the age of the victim. Relating the amount of the award to an average salary may be helpful, but this cannot be done mechanically. The aim of the damages is to compensate non-pecuniary harm which is very difficult to measure. Courts also emphasized that a high degree of the tortfeasor's fault should result in an increased quantum of damages.[603] Moral suffering may well be enhanced by the tortfeasor's insensible behaviour after the tortious event in failing to undertake an action mitigating the damage.[604]

361. The Supreme Court stressed that the improved living standards in Polish society ought to be material in determining the amount of damages for non-pecuniary losses awarded to a claimant who suffered physical and mental pain as a result of a wrong diagnosis and the resulting chemotherapy.[605] Damages for non-pecuniary loss purport to make the injured person whole (compensatory function). In certain cases this is the only type of damages received by the victim. In the judgment of 24 October 1968 the Supreme Court held that 'the amount of financial compensation should provide material support for the injured person, compensating him to some extent for the inflicted physical pain and moral harm, and yet it should also be moderate'. In general, in the present practice the sums awarded by Polish courts as compensation for non-pecuniary loss are increasingly high.[606]

362. Compensation also covers future harm which is certain to occur or which can be foreseen at the moment of deciding the case. A final adjudication may not be

602. SN of 25 Feb. 1972, [1972] OSPiKA 210.
603. SN of 27 Mar. 1973, [1973] ICR 73/73/.
604. SN of 9 Jan. 1978, [1978] OSN 210.
605. Judgment of 10 Mar. 2006. Kidney removal was assessed at 35% of health detriment, and the resulting depression and anxiety – at 10%. The Supreme Court assessed the non-pecuniary damage to be 150,000 PLN (around USD 50,000), which doubled what the district court awarded the claimant in the first instance.
606. I CR 383/68.

modified or reconsidered since it is subject to the principle of res judicata. Thus, in case of a further decline of the victim's health no additional award is allowed unless there appears a new injury that could not have been foreseen based on the facts of the adjudicated case.

363. The ability to obtain compensation for non-pecuniary damage caused by death of a close relative (bereavement damages) is a new addition to the Civil Code. It was introduced by the Act amending the Code of 30 May 2008 (in force since 3 August 2008), although throughout the 1970s, 1980s and 1990s courts utilized the ability to award compensation of pecuniary damage mentioned below to include some purely non-pecuniary losses as well.[607] Close relatives are entitled to bereavement damages if the victim of a tort died on or after 3 August 2008. In the light of the apparent discrimination of the relatives whose family member died as a result of a tort before 3 August 2008, the Supreme Court ruled that a tort resulting in the wrongful death before 3 August 2008 can constitute an infringement of personal interests of the victim's immediate family members and entitle them to demand damages for non-pecuniary loss on the ground of Article 448 KC.[608] The court supports the construction of a new personal interest – a right to family life and family ties. According to the court a 'special family tie between the living persons' may be violated by wrongfully causing death to one of the family members. This interpretation, however, has met with doctrinal criticism.[609]

The Supreme Court held that the death of an unborn child who was capable of living outside its mother's body gives ground to a bereavement claim on the basis of Article 446 §4 KC.[610] In the given case the child died together with her mother and father in a car accident two weeks before planned delivery. The parents and sister of the deceased woman demanded bereavement damages separately for the death of the mother and for the death of her unborn child (the granddaughter and niece in relation to the plaintiffs). On the contrary, a non-viable foetus cannot be declared a deceased according to Article 446 §4 KC and hence the claim for bereavement does not arise. This opinion, expressed in a judgment of 13 May 2015,[611] goes contrary to its previous decision of SN 9 March 2012,[612] which was strongly criticized by doctrine (in particular M Nesterowicz[613]). However, in 2015, the court emphasized that the parents of a viable foetus who died can still claim the violation of their personal right to uninterrupted family life on the basis of Article 24 in conjunction with

607. Act on the amendment of the Civil Code of 30 May 2008, in force since 3 Aug. 2008, Dz.U. 2008, No. 116, item 731. Smieja, p. 6, at 733 refers to examples of judicial decisions to this effect.
608. SN of 21 Oct. 2010, III CZP 76/10, OSP 9/2011, item 96; SN of 10 Nov. 2010, II CSK 248/10, OSNC-ZD B/2011; item 44; SN of 3 Jun. 2011, III CSK 279/10; SN of 13 Jul. 2011, III CZP 32/11, not published.
609. Comments by *M. Walachowska*, *M. Lolik*, *B Lackoronski* to the judgment SN of 21 Oct. 2010, III CZP 76/10, OSP 9/2011, 665, 669 and 672 respectively, cmt by *M Walachowska*, OSP 2/2011, item 15.
610. SN of 12 Nov. 2014, III CSK 307/13, OSNC 12/2015, item 147.
611. III CSK 286/14, OSNC 4 /2016 item 45, commented by E. Bagińska & K. Krupa-Lipińska, in *European Tort Law 2016*, Nos 40–49 (2017).
612. I CSK 282/11 commented by E. Bagińska & K. Krupa-Lipińska in: *European Tort Law* 2012, No. 8 (2013).
613. Comment by *M.Nesterowicz*, Przegląd Sądowy 1 (2013) 108.

Article 448 KC. Obviously, every tort which leads to the death of an unborn child dramatically interrupts family life, infringes upon the parental right to develop emotional bonds with the child and eliminates the possibility to continue life together with the child. In this case a strong, positive and deep emotional bond can exist between the plaintiffs and the deceased baby. As far as the mother is concerned, her moral harm flowing from her physical injuries should be separated from the harm stemming from the interruption of the emotional bond with the unborn child. Moreover, a court cannot discriminate between the parents as far as the amount of compensation goes. In the discussed case scenarios it could also be argued that the parents' claims should be classified as those of primary victims (on the ground of Article 445 §1 KC) if they have suffered moral damage (physical and mental pain) due to the death of their unborn baby, and not as secondary victims (on the ground of Article 446 §4 KC).

364. The Supreme Court has held that a bereavement claim governed by Article 446 §4 KC passes to heirs under the conditions laid down in Article 445 §3 KC.[614] The decision has been strongly criticized by legal scholars, because of the principle according to which a claim for compensation of non-pecuniary loss does not pass on to heirs due to its personal character. It is doubtful whether the lack of a legal provision on the inheritance of the bereavement claim (within Article 446 KC) was an intentional omission of the legislator, a normative gap or a simple mistake.

365. In the judgment of 22 February 2018,[615] the Supreme Court addressed the issue of how to interpret the concept of 'immediate members of the deceased's family' after the spouses have divorced. According to the court, a former spouse may be regarded as a close relative if, despite the divorce, the former spouses have re-established marital life, as well as a permanent and close personal, physical, emotional and economic relationship, similar to that which exists in a properly functioning marriage.

366. The problem of quantum of damages for non-pecuniary loss has been a recurring theme in the last decade. Naturally, it is a very difficult task to assess and express in money the scope of the moral damage caused by the death of closest relatives, and each case requires an individual assessment. Nevertheless, when determining the amount of compensation, one should take into account, among other things, the drama of the experience, moral pain, the feeling of emptiness, the mental shock caused by the death of the closest person, medical treatment of the trauma. The Supreme Court has stated that compensation must not lead to enrichment of the victim but should have a 'perceptible economic value'.[616]

614. Article 445 §3 reads: 'A claim for compensation for non-pecuniary harm shall pass to the heirs of the deceased only if this was agreed in writing or the action was commenced when the deceased was still alive.'
615. I CSK 377/17.
616. SN of 11 Jul. 2019, V CSK 179/18.

367. In the recent years the Supreme Court developed a line of case law,[617] which was based on the argument that the fact that indirect victims were vested with a right to demand bereavement damages in Article 446 § 4 KC does not mean that they had been prevented from seeking compensation pursuant to the rules on the protection of personal interests in other situations, especially in cases resembling death. There is no ethical ground to differentiate between the breach of family ties due to the victim's death and due to a serious irreversible injury. In the court's view, its decision is compatible with 'a European standard', which means a more intensive protection of the physical and mental integrity of a person (in particular Article 10:301 section 1 of the Principles of European Tort Law). The doctrine of the violation of family bonds as a ground for compensation to the closest family members in non-fatal accidents cases, approved of by three resolutions of the Civil Chamber of the Supreme Court dated on 27 March 2018,[618] was then unexpectedly questioned by a decision of 22 October 2019[619] by the Chamber of Extraordinary Control and Public Affairs[620]. In the legal scholarship, on the other hand, it is argued that besides a great controversy regarding the concept of the new type of a personal right (family bonds[621]) the new line of case law contradicts the traditional position of Polish law pursuant to which the injured party in the legal sense is the person who has suffered damage to be compensated and against whom the causative event (an act or omission fulfilling the conditions of a tort) was directed. The situation called for an intervention of the legislative. In 2021, a new rule of Article 446^2 was introduced to allow compensation for moral damage suffered by the next of kin when a direct victim has suffered serious and permanent injuries.[622] As it was explained in the bill, the purpose of the amendment was to remove the disparity regarding the possibility of awarding damage for moral harm caused to indirect victims; despite the Supreme Court's resolutions, a number of courts have not qualified family bonds as a particular personal interest and subsequently have denied compensation for moral harm caused by the violation of personal interest. Article 446^2 KC reads: In the event of a serious and permanent personal injury or disorder of health resulting in the inability to establish or continue a family relationship, the court may award the injured party's immediate family members an appropriate sum

617. SN of 9 Aug. 2016, II CSK 719/15, OSNC 5/2017, item 60, SN of 10 Feb. 2017, V CSK 291/16, OSP 12/2017, item 125, SN of 27 Mar. 2018, III CZP 36/17, OSNC 11/2018, item 103, SN of 27 Mar. 2018, III CZP 69/17, OSNC 11/2018, item 104.
618. Reported by E. Bagińska, I. Adrych-Brzezińska, in *E Karner/BC Steininger* (eds), European Tort Law 2018 (2019) 474, Nos 2–23
619. I NSNZP 2/19, Monitor Prawniczy 2019/23, 1250 and <www.sn.pl>. Interestingly, the decision cites a number of works of the European Group on Tort Law (on PETL) invoking their expressed doubts as well as the lack of uniformity in the European jurisdictions regarding the matter in question.
620. We should make a caveat that the appointment of judges to this chamber has been challenged on the grounds of the judges comprising that Chamber, given the manner of their appointment, did not offer the required guarantees of independence and impartiality. *See* Judgment of the CJEU (Grand Chambre) of 6 Oct. 2021, C-487/19, ECLI:EU:C:2021:798
621. See ia *T Grzeszak*, Dobro osobiste jako dobro zindywidualizowane [Personal interest as an individual interest], Przeglad Sadowy 4/2018.
622. by the Act of 24 Jun. 2021 amending the Civil Code, Dz.U. 2021 item 1509.

by way of financial compensation for the non-material harm suffered.[623] Several elements of the new claim will have to be resolved by the court practice and doctrine. The question refers, *inter alia*, to the understanding of a 'future relationship'. How to estimate whether a special bond between the direct and indirect victim could have been established in the future? It is also not clear who can be recognized as a closest family member to whom the bond could be tied. It is not clear whether there should be an adequate causal link between the permanent, serious personal injury of a direct victim and the impossibility to establish or continue a family relationship. Moreover, Article 446^2 KC shall apply to events which occurred prior to the date of entry into force of the amending act. Thus, the Polish legislator clearly introduced an exception to the *lex retro non agit* principle, because the new law has been granted a retrospective effect.

623. The Act of 24 Jun. 2021, Dz.U.2021 item 1509, in force from 19 Sep. 2021.

Chapter 5. Various Damages (Property)

§1. PROPERTY

I. Loss of Use of Property

368. The Polish Supreme Court rejected the idea that pure loss of the use of a certain good constitutes damage within the meaning of Article 361 KC. The loss of use of a vehicle is not an independent pecuniary loss related to the vehicle, regardless of its purpose. Reparation of such loss as non-pecuniary loss would also be impossible under Polish law. However, when the expenses for a replacement car are incurred (i.e., it is proven that the rental payment was made under a rental agreement), they constitute damage because it leads to a decrease in the victim's assets. The Supreme Court considers the inability to use the vehicle as a negative pecuniary outcome of a tort and the expenses that serve to mitigate this negative pecuniary outcome are treated as pecuniary losses. This view appeared first of all in cases where the cost of a replacement car used for business activity was at issue.[624]

Further, on 17 November 2011 the Supreme Court ruled[625] that the insurer's liability for damage or destruction of a vehicle under compulsory third-party liability motor insurance covered expenses related to rental of a replacement car irrespective of whether the victim used the car in the course of a business or not. However, the damage in question should be in an adequate causal connection with the damaging event. The liability was extended upon all purposeful and economically justified expenses, and was not necessarily conditional upon the accessibility of means of public transport. Whether the expense of renting a car was purposeful and economically justified should be evaluated on a case-by-case basis. To evaluate the economic justification of the expense, one has to take into account the victim's duty to prevent (or mitigate) the loss, his contribution to the loss, and the rule of *compensatio lucri cum damno*. The latter requires that, in awarding damages, the court should also account for any gain or benefit that the injured party obtained due to the wrong (*see also infra* no. 380 on insurance). Considerations of proportionality indicate that car rental should be considered unnecessary in certain situations, for instance when an owner did not in fact use his car or when he has another car. If the injured party rarely uses a car, it may be reasonable to expect him to use other, equivalent means of transport. In line with this decision the Supreme Court ruled on 22 November 2013,[626] that a compulsory third-party liability motor insurance policy covers purposeful and economically justified rental expenses for a replacement vehicle incurred by the injured party during the time needed for buying a new vehicle if damages were established in the amount of the difference between the value of the vehicle before the accident and the value of the severely damaged

624. For example SN of 6 Jan. 1999, II CKN 109/98, not published; SN of 8 Sep. 2004, IV CK 672/03, not published.
625. III CZP 5/11, OSP 1/2013, item 2, commented by E. Bagińska, K. Krupa-Lipińska in *Poland,* in *European Tort Law 2012*, Nos 5–15 (2013).
626. III CZP 76/13, OSN IC 9/2014 item 85, commented by E. Bagińska, K. Krupa-Lipińska, in *Poland,* in *European Tort Law 2014*, Nos 68–76 (2015).

value, whose repair was impossible or economically impractical ('total loss').[627] That approach was consequently confirmed in a resolution of the Supreme Court of 24 August 2017,[628] in which the court ruled that such car rental expenses are covered under the compulsory liability insurance contract if they were reasonable and economically justified; other expenses will not be considered as reparable damage. In its case law, the Supreme Court reiterates that 'loss of use of a thing' is not damage, but a pecuniary consequence of the existing material damage (i.e., destruction of a car). In the judgment of 13 March 2020[629] the Supreme Court openly admitted that a loss of use of a vehicle is not an independent, stand-alone loss. However, in the case at hand, it was problematic whether 'the cost of the loss' was actually incurred, as it was not paid in the traditional sense but subject to assignment to the repairment service entity.

II. Illicit Profits

369. As a general rule, calculation of an annuity requires taking into account only the income from legal sources and disregarding any income received in violation of the law, corruption (*lucrum illicitum vel inhonestum*), or contravening the principles of justice. It is not, however, always clear what kind of income this would be. There should be no doubt as to profits received from criminal acts, i.e., acts in violation of penal law (drug trafficking, dealing with stolen property, corruption). However, views differ as to income obtained in violation of administrative, taxation or social security law and in particular as to earnings received in the grey labour market.

In earlier cases, the Supreme Court presented a very restrictive approach. It held, for instance, that if legal provisions prohibited a pensioner from earning money in excess of a certain amount (resulting in the suspension of his social pension), this element of his whole loss would not be compensated.

In the case decided on 20 January 2004[630] a defendant questioned the inclusion into the computation of the annuity of the 'grey zone' income of the deceased. The income was not revealed in a personal income declaration, nor was it taxed. The Supreme Court held that although the phenomenon of 'grey zone' in the labour market should meet with disapproval, the computation of an annuity in wrongful death cases is not dependent on the taxed income but on the earning capacity of the deceased and on his financial standing, including but not limited to his actual income. However, on similar facts, the Court of Appeals in Bialystok in a judgment of 18 September 2002[631] ruled to the contrary. It held that regular illicit earnings received by the deceased victim within 'the grey zone' might not lead to an increase in the quantum of damages. The court stated that failure to pay personal income tax

627. *See also* E. Bagińska. 'Compensation for property damage in motor third party liability insurance', *Wiadomości Ubezpieczeniowe* 4 (2014).
628. III CZP 20/17, OSNC 2018/6, item 56.
629. III CZP 63/19, OSNC 2020/11, item 96.
630. II CK 360/02 Lex No. 173557.
631. I ACa 399/02, OSAB 2003, p. 7.

is a fiscal criminal offence. Such an income also contradicts the principles of community life (principles of equity and justice) (*see supra* no. 22).

§2. Damage Arising from Wrongful Birth

370. Polish courts accept claims for wrongful conception and wrongful birth.[632] However, as the courts have consistently held that the birth of a child with a genetic condition does not per se constitute damage to the parents, we may assume that Polish law rejects the doctrine of wrongful life.

Before the presentation of seminal cases on wrongful birth, we should mention that in Poland the right to abort is limited to three cases. The Law of 7 January 1993 on Family Planning, Protection of a Human Foetus and Conditions for Abortion Admissibility[633] allows in Article 4a subparagraph 1 abortion to be performed exclusively by a physician when:

(1) The pregnancy constitutes a hazard for the life or health of the pregnant woman.
(2) Prenatal examinations or any other medical tests indicate a significant probability of grave or irreversible retardation of the foetus or incurable disease threatening its life.
(3) There is a justified suspicion that the pregnancy occurred as a result of a criminal act.

As to the third case, it includes pregnancies resulting from an act that is regarded an offence or a crime under penal law, such as a rape, incest or statutory rape (even if the minor consented to a sexual intercourse).

There is no time limit for performing the abortion in the first case. In the case defined under point 2, the abortion may be performed only up to the moment when the foetus is capable of living independently outside the mother's organism. With regard to the second ground for abortion, the Supreme Court held that a genetic defect need not be established with certainty or only through prenatal examinations. It is sufficient that there is a high probability of such defects to occur, which may be shown on the basis of other medical preconditions (SN of 13 October 2005, IV CK 161/05, OSP 6/2006). In both cases abortion has to be carried out by a physician in hospital. In the case defined under point 3, abortion is admitted (also in a private surgery) if the pregnancy is not older than twelve weeks.

In accordance with the 'judgment' of the Constitutional Tribunal of 22 October 2020 (*Journal of Laws* of 2021, item 175). Article 4a section 1 item 2 has been deemed inconsistent with Article 38 in connection with Article 30 in connection with Article 31 section 3 of the Polish Constitution. It ceased to be in force on 27

632. *See* E. Bagińska, *The Liability for Wrongful Conception and Wrongful Birth in Polish Law*, Lex Medicinae. Revista Portuguesa de Direito da Saude Issue 10, 2009, 46; and E. Bagińska, *Wrongful Birth and Non-pecuniary Loss: Theories of Compensation*, J. of Eur. Tort L., Issue 2, 171–203 (2010).
633. Dz.U. No. 17, item 78, with later amendments.

January 2021. However, the judges who delivered the judgment can be legally challenged due to the incorrect nomination of the tribunal's judges.[634]

371. Violation of someone's right to plan a family is a basis for seeking compensation using Article 448 KC (compensation of non-pecuniary loss – *see supra* nos 296–301).[635] In the judgment of 22 February 2006[636] the Supreme Court ruled that 'in case where an abortion was wrongfully denied to a raped woman and the offender has not been identified, the person responsible for the denial of abortion is liable to cover the child support to the extent that cannot be covered by the mother exercising personal care of the child'. Thus, the court separated the issue of giving birth to a child, which is not seen as damage, from the costs of maintenance. The latter are expenses that the mother did not want to incur but she is now obliged to pay. The court's view was widely accepted by scholars. However, it is considered arguable whether the court should have limited the pecuniary damages to the increased costs of child maintenance instead of the full costs because the child, after all, was not 'planned', but conceived and born as a result of duress.[637]

372. Courts hearing wrongful birth claims of parents of handicapped children tend to award the parents damages for non-pecuniary loss and an annuity to cover pecuniary damage. It is emphasized that the birth of a child with a genetic condition does not per se constitute damage to its parents. However, it is the parents' loss to have to bear the additional costs of raising a handicapped child, 'which they did not plan nor agree to bear and which they would not have had to bear had their right to plan a family and to decide about aborting the pregnancy not been breached'.[638] Both the parents are thus entitled to a monthly annuity to cover the additional cost of the treatment and the maintenance of the handicapped child (i.e., the difference in expenses in comparison to the maintenance costs of an average healthy child). The basis for the claim is Article 415 KC in conjunction with Article 361 §2 KC (the latter concerning the principle of full compensation – *see supra* no. 277).

373. Most importantly, a pregnant woman has a right to free prenatal tests, as well as a right to choose to abort a child. Violation of these rights by a doctor constitutes moral harm which entitles the woman to compensation pursuant to Article

---

634. According to the judgment of the European Court of Human Rights in Xero Flor in *Poland v. Poland* (No. 4907/18) of 7 May 2021 the actions of the authorities in appointing one of the judges who had been on the bench in the applicant company's case and the ignoring of the Constitutional Court's judgments in that connection had meant that the panel that had tried the case had not been a 'tribunal established by law'. The ECtHR held, unanimously, that there had been a violation Art. 6 §1 of the ECHR as regards the right to a tribunal established by law. Therefore, in the light of the above judgment, the legal force of the TK judgment in which the Tribunal abolished the ground for medical abortion in Poland is subject to challenge (a non-existent or invalid judgment), albeit it de facto creates the harsh reality for women in relations with their physicians who follow the judgment.
635. SN of 21 Nov. 2003 V CK 16/03, OSP 10/2004, at 125, OSNC 6/2004, at 104.
636. III CZP 8/06, OSNC 7–8/2006, item 123.
637. *See* E. Bagińska & M. Nesterowicz, *Comment to the case in Digest of European Tort Law*, Essential Cases on Damage, vol. 2, at 21.22/No. 12.
638. SN of 13 Oct. 2005, IV CK 161/05, OSP 6/2006, item 71.

448 KC. The compensation award should take into account the gravity of anguish and suffering and the conduct of doctors.[639] In such situations, a mother may also claim damages for the lost income and medical expenses linked to her mental breakdown suffered after the child's birth.[640] In a judgment of 12 May 2015, I ACa 204/15, the Court of Appeals in Kraków acknowledged that a right to plan a family and a right to legal abortion stemming therefrom is a personal right protected by the Civil Code (Article 23 KC). The plaintiff demanded PLN 500,000 but the court awarded half of this sum as compensation for non-pecuniary loss.

§3. Loss of Enjoyment of Holidays

374. As mentioned above, pecuniary reparation of non-pecuniary harm is permitted only when a statute so provides and solely in the regime *ex delicto*. Because there exists no such provision in the Civil Code as regards loss of enjoyment of holidays, Polish courts have long dismissed such claims.[641] Nevertheless, after the ECJ judgment in *Simone Leitner v. TUI Deutschland GmbH & Co KG* [642] a Polish court can no longer dismiss loss of enjoyment of holiday claims.

375. Some courts have since applied the rules concerning protection of personal interests (Articles 23, 24, 448 KC – *see supra* nos 116 and 299) through the construction of a new personal interest in the context of holidays – a right to full satisfaction from a package holiday. This position was however criticized by scholars.[643]

The problem was ultimately resolved by the Supreme Court.[644] Following the Leitner case the court held that the legal basis of the tour operator's liability for loss of holidays was found in Article 11a section 1 of the Law on Travel Services (1997), which implements Article 5 of the EC Directive 90/314/CEE on package travel, package holidays and package tours.[645] According to the Supreme Court, Article 11a section 1 regulates the reparation of the whole damage suffered by a tourist, hence it includes both pecuniary and non-pecuniary losses. This provision should be seen as *lex specialis* to the general rule of Article 471 KC[646] as far as the claim for non-pecuniary loss is concerned. The court rejected the theory suggesting that the right

639. SN of 12 Jun. 2008, III CSK 16/08, OSNC 3/2009, item 48, reported by E. Bagińska, in *European Tort Law 2009*, Nos 51–56 (2010).
640. *See also* SN of 6 May 2010, II CSK 580/09, OSP 2/2011, item 13 cmt M. Nesterowicz.
641. The Law on Travel Services (1997) lacks any explicit basis for the claim for compensation of immaterial loss due to the non-performance of a contract of travel. *See* M. Nesterowicz, *Prawo turystyczne* (2009) 100.
642. C-168/00, ECR 2002, I-2631.
643. *See* J. Luzak & K. Osajda, *Odpowiedzialnosc za zmarnowany urlop w prawie polskim*, Kwartalnik Prawa Prywatnego 2 (2005) 309, 84; M. Walachowska, *Zadoscuczynienie pieniezne za doznana krzywdę* (2007) 388.
644. SN of 19 Nov. 2010, III CZP 79/10, OSNIC 4/2011, item 41; SN of 24 Mar. 2011, I CSK 372/10, OSP 1/2012, item 3.
645. O.J. L 158 of 23 Jun. 1990.
646. Article 471 KC establishes the rule of contractual liability based on presumed fault.

to holidays should be seen as a new personal interest. It is, in its opinion, an artificial construct and contrary to the provisions of the Civil Code. This notwithstanding, the court classified loss suffered by tourists as non-pecuniary loss. The incentives to buy a package tour relate to the need for immaterial gains (relaxation, peace, comfort, etc.). Failure to obtain these gains due to negligence of the organizer amounts to wasted pleasure (loss of holidays), which is sometimes the sole harm suffered by the client.

376. However, it is also important to point out that the conduct of a tour operator may in a particular case lead to infringements of the personal interests listed in Article 23 KC.

Chapter 6. Interference with Collateral Benefits

377. Tort law operates alongside several other mechanisms of a substantive or procedural nature performing similar functions. Here the focus is on the compensatory function and the question of possible deductions from the scope of tort liability (and tort compensation in particular) of certain collateral benefits received through these other mechanisms. They include insurance, social security benefits, compensation received through workers' compensation scheme, as well as other mechanisms for obtaining redress outside the scope of ordinary tort litigation.

§1. Insurance

378. When property damaged by tortious conduct is covered by a property insurance policy, benefits received on account of the insurance policy are included when the scope of damage is being determined. The principle of *compensation lucre cum damno* is applied here. Thus, the damage will be seen as appropriately smaller, and compensation as reduced in relation to what it would be if there was no insurance payment. The latter payment is seen as fulfilling a compensatory function. By reducing the scope of compensable damage the law accounts for the presence of two compensatory mechanisms covering the same damage.[647]

However, in cases where a person is covered by a personal insurance policy, payments on account of personal injury or death are normally not seen as playing a compensatory role. Thus, the payment is not included within the consideration of the scope of loss to be compensated by the tortfeasor, provided that the tortfeasor was not the insuring party (*ubezpieczajacy*) (such as in the work accidents scenarios) who paid the premium. Thus, for instance, annuities received by family members in case of death (*see* nos 338–339) are not reduced by amounts of insurance payments they receive on account of the death of the victim who paid the premium herself.[648] In a case where the tortfeasor insured himself against certain risks, the rule of *compensation lucre cum damno* applies. The majority of scholars see this as the only fair approach: the victim ought not to be in the same position as someone who did not suffer the costs of the insurance policy.[649] Further, payment on account of an insurance policy and compensation for tort are not seen as playing the same functions.

379. Article 822 §4 KC permits the injured person to bring an *actio directa* against the insurer if the person liable for the damage has a civil liability insurance policy.

647. M. Kalinski, *Odpowiedzialnosc odszkodowawcza,* 159.
648. *Ibid.*
649. A. Smieja, *Szczegolne zasady ...* , 680.

§2. Social Security

380. In tort cases, Polish courts make deductions from damages awards for received collateral benefits on account of social security insurance. The social security insurance system, coordinated by the Office for Social Insurance (ZUS) is very comprehensive. It includes the following types of benefits:

(1) In cases of sickness and childbirth:
   (a) Sickness benefits;
   (b) Maternity benefits;
   (c) Care benefits;
   (d) Rehabilitation benefits;
   (e) Shortfall benefits.
(2) In cases of inability to work:
   (a) Inability to work benefits;
   (b) Work training benefits.
(3) Old age benefits:
   (a) Pensions;
   (b) Care benefit.
(4) Benefits for persons who lost a family member maintaining them:
   (a) Family pensions;
   (b) Additional benefits for orphans.
(5) Benefits for victims of work accidents and occupational diseases:
   (a) A lump sum compensation;
   (b) Annuities for occupational diseases, loss of ability to work and loss of a family member;
   (c) Dental and vaccination benefits;
   (d) Reimbursement of costs of orthopaedic devices.
(6) Others:
   (a) Funeral benefit;
   (b) Pensions.

The system of social security insurance is funded by contributions of potential beneficiaries, many of which are mandatory, for instance all employees are obliged to pay work accident and occupational disease contributions.[650]

§3. Worker's Compensation

381. Work-related accidents and occupational diseases are regulated by a compensation scheme which is independent of the Civil Code. This special system of liability was established by Act of 12 June 1975 on Payments for Work Accidents

650. The system of social security insurance is regulated by the Act of 13 Oct. 1998, later amended (the amended version was published in Dz.U. of 1998, No. 205, item 1585), and a number of other acts.

and Sickness, and is now regulated by the Act on Social Insurance for Work Accidents and Occupational Diseases of 30 October 2002.[651] The employer's liability is strict, with the only exonerating circumstances being intentional fault or gross negligence of the employee who suffered injury, and a situation when the employee greatly contributed to the accident by being intoxicated or under the influence of another substance (Article 21 of the Act). Force majeure or exclusive fault of a third person constitutes no defence. Compensation is based on a fixed-rate tariff system. The tariff is determined using the percentage disability schedule or, in case of the employee's death, it is set proportionally to the number of family members of the deceased worker depending on the degree of consanguinity. As a result, the indemnification is not necessarily equivalent to the damage, and tends to be either lower or, in some cases, higher than the damage suffered.

A worker who sustained bodily harm arising out of a work accident or a work-related disease has a right to claim an annuity for loss of capacity to work, and a lump sum compensation for pecuniary and non-pecuniary loss. The exact amount of the lump sum depends on the percentage of bodily injury sustained by the worker. A minimum compensation is provided for 4% of health loss. The compensation rises by a given sum (pertaining to 20% of health loss) if the worker has been classified a first degree invalid as a result of the accident. In the case of the worker's death a lump sum compensation is paid to the members of his family and its quantum depends on the degree of blood relationship (a spouse and children are entitled to the highest sum) and the number of relatives (Article 13 of the Act). Family members of the deceased worker are also entitled to an annuity (Article 17).

382. Employees whose injuries or sickness were not entirely compensated by the scheme, or families in case injuries or sickness led to death, can bring claims for the reminder of the compensation before a labour court. Here, compensation paid to the injured employee by the workers' compensation scheme is deducted from the total compensation which would be payable under tortious liability. Normal rules of tortious liability apply (depending on the circumstances of the particular case, fault liability, strict liability, or liability based on equity will be relevant). Articles 444–446 of the Civil Code, which were analysed above and which concern compensation, are also applicable. Such additional claims cover additional sums of money for cost of treatment, or costs of equipment or other improvements necessary for the injured employee. For example, the Supreme Court decision of 14 May 1997[652] covered the costs of a car designed especially for the disabled, which was indispensable for continuation of treatment and carrying out business by the employee.

651. Dz.U. of 2002, No. 199, item 1673.
652. OSN, 1998, item 121.

§4. Compensation Funds

383. In Poland we have compensation funds which are regulated by public law (such as in labour relations), or specific fields of law, such as nuclear law and maritime law (*see* no. 229).

More importantly, the Insurance Guarantee Fund (*Ubezpieczeniowy Fundusz Gwarancyjny*) and the Central Record for Vehicles and Drivers (CEPiK – *Centralna Ewidencja Pojazdów i Kierowców*) are significant for the functioning of compulsory traffic insurance. Further, according to Article 113 of the Act on Compulsory Insurance, the Insurance Guarantee Fund and Polish Motor Insurers' Bureau, if the insurance company declares bankruptcy, the fund meets all the claims of the persons entitled to them. The insurance protection on account of all compulsory liability insurance is a solution that is not found in other legal systems.[653]

653. *See* E. Bagińska & E. Kowalewski, *The shaping of insurance law in Poland after 1990 – a critical analysis*, Wiadomosci Ubezpieczeniowe 3/2013.

Chapter 7. Other Remedies

§1. Restitution (Unjust Enrichment)

384. Unjust enrichment is regulated in the Civil Code in a separate Title V 'Unjust Enrichment'. Under the general rules of Article 405:

> Anyone who without legal grounds has gained a financial benefit at the expense of another person is obliged to hand over the benefit in kind, and if this is not possible, to return its value.

The provisions of Title V do not prejudice the provisions on the obligation to remedy damage (Article 415).

385. The Civil Code provides for *condictiones* (undue performance) in Article 410. The performance is undue in the following circumstances:

- if the person who rendered performance was not obliged;
- if he was not obliged towards the person to whom he rendered the performance;
- if the basis for the performance ceased to be binding;
- if the intended purpose of the performance has not been attained;
- if the legal act binding him to render performance was void and has not become valid after the performance was rendered.

However, the return of a performance cannot be demanded:

- if the person rendering the performance knew that he was not obliged to perform, unless he performed with the reservation of return, or in order to avoid duress, or when performance arose from a void legal act;
- if the performance satisfies the principles of community life;
- if the performance was rendered in order to satisfy a claim barred by the statute of limitations;
- if it was rendered before a receivable became mature.

386. As to the scope of the restitution one should pay attention to the following rules:

- The obligation to release the benefit includes not only the directly obtained benefits, but also everything which in the case of alienation, loss, or damage was obtained in exchange for the benefit or as the redress of the damage (Article 406 KC).
- A person obliged may demand reimbursement of necessary expenditures inasmuch as they have not been matched by the use which he obtained from them. He may demand that other expenditures be reimbursed inasmuch as they increase the value of the benefit at the time it is handed over. However, he may take away these expenditures, restoring the former state (Article 408 KC). Furthermore,

anyone who knew that he was not entitled to the benefit may demand the reimbursement of the expenditures only inasmuch as they increase the value of the benefit at the moment of its release.

387. If the obliged party disposed of the benefit gratuitously for the benefit of a third party, the obligation to hand over the benefit passes onto the third party.

The obligation to release the benefit or to reimburse its value shall expire if a person who obtained the benefit consumed it or lost it in such a manner that he is no longer enriched, unless he should have taken into account the duty to return it when relinquishing the benefit or consuming it (Article 409).

§2. Injunctive Relief

388. There are a number of instances where a party can demand injunctive relief.

First of all it is possible in the case of violation of personal interests under Article 24 §1 KC (*see supra* no. 116).

389. Second, the general rule of Article 439 KC, situated in the Title on Torts should be mentioned. According to this provision, a person who is directly exposed to the risk of damage resulting from the behaviour of another person, in particular due to lack of proper supervision of the operation of an enterprise or business controlled by him, or of the condition of a building or any other installation possessed by him, may demand that that person undertake any measures necessary to avert the immediate danger, and, if necessary, also to give adequate security (e.g., to place a sum of money in the court deposit). The claim of the person who is endangered is dependent on the proof of concrete danger (e.g., a disintegrated house close to collapsing). Nevertheless, Article 439 KC has rarely been used in the court practice.

390. Third, the 'neighbourhood law' (nuisance law) prescribes a possibility of demanding injunctive relief. Indeed, the nature of liability in the neighbourhood law is not entirely clear. There are many plausible arguments for qualifying the liability as delictual, as it is usually described in legal writings.[654]

391. Further, according to Article 144 KC, the owner of immovable property should, when exercising his right, refrain from activities which interfere with the use of the neighbouring immovable properties and which exceed normal use resulting from the socio-economic purpose of the immovable property and the local conditions. A claim based on this provision, which may lead to injunctive relief being granted, can be brought by owners as well as persons enjoying other proprietary rights. Conduct which disturbs the neighbouring land beyond the acceptable local standards is illegal, and thus it creates a claim for damages based on the general rules of the Civil Code. However, the illegality of the activity carried out on the neighbouring land would not be relevant for the action for compensation based on

---

654. *See* W. Katner, *Ochrona wlasnosci nieruchomosci przed naruszeniami posrednimi* (1982) 130.

Article 435 KC (strict liability of an enterprise), even if the claim based on Article 144 KC could not be raised (*see supra* no. 205).

392. A short reference to environmental protection laws should be made here. Article 18 PREP (*supra* no. 210) allows the land holder to demand indemnity if the preventive or remedial measures that were carried out on his land caused him (individual) damage. Further, under Article 323 of Environmental Protection Law, anyone who is exposed to the risk of damage, or who incurred damage through another's illegal influence on the environment, may demand from the person liable that he restores the lawful state and takes preventive measures, such as installing safety appliances or machines. Where the preventive action is impossible or unreasonably difficult, the claimant may demand that the actor abstains from the infringement. The relations between Article 323 EPL and the 'neighbourhood law' in the Civil Code are debatable. The opinion that the EPL broadens the remedies available in the Code, quite rightly, prevails.[655] Both *actio negatoria* (Article 222 §2 KC) and a claim to abstain from infringement on the basis of Article 144 KC may be brought against any person who infringes upon the environment.

393. Another instance of judicial injunctions concerns cases of unfair competition, regulated by Articles 18 and 19 of the Act on Combating Unfair Competition of 16 April 1993.[656] Actions for injunction are possible as regards many types of unfair practices specified in the Act, for example misleading or false indication of geographical origin, geographical indications and information relating to the name or characteristics of goods or services. A court may rule that the unlawful act be stopped, its effects be removed and that the competitor breaking the law make a single or multiple declarations of an appropriate form and contents (in addition to monetary compensation). As a part of its interim ruling, the court may also put a ban on the sale of specific goods, their introduction into trade and advertising thereof. A temporary order may be requested from the court in whose district the unfair competitor's property is located.[657] Moreover, the Act does not prejudice claims under other legal provisions (such as the Civil Code, copyright law, patent law or trademark law).

§3. Punitive Damages

394. Polish law does not accept the concept of punitive damages. Courts have held that damages are not intended to amount to a penalty since compensation awarded in civil proceedings may not, in any case, exceed the actual damage. Punitive damages are not the same as compensatory sanctions provided for in the area of the protection of intellectual property. Machnikowski has argued persuasively

655. *See* J.J. Skoczylas, *Odpowiedzialnosc cywilna na podstawie ustawy – prawo ochrony srodowiska,* [2003] Przegląd Sądowy [PS] 4, 68.
656. Dz.U. 2003, No. 153, at 1503 with amendments.
657. *See* in general J. Szwaja (ed.), *Ustawa o zwalczaniu nieuczciwej konkurencji. Komentarz* (Warszawa, 2001).

that pre-determined damages are not a type of punitive damages, as their assessment does not depend on the nature of the perpetrator or his conduct.[658] Punitive damages are classified as such by their purpose (punishment and deterrence in cases of particularly gross negligence or wilful conduct) and not solely by their method of calculation.

395. The Court of Appeals in Warsaw quashed a motion for the recognition and enforcement of a judgment of a US court in Poland, in which the plaintiffs were awarded USD 1,000,000 as compensatory damages and USD 4,000,000 as punitive damages.[659] The court held that a foreign judgment under examination in the enforcement proceedings cannot be divided into parts in the sense that it would be enforced as to a part of the award. The court emphasized that compensation of non-pecuniary damage is determined by several individual circumstances and must not exceed the amount of the damage, or be disproportionately high or low. Hence, the examined award clearly violated public policy (Article 1146 §1(7) and Article 1150 of the Code of Civil Procedure). The court also stated that the sole aim of punitive damages is to penalize the tortfeasor, which is not an accepted function of a civil law sanction in Polish law. This point is particularly crucial in the light of the compensatory nature of damages for non-pecuniary loss. Punitive damages may not be considered as a penal sanction that a criminal court may impose on the basis of Article 46 of the Penal Code (*see supra* no. 28). Moreover, the amount awarded by the American jury was so excessively high that it clearly violated public policy. Hence, both the award of exorbitant compensation for non-pecuniary loss and the award of punitive damages justified the conclusion that the enforcement of the judgment would run against *l'ordre public.*

On cassation, however, the Supreme Court reversed the judgment of the Court of Appeals.[660] The court held that a foreign judgment could be enforced with respect to a part of the claim, provided that the claim is divisible. The Polish public policy clause does not support a denial of *exequatur* based solely on existing discrepancies, whether minor or significant, between the legal systems involved. What matters are the cardinal, patent violations of public policy by the consequences of the enforcement of a foreign judgment (the effects of the judgment) in the country where *exequatur* is demanded. The court stated that punitive damages are unknown to most continental European jurisdictions. They were rejected as an institution of civil law in several international and European acts aiming at the harmonization of procedural law and substantive private international law. The court also referred to the reported decisions of other highest European courts which refused to recognize American judgments rendering punitive damages.

The requirement of proportionality of civil sanctions that are deployed against a wrongdoer is a fundamental principle of the Polish legal system. Hence, deviation

---

658. *See* P. Machnikowski, *Damages for the Infringement of Intellectual Property Rights under EU Law*, in *Compensation for private losses, The Evolution of Torts in European Business Law*, 88–89 (R Schulze ed., 2011).

659. Court of Appeals of 26 Jan. 2012, I ACz 2059/11, reported in E. Bagińska, *European Tort Law 2012*, Nos 36–42 (2013).

660. SN of 11Oct. 2013, I CSK 697/12, OSNIC 1/2014, item 9, commented by E. Bagińska & K. Krupa-Lipińska, in: *European Tort Law 2014* Nos 14–23 (2015).

from the principle of *restitutio in integrum* will be permitted only if the level of the award meets the test of proportionality. In this case, the level of punitive damages clearly violated public policy. The stronger the links with the national legal order, the greater the influence of the public policy clause on the possible acceptance of the effects of the foreign judgment in the given jurisdiction. The court also suggested that the level of damages awards in Poland is of relevance here in the light of the fact that broad jurisdictional bases of the US courts can be used as a vehicle to obtain high pecuniary awards, later to be enforced in Poland. Contrary to the opinion of the Court of Appeal, the Supreme Court held that partial recognition and enforcement of a divisible award or of a divisible claim is allowed (citing *inter alia* Article 48 (2) Regulation 44/2001 Brussels I and Article 11 (1) the Hague Convention on Choice of Court Agreements[661]). Consequently, on remand, the award of 'compensatory damages' should be analysed with respect to possible violations of public policy. The importance of the presented judgment lies in the fact that the Supreme Court permitted partial execution of a foreign judgment insofar as the awarded amount is not disproportionate to the loss incurred. Moreover, the public policy clause can only apply to exceptional situations. A foreign award of compensatory damages is not to be automatically 'reduced' to the level matching the maximal level of damages which would be adjudicated by Polish courts in similar cases. Close ties between the facts of a case and the territory of a foreign *fori* can support the recognition of higher damages.

661. Convention of 30Jun. 2005, signed by the EU (OJ L 133, 29.5.2009, 1–13).

Selected Bibliography

Selected General Works

E. Baginska. 'The Meandres of Polish Tort law (1933–2015)' in J. Potgieter, J. Knobel & R.-M. Jansen (eds) *Essays in Honour of / Huldigingsbundel vir Johann Neethling,* Durban: LexisNexis 2015.

G. Bieniek. *Komentarz do kodeksu cywilnego, Ksiega trzecia, Zobowiazania.* Vol. 1. 2007.

W. Czachorski. *Zobowiazania. Zarys wykladu* [*The Law of Obligations. The Teaching Framework*]. Warszawa: Lexis Nexis, 8th edition, 2002, 9th edition 2004.

N. Davies. *Heart of Europe. The Past in Poland's Present*, Oxford University Press, 2001, 249.

T. Dybowski. In Z. Radwański (ed.), *System prawa cywilnego* [*The System of Civil Law*]. Vol. III, part 1. Wyd. PAN, 1981.

E. Gniewek & P. Machnikowski (eds). *Kodeks cywilny. Komentarz* [*Commentary to the Civil Code*]. 5th edition. CH Beck, 2013.

H. Izdebski. 'General Survey of Developments in Eastern Europe in the Field of Civil Law'. In Ginsburgs, Barry & Simmons (eds), *The Revival of Private Law in Central and Eastern Europe: Essays in Honor of F.J.M. Feldbrugge*. Institute of East European Law and Russian Studies, Leiden University Faculty of Law, No. 46. The Hague, London and Boston, MA: Martinus Nijhoff Publishers and Kluwer, 1996.

T. Justynski. *Naduzycie prawa w polskim prawie cywilnym* [*Abuse of a Right in Polish Civil Law*]. Krakow, 2000.

M. Kalinski. *Odpowiedzialnosc odszkodowawcza* [*Compensatory Liability*]. In A. Olejniczak (ed.), *System Prawa Prywatnego: Prawo Zobowiazan. Część Ogolna.* Vol. 6. Warszawa: Wydawnictwo C.H. Beck, Instytut Nauk Prawnych PAN, 2009.

E. Kowalewski, *Prawo ubezpieczen gospodarczych* [*Economic Insurance Law*]. 3rd edition. 2006.

Z. Kühn. 'Worlds Apart: Western and Central European Judicial Culture at the Onset of the European Enlargement'. *American Journal of Comparative Law* 52 (2004): 531–567.

R. Longchamps de Berier. *Zobowiazania* [*Obligations*]. Poznan, 1948.

D. Lasok. 'Polish Civil Law'. In Z. Szirmai (ed.), *Law in Eastern Europe.* A.W. Sijthoff, 1973.

J. Lukowski & H. Zawadzki. *A Concise History of Poland.* Cambridge University Press, 2001.

M. Nesterowicz. *Kodeks cywilny z komentarzem* [*The Civil Code with Commentary*]. Vol. 1, 2nd edition. Warszawa: Wydawnictwo Prawnicze, 1989.
A. Ohanowicz & J. Gorski. *Zarys prawa zobowiazan* [*General Framework of the Law of Obligations*]. Warszawa, 1970.
W. Posch. *Austria*. International Encyclopaedia of Laws Series. Kluwer Law, 2004.
M. Pyziak-Szafnicka. 'Prawo podmiotowe' ['Rights']. In M. Safjan (ed.), *System Prawa Prywatnego. Tom I. Część Ogolna* [*The System of Private Law. VolumeI. General Part*]. 2nd edition. Warszawa: C.H. Beck, Instytut Nauk Prawnych PAN, 2012.
Z. Radwański & M. Zielinski. *Normy i przepisy prawa cywilnego* [*Norms and Rules of Civil Law*]. In M. Safjan (ed.), *System Prawa Prywatnego. Tom I. Część Ogolna*. 2nd edition. Warszawa: C.H. Beck, Instytut Nauk Prawnych PAN, 2012.
Z. Radwański & A. Olejniczak. *Prawo cywilne: Część Ogolna* [*Civil Law. General Part*]. 11th edition. Warszawa: C.H. Beck, 2011.
Z. Radwański & A. Olejniczak. *Zobowiazania – Część Ogolna* [*Obligations – General Part*]. 9th edition. 2010.
Z. Radwański. *Zobowiazania – Część Ogolna* [*The Law of Obligations – General Part*]. Warszawa: C.H. Beck, 2004.
M. Safjan. *Źrodla Prawa Prywatnego* [*The Sources of Private Law*]. In M. Safjan (ed.), *System Prawa Prywatnego. Tom I. Część Ogolna* [*The System of Private Law. VolumeI. General Part*]. 2nd edition. Warszawa: C.H. Beck, Instytut Nauk Prawnych PAN, 2012.
M. Safjan. In K. Pietrzykowski (ed.), *Kodeks cywilny. Komentarz* [*The Civil Code. Commentary*]. 4th edition. C.H. BECK, 2005.
R. Siemienska & A. Domaradzka. 'Welfare State in Poland: Transformation with Difficulties'. In K. Schubert, S. Hegelich & U. Bazant (eds), *The Handbook of European Welfare Systems*. Routledge, 2009.
A. Stepkowski. *Naduzycie prawa a rozwoj prawa* [*Abuse of a Right and an Evolution of a Right*]. In H. Izdebski & A. Stepkowski (eds), *Naduzycie Prawa: Konferencja Wydzialu Prawa i Administracji 1 Marca 2002 roku* [*Abuse of a Right: Conference of the Law and Administration Department, 1 March 2002*]. Wydzial Prawa i Administracji Uniwersytetu Warszawskiego: Konferencje Naukowe. Warszawa: Liber, 2003, 49–76.
M. Tulibacka. *The Ethos of the Woolf Reforms in the Transformations of Post-socialist Civil Procedures: Case Study of Poland*. In D. Dwyer (ed.), *The Civil Procedure Rules. Ten Years On*. Oxford University Press, 2009.
M. Tulibacka. *Poland*. In D.R. Hensler, C. Hodges & M. Tulibacka (eds), *The Globalization of Class Actions*. The Annals of the American Academy of Political and Social Science. Vol. 622. Sage, 2009, 190.
W. Warkallo, *Odpowiedzialnosc odszkodowawcza* [*Liability for Damages*]. Warszawa, 1972.
T. Wisniewski. *Commentary to Civil Code Obligations*. Vol. I. LexisNexis 2002.

Selected Bibliography

General Principles and Prerequisites of Tort Liability

E. Bagińska. Odpowiedzialnosc deliktowa w razie niepewnosci zwiazku przyczynowego [Tort Liability under Uncertainty and Complexity of Causation]. Dom Organizatora TNOiK Toruń, 2013.

E. Bagińska. 'Causal uncertainty and proportional liability in Poland', in: I. Gilead, M.D. Green, B.A. Koch (eds.). Proportional liability: Analytical and Comparative Perspectives. De Gruyter Berlin 2013.

E. Bagińska & K. Krupa-Lipińska. 'Hypothetical causation (causa superveniens) in modern court practice', 2 (vol. 38) Gdańskie Studia Prawnicze 2017.

M. Balwicka-Szczyrba. Przedawnienie roszczen z tytulu odpowiedzialnosci deliktowej za szkody przyszle na osobie [Limitation of Tortious Personal Injury Claims for Future Loss]. Poznan, 2008.

Z. Banaszczyk. 'O odpowiedzialnosci deliktowej osoby maloletniej za czyn wlasny na zasadzie winy' ['On Tortious Fault Liability of a Minor for Own Conduct']. In M. Pyziak-Szafnicka (ed.), Odpowiedzialnosc cywilna. Ksiega pamiatkowa ku czci Profesora Adama Szpunara (Civil liability. Ad memoriam Professor Adam Szpunar). Krakow, 2004.

M. Bosakirska. Dochodzenie roszczen o naprawienie szkody wyrzadzonej czynem niedozwolonym w procesie cywilnym [Seeking Claims for Reparation of Losses Caused by an Illicit Act in Civil Proceedings]. Warszawa, 1983.

H. Cousy. 'Tort Liability and Liability Insurance: A Difficult Relationship'. In H. Koziol & B. Steininger (eds), European Tort Law 2001. Springer, 2002, 18–55.

J. Dabrowa. Wina jako przeslanka odpowiedzialnosci cywilnej [Fault as a Requisite of Civil Liability]. Wroclaw, 1968.

M. Jagielska & G. Zmij. 'Tort and Regulatory Law in Poland'. In: W. Van Boom, M. Lukas & C. Kissling (eds), Tort Law and Regulatory Law. Springer, 2007.

M. Kalinski. Odpowiedzialnosc odszkodowawcza [Compensatory Liability]. In A. Olejniczak (ed.), System Prawa Prywatnego: Prawo Zobowiazan. Część Ogolna [The System of Private Law: The Law of Obligations. General Part]. Vol. 6. Warszawa: C.H. Beck, Instytut Nauk Prawnych PAN, 2009.

A. Koch. Zwiazek przyczynowy jako podstawa odpowiedzialnosci odszkodowawczej w prawie cywilnym [Causal Link as a Base for the Liability for Damage in Civil Law]. 1975.

J.M. Kondek. Bezprawność jako przesłanka odpowiedzialności odszkodowawczej [Unlawfulness as a prerequisite for liability in damages] CH Beck, Warsaw 2013.

J. Kuźmicka-Sulikowska. Zasady Odpowiedzialnosci Deliktowej w Swietle Nowych Tendencji w Ustawodawstwie Polskim [The Principles of Delictual Liability in the Light of New Tendencies in Polish Legislation]. Warszawa: Wolters Kluwers Polska, 2011.

B. Lewaszkiewicz-Petrykowska. 'Zasada pelnego odszkodowania (mity i rzeczywistosc)'. (The Principle of Full Compensation – The Myths and Reality). In Rozprawy prawnicze, Ksiega pamiatkowa Profesora Maksymiliana Pazdana. Zakamycze, 2005.

B. Lewaszkiewicz-Petrykowska. 'Nowe tendencje w zakresie cywilnej odpowiedzialnosci zawodowej' ['New Currents in the Field of Professional Civil Liability']. In Rozprawy z polskiego i europejskiego prawa prywatnego. Ksiega pamiatkowa ofiarowana Profesorowi Jozefowi Skapskiemu [Treatises on Polish and European Private Law. Memorial Book for Professor Jozef Skapski]. Krakow, 1994.

B. Lewaszkiewicz-Petrykowska. Wyrzadzenie szkody przez kilka osob [Damage Caused by Several Persons]. 1978.

B. Lewaszkiewicz-Petrykowska. 'Wina jako podstawa odpowiedzialnosci z tytulu czynow niedozwolonych' ['Fault as a Pre-requisite of Tortious Liability']. Studia Prawno-Ekonomiczne 2 (1969).

P. Machnikowski. 'Odpowiedzialnosc za wlasne czyny' ['Liability for Own Actions']. In A. Olejniczak (ed.), System Prawa Prywatnego: Prawo Zobowiazan. Część Ogolna [The System of Private Law: The Law of Obligations. General Part]. Vol. 6. Warszawa: C.H. Beck, Instytut Nauk Prawnych PAN, 2009.

M. Nesterowicz. 'Adekwatny zwiazek przyczynowy jako przeslanka odpowiedzialnosci cywilnej w swietle orzecznictwa sadowego' ['Adequate Causal Link as a Pre-requisite of Civil Liability in the Light of Judicial Decisions']. In A. Nowicka (ed.), Prawo prywatne czasu przemian. Ksiega pamiatkowa dedykowana Profesorowi Stanislawowi Soltysinskiemu [Private Law in Transition. In Memoriam Professor Stanislaw Soltysinski]. Poznan, 2005.

M. Nesterowicz (ed.). Czyny niedozwolone w prawie polskim i prawie porownawczym [Torts in Polish Law and in Comparative Law]. Warszawa: Wolters Kluwer, 2012.

M. Nesterowicz & E. Bagińska. 'Strict Liability in Poland'. In B.A. Koch & H. Koziol (eds), Unification of Tort Law: Strict Liability. Kluwer Law International, 2002.

M. Nesterowicz & E. Bagińska. Contributory Negligence under Polish Law. In U. Magnus & M. Martín-Casals (eds), Unification of Tort Law: Contributory Negligence. Kluwer Law International, 2004.

M. Nesterowicz & E. Bagińska, Liability for Damage Caused by others under Polish Law. In J. Spier (ed.), Unification of Tort Law: Liability for Damage Caused by Others. Kluwer Law International, 2003.

M. Nesterowicz & E. Bagińska. Multiple Tortfeasors under Polish Law. In W.V.H. Rogers (ed.), Unification of Tort Law: Multiple Tortfeasors. Kluwer Law International, 2004.

N. Perram. 'The Law of Torts in Eastern Europe and the Vital Role of Liability Insurance in an Emerging Market Economy'. Central and East European Law 18, no. 3 (1992): 253.

M. Pyziak-Szafnicka (ed.). Odpowiedzialnosc cywilna. Ksiega pamiatkowa ku czci Profesora Adama Szpunara [Civil Liability. In Memoriam Professor Adam Szpunar]. Zakamycze, 2004.

Z. Radwański. 'Przedawnienie roszczen z czynow niedozwolonych w swietle znowelizowanego art. 442 kc' ['Limitation of Tort Claims in the Light of the Amended Art. 442 of the Civil Code']. Monitor Prawniczy 11 (2007): 591.

M. Safjan. 'Odpowiedzialnosc deliktowa osob prawnych. Stan obecny i kilka uwag de lege ferenda' ['Tortious liability of legal persons. Current rules and some comments de lege ferenda']. Studia Iuridica XXI (1994).

M. Sosniak. Bezprawnosc zachowania jako przeslanka odpowiedzialnosci cywilnej za czyny niedozwolone [Unlawfulness of Conduct as a Pre-requisite of Civil Liability in Tort]. Krakow, 1959.

L. Stecki. 'Problematyka odpowiedzialnosci za szkode posrednia' ['The Issue of Liability for Indirect Loss']. In S. Soltysinski (ed.), Problemy kodyfikacji prawa cywilnego (studia i rozprawy)[The Problems of Codification of Civil Law (Studies and Treatises)]. Poznan, 1990.

A. Szpunar. 'Uwagi o funkcjach odpowiedzialnosci odszkodowawczej' ['Remarks on Functions of Compensatory Liability']. Panstwo i Prawo 1 (2003).

A. Szpunar. Odszkodowanie za szkode majatkowa [Compensation for Pecuniary Loss]. Warszawa, 1998.

A. Szpunar. Wina poszkodowanego w prawie cywilnym [Victim's Fault in Civil Law]. Warszawa, 1971.

A. Szpunar. 'Czyny niedozwolone w kodeksie cywilnym' ['Illicit Acts in the Civil Code']. Studia Cywilistyczne 15 (1970).

A. Smieja. 'Umowna modyfikacja deliktowego stosunku odszkodowawczego' ['A Contractual Modification of a Delictual Obligation Relationship]. In A. Olejniczak (ed.), System Prawa Prywatnego: Prawo Zobowiazan. Część Ogolna [The System of Private Law: The Law of Obligations. General Part]. Vol. 6. Warszawa: C.H. Beck, Instytut Nauk Prawnych PAN, 2009.

A. Smieja. 'Czyny niedozwolone' ['Illicit Acts']. In A. Olejniczak (ed.), System Prawa Prywatnego: Prawo Zobowiazan. Część Ogolna [The System of Private Law: The Law of Obligations. General Part]. Vol. 6. Warszawa: C.H. Beck, Instytut Nauk Prawnych PAN, 2009.

A. Smieja. 'Wiek sprawcy szkody jako przeslanka odpowiedzialnosci cywilnej z tytulu czynow niedozwolonych' ['The Age of the Wrongdoer as a Condition of Civil Tortious Liability']. Panstwo i Prawo (1979).

W. Wagner. 'Obligations in Polish Law'. In D. Lasok (ed.), Polish Civil Law. Vol. II. A.W. Sijthoff-Leiden, 1974.

W. Warkallo. Odpowiedzialnosc odszkodowawcza: funkcje, rodzaje, granice. Warszawa, 1972.

B. Wiezowska. Odpowiedzialnosc cywilna na zasadzie slusznosci [Civil Liability Based on the Principle of Equity]. Warszawa, 2009.

Reparation of Damage

E. Bagińska. 'Zadoscuczynienie po nowelizacji art 446 Kodeksu cywilnego na tle doswiadczen europejskich' ['Compensation of Non-pecuniary Losses after the Amendment of Article 446 of the Civil Code from the Perspective of European Experiences]. In Z. Strus, J. Pokrzywniak & K. Ortynski (eds), *Wiadomosci Ubezpieczeniowe*, Special issue 2 (2010): 53.

E. Bagińska. 'Droit polonais (La réparation intégrale)'. In F. Leduc & P. Pierre (eds), *La réparation intégrale en Europe. Études comparatives des droits nationaux*. Larcier, 2012.

E. Bagińska. 'Compensation for property damage in motor third party liability insurance', *Wiadomości Ubezpieczeniowe* 4 (2014)

Selected Bibliography

E. Bagińska. *Poland: Developments in Personal Injury Law in Poland: Shaping the Compensatory Function of Tort Law*, 8 J. Civ. L. Stud. [Journal of Civil Law Studies] (2015).

M. Kaliński. *Szkoda na mieniu i jej naprawienie* [*Damage to Property and Its Reparation*]. Warszawa: C.H. Beck, 2008.

M Kaliński, *Szkoda na osobie i jej naprawienie* [Personal injury and its reparation] (Beck 2021)

E. Kowalewski (ed.). *Odszkodowanie za ubytek wartosci handlowej pojazdu poddanego naprawie* [*Compensation for Loss of a Vehicle's Market Value after Repairs*]. Toruń: TNOIK, 2012.

E. Kowalewski (ed.). *Odszkodowanie za niemoznosc korzystania z pojazdu uszkodzonego w wypadku komunikacyjnym* [*Compensation for Loss of Use of a Motor Vehicle Damaged in a Traffic Accident*]. Toruń: TNOIK, 2011.

E. Kowalewski. *Odszkodowanie ubezpieczeniowe za utracone korzysci* [*Insurance Compensation for Lost Profits*]. PA No. 3 (1996).

B. Lackoroński. *Odpowiedzialność cywilna za pośrednie naruszenia dóbr* [*Civil liability for indirect infringements of interests*] (Lexis Nexis, Warszawa 2013).

J. Matys. *Model zadoscuczynienia pienieznego z tytulu szkody niemajatkowej w kodeksie cywilnym* [*The Model of Pecuniary Compensation for Non-pecuniary Loss in the Civil Code*]. Wolters Kluwer, OFICYNA, 2009.

M. Nesterowicz & E. Bagińska. 'Non-pecuniary Loss under Polish Law'. In H. Rogers (ed.), *Damages for Non-pecuniary Loss in a Comparative Perspective*. Springer, 2001.

M. Nesterowicz, *Zadoscuczynienie pieniezne za doznana krzywdę w 'procesach lekarskich'* [*Compensation for Moral Harm in Medical Malpractice Cases*]. PiP 3 (2005).

T. Pajor. 'Poland'. in V.V. Palmer & M. Bussani (eds), *Pure Economic Loss. New Horizons in Comparative Law*. Routledge Cavendish, 2008.

M. Pazdan. 'Dobra osobiste i ich ochrona' ['Personal Interests and Their Protection']. in Marek Safjan (ed.), *System Prawa Prywatnego. Tom I. Część Ogolna*, 2nd ed. Warszawa: C.H. Beck, Instytut Nauk Prawnych PAN, 2012, 1286.

Z. Radwański. *Zadoscuczynienie pieniezne za szkode niemajatkowa. Rozwoj i funkcja spoleczna* [*Pecuniary Redress of Non-pecuniary Loss. Evolution and Social Function*]. Poznan, 1956.

J. Rezler. *Naprawienie szkody wyniklej ze spowodowania uszczerbku na ciele lub zdrowiu (wedlug prawa cywilnego)*[*Reparation of Losses Resulting from Damage to Health or Body (according to Civil Law)*]. Warszawa, 1968.

A. Szpunar. *Wynagrodzenie szkody wyniklej wskutek smierci osoby bliskiej* [*Compensation for Wrongful Death Cases*]. Branta, 2000.

A. Szpunar, *Zadoscuczynienie za szkode niemajatkowa* [*Compensation of Non-pecuniary Loss*]. Branta, 1999.

A. Szpunar. *Odszkodowanie za szkode majatkowa. Szkoda na mieniu i osobie* [*Compensation for Pecuniary Loss. Property Damage and Personal Injury*]. Branta, 1998.

A. Szpunar. *Ustalenie odszkodowania w prawie cywilnym* [*The Determination of Damages in Civil Law*]. Warszawa, 1975.

A. Smieja. 'Szczegolne zasady naprawienia deliktowej szkody na osobie' ['Specific Principles of Compensating Personal Injuries Resulting from Torts]. In A. Olejniczak (ed.), *System Prawa Prywatnego: Prawo Zobowiazan. Część Ogolna.* Vol. 6. Warszawa: Wydawnictwo C.H. Beck, Instytut Nauk Prawnych PAN, 2009.

M. Walachowska. *Zadoscuczynienie pieniezne za doznana krzywdę [Pecuniary Compensation for Non-pecuniary Loss*]. Toruń: Dom Organizatora, 2007.

M. Wałachowska. Wynagrodzenie szkód deliktowych doznanych przez pośrednio poszkodowanych [Compensation of damage suffered by indirect victims as a result of the death or personal injury of a close person] LexisNexis, Warsaw 2014.

J. Winiarz. *Obowiazek naprawienia szkody* [*The Obligation to Repair Damage*]. Warszawa, 1970.

J. Winiarz. *Ustalenie wysokosci odszkodowania* [*Assessment of Damages*]. Warszawa, 1962.

Specific Torts in the Civil Code

E. Bagińska & J. Parchomiuk. 'Odpowiedzialnosc odszkodowawcza w administracji' ['Compensatory Liability in Administration'], In R. Hauser, Z. Niewiadomski & A. Wrobel (eds), *System Prawa Administracyjnego* [*The System of Administrative Law*]. Vol. 12. 2nd ed. Warszawa, 2015.

E. Bagińska. *Odpowiedzialnosc odszkodowawcza za wykonywanie wladzy publicznej* [*Tort Liability of Public Authorities*]. Warszawa, 2006.

E. Bagińska, 'Liability of Public Authorities for Damage to Individuals: Is Article 77 of the Polish Constitution a Model Solution?'. In A. Bodnar, M. Kowalski, K. Raible & F. Schorkopf (eds), *The Emerging Constitutional Law of the European Union – German and Polish Perspectives*. Beiträge zum ausländischen öffentlichen Recht und Völkerrecht, 2003, 163.

E. Bagińska. *Nowe unormowanie odpowiedzialnosci cywilnej za product* [*The New Civil Product Liability Rules*]. PS No. 9 (2000): 47.

E. Bagińska, 'Product liability in Poland', in: *European product liability: an analysis of the state of the art in the era of new technologies* (P. Machnikowski ed.), Cambridge; Antwerp; Portland: Intersentia 2016.

E. Bagińska, 'The development of liability for 'reproductive torts' in Polish law', in: H. Koziol, U. Magnus (eds.) *Essays in honor of Jaap Spier*. Jan Sramek Vienna 2016.

E. Bagińska. 'The Liability of Public Authorities in Poland, in K. Oliphant (ed.) *The Liability of Public Authorities in Comparative Perspective*, Intersentia 2016.

G. Bieniek. *Odpowiedzialnosc cywilna za wypadki drogowe* [*Civil Liability for Traffic Accidents*]. 2nd ed. LexisNexis, 2007.

L. Bosek. *Bezprawie legislacyjne* [*Legislative Illegality*]. Warszawa, 2007.

M. Jagielska. *Odpowiedzialnosc za produkt. Dostosowanie prawa wewnetrznego panstw Unii Europejskiej do wymogow Dyrektywy 374/85*[*Product Liability. Adjustment of Internal Laws of EU Member States to the Requirements of Directive 374/85*]. Krakow, 1999.

M. Jagielska. *Odpowiedzialnosc za produkt* [*Product Liability*]. In A. Olejniczak (ed.), *System Prawa Prywatnego: Prawo Zobowiazan. Część Ogolna* [*The System of Private Law: The Law of Obligations. General Part*]. Vol. 6. Warszawa:

C.H. Beck, Instytut Nauk Prawnych PAN, 2009.
M. Jagielska. *Podstawy odpowiedzialnosci za product* [*The Fundamentals of Product Liability*]. Warszawa: C.H. Beck, 2004.
B. Lewaszkiewicz-Petrykowska. *Odpowiedzialnosc cywilna prowadzacego przedsiebiorstwo wprawiane w ruch przy pomocy sil przyrody (art 435 kc)* [*Civil Liability for an Enterprise Set into Motion by the Forces of Nature (Article 435 KC)*]. Wyd Prawnicze, 1967.
K. Ludwichowska. *Odpowiedzialnosc cywilna i ubezpieczeniowa za wypadki samochodowe* [*Civil and Insurer's Liability for Traffic Accidents*]. Dom Organizatora TNOiK, 2008.
J. Lopuski. 'Odpowiedzialnosc za szkody wyrzadzone w zwiazku z uzyciem sil przyrody (art 152 KZ): jej znaczenie i ewolucja w perspektywie minionego 70-lecia' [Liability for Damage Caused with the Use of Forces of Nature: Its Implications and Evolution within the Past 70 Years']. KPP 3 (2004).
E. Łętowska. *Ochrona niektorych praw konsumentow. Komentarz* [*Protection of certain consumer rights. Commentary*]. Warszawa, 2001.
P. Machnikowski & A. Smieja. 'Odpowiedzialnosc za szkody wyrzadzone przez zwierzeta' ['Liability for Damage Caused by Animals']. In A. Olejniczak (ed.), *System Prawa Prywatnego: Prawo Zobowiazan. Część Ogolna* [*The System of Private Law: The Law of Obligations. General Part*]. Vol. 6. Warszawa: C.H. Beck, Instytut Nauk Prawnych PAN, 2009, 489.
M. Nesterowicz. 'Odpowiedzialnosc za szkody wyrzadzone wprowadzeniem do obrotu rzeczy niebezpiecznych z wadami' ['Liability for Damage Caused by the Introduction into Circulation of Dangerously Defective Products']. *Palestra* 11 (1979): 16.
M. Pyziak-Szafnicka. 'Odpowiedzialnosc cywilna prowadzacego przedsiebiorstwo za szkode ekologiczna' ['Civil Liability of Owner of an Enterprise for Ecological Damage']. In *Studia z prawa prywatnego. Ksiega pamiatkowa ku czci Profesor Biruty Lewaszkiewicz-Petrykowskiej* [*Studies in Private Law. In Memoriam Professor Biruta Lewaszkiewicz-Petrykowska*]. Wyd. U.L., 1997.
J. Rajski. 'Odpowiedzialnosc za produkt niebezpieczny w swietle nowych przepisow kodeksu cywilnego' ['Liability for a Dangerous Product in the Light of the New Provisions of the Civil Code']. PPH No. 100 (2001): 24.
A. Rembielinski. *Odpowiedzialnosc cywilna za szkode wyrzadzona przez podwladnego* [*Civil Liability for Damage Caused by an Employee*]. Warszawa, 1971.
M. Safjan & K. Matuszyk. *Odpowiedzialnosc odszkodowawcza wladzy publicznej za szkode* [*Compensatory Liability of Public Authorities for Damage*]. 2nd ed. Warszawa: Lexis Nexis, 2009.
M. Safjan. 'Odpowiedzialnosc odszkodowawcza z tytulu bezprawia normatywnego' ['Liability for Damage in Cases of Normative Wrongs']. *Ruch Prawniczy, Ekonomiczny i Socjologiczny (RPEiS)* 1 (2005): 13.
J. Skoczylas. *Odpowiedzialnosc za szkody wyrzadzone przez wladze publiczna* [*Liability for Damage Caused by Public Authorities*]. Warszawa, 2005.
A. Smieja. 'Odpowiedzialnosc za wyrzucenie, wylanie lub spadniecie przedmiotu z pomieszczenia' ['Liability for Ejection, Emission or Fall of an Object from Premises']. In A. Olejniczak (ed.), *System Prawa Prywatnego: Prawo Zobowiazan. Część Ogolna* [*The System of Private Law: The Law of Obligations. General*

Part]. Vol. 6. Warszawa: C.H. Beck, Instytut Nauk Prawnych PAN, 2009.
A. Smieja. 'Odpowiedzialnosc za szkode wyrzadzona przez zawalenie sie budowli' ['Liability for Damage Caused by a Collapse of a Building']. In A. Olejniczak (ed.), *System Prawa Prywatnego: Prawo Zobowiazan. Część Ogolna* [*The System of Private Law: The Law of Obligations. General Part*]. Vol. 6. Warszawa: C.H. Beck, Instytut Nauk Prawnych PAN, 2009.
A. Smieja. *Odpowiedzialnosc odszkodowawcza z tytulu nienalezytego sprawowania nadzoru nad maloletnim* [Civil Liability for Negligent Supervision over Minors]. Wroclaw, 1982.
A. Szpunar. *Odpowiedzialnosc Skarbu Panstwa za funkcjonariuszy* [*Liability of State Treasury for Functionaries*]. 1985.
A. Szpunar. *Odpowiedzialnosc osob zobowiazanych do nadzoru* [*The Liability of Supervisors*]. 1978.
M. Tulibacka. *Product Liability Law in Transition: A Central European Perspective*. Ashgate Publishing, 2009.
W.J. Wagner. *Recent Developments in State Tort Liability in Poland*. AJCL 20 (1971): 247.

Medical Liability

E. Bagińska. 'The New Extra-Judicial Compensation System for Victims of Medical Malpractice and Accidents in Poland'. JETL 3 (2012): 101.
E. Bagińska. 'Remedying Patients for Moral Harm Arising from an Infringement of Patients' Rights'. *Comparative Law Review* 15 (Toruń: ED. UMK, 2013).
E. Bagińska. 'Medical Liability in Poland'. In B.A. Koch (ed.), *Medical Liability in Europe. A Comparison of Selected Jurisdictions, Tort and Insurance Law Series*. Vol. 29. Berlin: de Gruyter, 2011.
E. Bagińska. *Wielka Encyklopedia Prawa. tom X: Prawo medyczne* [The Great Encyclopaedia of Law. vol. X. Medical Law]. E. Bagińska (ed.). Ubi societas ibi ius Warsaw 2016.
E Bagińska (ed), *Odpowiedzialność prywatnoprawna. System Prawa Medycznego* [Private Law Liability. The System of Medical Law] vol. 5, M. Safjan/L. Bosek (gen eds). Warsaw: CH Beck 2021.
K. Bączyk-Rozwadowska. *Odpowiedzialnosc cywilna za szkody wyrzadzone przy leczeniu* [*Civil Liability for Damages Caused by Medical Malpractice*], 2nd edn. Toruń: Dom Organizatora TNOiK, 2013.
K. Bączyk-Rozwadowska. 'Medical Malpractice and Compensation in Poland'. *Chicago-Kent Law Review* 86 (2011): 1251.
T. Justynski. *Poczecie i urodzenie dziecka jako źrodlo odpowiedzialnosci cywilnej* [*Conception and Birth of a Child as a Source of Civil Liability*]. 2003.
S. Kalus. 'Liability for Medical Damages in Polish Law'. In B. Heiderhoff & G. Zmij (eds), *Tort Law in Poland, Germany and Europe*. Sellier, 2009.
M. Nesterowicz. *Prawo medyczne* [*Medical Law*]. 9th ed. TNOiK, 2010.
M. Nesterowicz. *Prawo medyczne. Komentarze i glosy do orzeczen sadowych* [*Medical Law. Commentaries to Judicial Decisions*]. Warszawa, 2012.
M. Nesterowicz, E. Bagińska & A. den Exter. *Medical Law in Poland*. Wolters Kluwer, 2011.

M. Sosniak. *Cywilna Odpowiedzialnosc lekarza* [*Civil Liability of Physicians*]. 2nd ed. Wyd. Prawnicze, 1977.

Tort Rules outside the Civil Code

E. Bagińska. 'Economic Loss Caused by GMOs in Poland'. In B.A. Koch (ed.), *Economic Loss Caused by Genetically Modified Crops. Liability and Redress for the Adventitious Presence of GMOs in Non-GM Crops*, Tort and Insurance Law. Vol. 24. Springer, 2008.

M. Baczyk. 'Liability of a Notary under Polish Law According to the Latest Judicature of the Supreme Court of the Republic of Poland'. In M. Kolasinski (ed.), *Civil Liability of a Notary and its Insurance in Poland and Other Selected Member States of the European Union*. Toruń, 2012.

M. Kolasinski (ed.). *Odpowiedzialnosc cywilna notariusza i jej ubezpieczenie w Polsce i innych wybranych panstwach Unii Europejskiej* [*Civil Liability of a Notary and its Insurance in Poland and Other Selected Member States of the European Union*]. Toruń, 2012.

M. Kolasinski. *Odpowiedzialnosc cywilna notariusza* [*Civil Liability of a Public Notary*]. Toruń: TNOiK, 2005.

A. Konert. *Odpowiedzialnosc cywilna przewoznika lotniczego* [*Civil Liability of Air Carriers*]. Oficyna/Wolters Kluwer, 2010.

B. Lewaszkiewicz-Petrykowska. 'Uwagi o zasadach rzadzacych cywilna odpowiedzialnoscia notariusza' ['Remarks on the Principles Governing Civil Liability or a Notary]. PS no. 2 (1995): 29.

B. Lewaszkiewicz-Petrykowska. 'Cywilna odpowiedzialnosc za szkode jadrowa w polskim prawie atomowym' ['Civil Liability for Nuclear Loss in the Polish Nuclear Law']. 4 PiP (1987).

R. Mikosz. *Odpowiedzialnosc za szkody wyrzadzone ruchem zakladu gorniczego* (*The Liability for Damage Caused through the Activity of a Mining Enterprise*). Zakamycze-Wolters Kluwer, 2006.

A. Oleszko. 'Starannosc zawodowa notariusza jako przeslanka odpowiedzialnosci za szkode wyrzadzona przy wykonywaniu czynnosci notarialnej' ['Professional Diligence of a Notary as a Requisite of Compensatory Liability for Damage Caused While Performing Duties of a Notary']. *Rejent* no. 11 (1999).

T. Pajor. 'Odpowiedzialnosc cywilna organizatora imprezy sportowej' ['Civil Liability of the Sport Organizer']. PS No. 10 (2002).

W. Radecki. *Odpowiedzialnosc cywilna w ochronie srodowiska* [*Civil Liability in Environmental Protection*]. Wyd. PAN, 1987.

T. Siemiatkowski. *Odpowiedzialnosc cywilnoprawna w spolkach kapitalowych* [*Civil Liability in Companies*]. Warszawa: C.H. Beck, 2007.

Index

The numbers here refer to paragraph numbers.

Index